TWO-YEAR COLLEGE EDITION

YOUR COLLEGE
EXPERIENCE

Strategies for Success

TWO-YEAR COLLEGE EDITION

YOUR COLLEGE EXPERIENCE

Strategies for Success

John N. Gardner

President, John N. Gardner Institute for Excellence in
    Undergraduate Education
Brevard, North Carolina

Distinguished Professor Emeritus, Library and Information Science
    Senior Fellow, National Resource Center for The First-Year Experience
    and Students in Transition
University of South Carolina, Columbia

Betsy O. Barefoot

Senior Scholar
John N. Gardner Institute for Excellence in Undergraduate Education
Brevard, North Carolina

Negar Farakish

Provost/Assistant Vice President for Academic Affairs
    and Dean of American Honors
Union County College, New Jersey

Bedford/St. Martin's
Boston ■ New York

For Bedford/St. Martin's

Vice President, Editorial, Macmillan Higher Education Humanities: Edwin Hill
Publisher for College Success: Erika Gutierrez
Senior Executive Editor for College Success: Simon Glick
Developmental Editor: Jennifer Jacobson of Ohlinger Publishing Services
Production Editor: Kerri A. Cardone
Senior Production Supervisor: Dennis J. Conroy
Senior Marketing Manager: Christina Shea
Associate Editor: Bethany Gordon
Copy Editor: Janet Renard
Indexer: Steve Csipke
Photo Researcher: Sue McDermott Barlow
Senior Art Director: Anna Palchik
Text Design: Jerilyn Bockorick, Cenveo Publisher Services
Cover Design: Billy Boardman
Cover Photo: College students having group discussions. Photograph by
Stephen Simpson. © Getty Images
Composition: Cenveo Publisher Services
Printing and Binding: RR Donnelley and Sons

Manufactured in the United States of America.

9 8 7 6 5 4
f e d c b a

For information, write: Bedford/St. Martin's, 75 Arlington Street, Boston, MA 02116
(617-399-4000)

ISBN 978-1-4576- 6576-9 (Two-Year College Student Edition)
ISBN 978-1-4576-9018-1 (Loose-leaf Edition)

Acknowledgments
Acknowledgments and copyrights appear at their source throughout the text, which constitutes an extension of the copyright page. It is a violation if the law to reproduce these selections by any means whatsoever without written permission of the copyright holder.

Chapter Opening Images: Chapter 1: p. 3, A Aleksii/Shutterstock; Chapter 2: p. 23, lisboaimagelab/Shutterstock; Chapter 3: p. 51, Introwiz1/Shutterstock; Chapter 4: p. 73, VoodooDot/Shutterstock; Chapter 5: p. 95, WonderfulPixel/Shutterstock; Chapter 6: p. 117, Introwiz1/Shutterstock; Chapter 7: p. 133, Introwiz1/Shutterstock; Chapter 8: p. 157, Palsur/Shutterstock (computer), Kapreski/Shutterstock (book cart); Chapter 9: p. 175, Vector Icon/Shutterstock; Chapter 10: p. 193, Palsur/Shutterstock; Chapter 11: p. 213, Happy Art/Shutterstock; Chapter 12: p. 245, Introwiz1/Shutterstock.

At the time of publication all Internet URLs published in this text were found to accurately link to their intended Web site. If you do find a broken link, please forward the information to collegesuccess@bedfordstmartins.com so that it can be corrected for the next printing.

Dear Student,

More than ever before, a college education is an essential step in preparing you for almost any career. A few years ago, many well-paying jobs required only a high school diploma, but most employers today require that job applicants have some form of education beyond high school. This can be a college degree or a certificate in a particular vocation.

The higher education is becoming more expensive, and some people are questioning whether a college degree is worth the cost. Yes, college is expensive, but the benefits of a college education are well worth the price tag. A college educated person receives a better salary and enjoys a healthier life, more confidence, and a greater future for his or her children. Of course we can all name a few exceptions: Mark Zuckerberg of Facebook and Steve Jobs of Apple were college dropouts who still managed to be highly successful. Such success stories are rare.

While you might have many reasons for being in college, we hope your primary goal is graduation. And you will be more likely to graduate if you have a successful first year. When we were in our first year of college, college success courses did not exist. Colleges and universities just allowed new students to sink or swim. As a result, some students did well, some hardly survived, and some dropped out or flunked out.

As college professors, researchers, and administrators with many years of experience working with first-year students, we know that starting college can be challenging. Today, most colleges offer success courses to help students to be successful in the first year and to eventually graduate.

You are likely reading *Your College Experience* because you are enrolled in a college success course. Although this book might seem different from your other textbooks, we believe that it could be the most important book you read this term because it's all about improving your chances for success in college and in your career. This book will help you discover your own strengths and your needs for improvement. We know that if you apply the ideas in this book to your everyday life, you are more likely to enjoy your time in college, graduate, and achieve your life goals. Welcome to college!

John N. Gardner
Betsy O. Barefoot
Negar Farakish

About the Authors

John N. Gardner brings unparalleled experience to this authoritative text for first-year seminar courses. He is the recipient of the University of South Carolina's highest award for teaching excellence. He has twenty-five years of experience directing and teaching in the most respected and most widely emulated first-year seminar in the country, the University 101 course at the University of South Carolina. He is recognized as one of the country's leading educators for his role in initiating and orchestrating an international reform movement to improve the beginning college experience. He is also the founding leader of two influential higher education centers that support campuses in their efforts to improve the learning and retention of beginning college students: the National Resource Center for The First-Year Experience and Students in Transition at the University of South Carolina (**www.sc.edu/fye**) and the John N. Gardner Institute for Excellence in Undergraduate Education (**www.jngi.org**) based in Brevard, North Carolina. The experiential basis for all of John Gardner's work is his own miserable first year of college on academic probation, an experience that he hopes to prevent for this book's readers.

Betsy O. Barefoot is a writer, researcher, and teacher whose special area of scholarship is the first year of college. During her tenure at the University of South Carolina from 1988 to 1999, she served as co-director for research and publications at the National Resource Center for The First-Year Experience and Students in Transition. She taught University 101, in addition to special-topics graduate courses on the first-year experience and the principles of college teaching. She conducts first-year seminar faculty training workshops around the United States and in other countries, and she is frequently called on to evaluate first-year seminar outcomes. She currently serves as Senior Scholar in the Gardner Institute for Excellence in Undergraduate Education. In her Institute role she led a major national research project to identify institutions of excellence in the first college year. She currently works with both two- and four-year campuses in evaluating all components of the first year.

Negar Farakish is an educator and administrator with years of experience in teaching and working with community college students from diverse backgrounds and academic abilities. In her various roles, she has taught and assisted wide-ranging groups of students from the academically underprepared to those pursuing highly competitive majors and careers at these institutions. She currently serves as the Provost and Assistant Vice President for Academic Affairs and Dean of American Honors at Union County College in New Jersey and teaches as an Adjunct Assistant Professor at Teachers College, Columbia University.

Brief Contents

Contents

PART ONE · FIRST STEPS

1 Making the Transition to College and Planning Your Academic Journey   3

2 Managing Time, Energy, and Money 23

3 Discovering How You Learn 51

PART TWO STUDY STRATEGIES

4 Getting the Most Out of Class 73

5 Reading to Learn from College Textbooks 95

6 Studying, Understanding, and Remembering 117

7 Taking Tests Successfully 133

9   **Writing and Speaking**   175

PART THREE   YOUR PATH TO SUCCESS IN COLLEGE AND BEYOND

10   **Thinking Critically**   193

11 Managing Your Health, Emotions, and Relationships in a Diverse World 213

12 Making the Right Career Choice   245

Preface

Anyone who teaches beginning college students knows how much they have changed in recent years. Today's students are increasingly job-focused, skilled in using technology, and concerned about the future. And more than ever, students are worrying about how they will pay for college. Recently, popular media sources such as *USA Today* have raised questions about whether the money spent on a college degree would be better invested in a start-up business or travel.[1] While it is tempting to focus on the few individuals who can find an alternate path to a successful future, we know that for the overwhelming majority of individuals, a college degree is more essential than ever before.

Today, we see diverse students of all ages and backgrounds enrolling in two-year colleges, bringing with them hopes and dreams as well as expectations that may or may not be realistic. *Your College Experience,* Two-Year College Edition is designed specifically to give students in these colleges the practical help they need to gain self-knowledge, set goals, succeed, and persist so that those hopes and dreams have a better chance to become realities.

While keeping its approach on goal setting, the Two-Year College Edition adds skills and strategies in areas where two-year students often need the most support. These skills, such as time management, academic reading, and career preparation, are important for college courses and for the workplace. At a time when institutions are increasing class sizes and mainstreaming developmental students, students will need more, not less, individual attention and skills so that they can ask for the help they need. Of course concerns about student retention remain, as do pressures on college success administrators to do more with less. These realities of college life mean that giving students strategies they can use immediately is more important than ever.

To help you meet the challenges of engaging and retaining today's students, we have created a complete package of support materials, including an Instructor's Annotated Edition and an Instructor's Manual and Test Bank. In the Instructor's Annotated Edition, you will find clearly marked retention strategies and activities to help you engage and retain students. These activities, and all of the instructor support materials, will help both new and experienced instructors as they prepare to teach the course.

What has not changed in the forty years since the inception of the college success course is our level of commitment and deep understanding of our students. Although this edition of *Your College Experience* focuses specifically on the two-year college audience, it is still based on feedback from generations of users and our collective knowledge and experience in teaching new students. It is grounded in the growing body of research

[1] "Kids skip college–not worth the money." USA Today online, April 22, 2013, Oliver St. John (author).

on student success and retention and includes many valuable contributions from leading experts in the field. Our contributors were chosen for their knowledge and currency in their fields as well as their own deep commitments to their students and to the discipline. Most of all, it is a text born from our devotion to students and to their success. Simply put, we do not like to see students fail. We are confident that if students read and heed the information herein, they will become engaged in the college experience, learn, and persist to graduation.

We have written this text for students of any age specifically at two-year commuter institutions. Our writing style is intended to convey respect and admiration for students while recognizing their continued need for challenge and support. We have addressed every topic that our experience, our research, and our reviewers tell us is a concern for students at any type of two-year college with any kind of educational background. We have also embedded various reading and writing strategies to scaffold students' efforts in comprehension of the material and application of skills presented in each chapter and included technology tools and tips that can enhance students' studying experience.

This version of *Your College Experience* uses a simple and logical organization. Part One, First Steps, sets the stage by challenging students to explore their purpose for attending college, by helping them learn how to apply that purpose to both short- and long-term goal setting and to managing their complex lives. Students are armed with solid time, energy, and money management strategies in Chapter 2, and then they explore the topic of learning styles. Part Two, Study Strategies, enumerates essential study skills like, reading, note taking and test taking and guides students in finding information, writing and speaking. Part Three, Your Path to Success in College and Beyond, emphasizes critical thinking, and practical and realistic considerations such as managing emotional and physical health, and relationships in the diverse environments where students live and work. Part Three also includes a comprehensive chapter on majors and careers with a wealth of tools and strategies that students can use now and in the future.

Whether you are considering this textbook for use in your first-year seminar or have already made a decision to adopt it, we thank you for your interest, and we trust that you will find it to be a valuable teaching aid. We also hope that this book will guide you and your campus in understanding the broad range of issues that can affect student success.

AN EDITION DEVELOPED WITH TWO-YEAR STUDENTS IN MIND

- **Language and reading level** are appropriate for first-year students, many of whom are enrolled in developmental education courses. Reading strategies are embedded throughout the book.
- **Examples, models, and art program** reflect the reality of the broad range of traditional and non-traditional two-year students, For example, photos and wording are in the context of two-year colleges, and sample calendar templates reflect the schedules of two-year students and, the real priorities of all two-year students: work, family, and college.

- **Increased coverage of campus involvement** particular to open-enrollment colleges (e.g., extracurricular activities and examples of such activities are added, and students are encouraged to consider such activities when planning their days, weeks, and terms). The importance of joining study groups is particularly stressed.
- **Key topics** that are most essential to students at two-year colleges are included in each chapter.
- **All data** have been updated to reflect two-year colleges.

KEY FEATURES OF THIS EDITION

- **Powerful LearningCurve online assessment system available with every new book.** When it comes to retaining new information, research shows that self-testing with small, bite-sized chunks of information works best. *LearningCurve for College Success,* a new adaptive online quizzing program, helps students focus on the material they need the most help with. With LearningCurve, students receive as much practice as they need to master a given concept and are provided with immediate feedback and links back to online instruction. A personalized study plan with suggestions for further practice gives your students what they need to thrive in the college success course, in their college, career, and beyond!
- **A pre-reading activity** kicks off each chapter to get students thinking about and looking at the content that is to come and how it relates to them.
- **Chapter-opening profiles that help students see themselves in the text.** Each chapter of the text opens with a story of a recent first-year student at a two-year college who has used the strategies in the chapter to succeed. The profiled students come from diverse backgrounds and attend all kinds of two-year colleges around the country.
- **Your Turn activities** in each chapter encourage students to build communication, collaboration, critical thinking, organization, and self-assessment skills by asking them to reflect on or apply content introduced in the chapter. Your Turn activities are broken into four types: On Your Own; Try It; Discuss It; and Work Together. Some include space for students' responses.
- **Key terms** are boldfaced and defined within the narrative so as not to disturb the flow of reading. In addition, a glossary of key terms appears at the end of the book.
- **An increased focus on technology and learning.** Tech Tips in every chapter ask students to apply many of the technology skills they likely already have and use in their personal lives in an academic setting. For some readers, the Tech Tips teach new skills. This application-based feature appears at the end of the chapter so as not to disturb the flow of the main narrative.
- **Chapter-ending activities encourage communication, critical thinking, organization, application, and self-assessment skills** by asking students to THINK, WRITE, and APPLY concepts introduced in the chapter.

- **Where to Go for Help boxes connect the text to student experiences at their specific institution** to help students take more control of their own success, every chapter includes a quick overview of college and online resources for support, focusing on those available at open-enrollment colleges, including learning assistance centers, library, Web sites, professional staff, and fellow students. The box ends with a prompt for students to write in their own ideas and resources at their college.
- **A carefully executed design and art program** keep students focused on the content while keeping them engaged by including images of current students and pop culture help make students feel comfortable and connected. Captions invite students to think critically.
- **Models (including digital models) let students see principles in action** because many students learn best by example, full-size models—more than in any competing book—show realistic examples of annotating a textbook, creating a mind map, multiple styles of note taking, and other strategies for academic success. This edition includes digital models to reflect the tools students will be using in their everyday lives.
- **Retention Strategies in every chapter of the Instructor's Annotated Edition (IAE) offer best practices** from the authors to help students persist in the first year. In addition, a 16-page insert at the beginning of the IAE includes chapter-specific exercises and activities designed as retention strategies to support writing, critical thinking, working in groups, planning, reflecting, and taking action.

KEY CHAPTER-BY-CHAPTER CONTENT

Chapter 1 "Making the Transition to College and Planning Your Academic Journey," discusses the benefits of the course and the textbook in making a successful transition to college, emphasizes the benefits of a college education, and introduces students to the concepts of academic and career planning. The chapter concludes with college terminology that may be unfamiliar to most students and particularly those who are the first in their families to attend college.

Chapter 2 "Managing Your Time, Energy, and Money," presents students with strategies to coordinate the use of these valuable resources. The chapter starts with time management techniques and continues to offer suggestions for managing energy and money in conjunction with time. Multiple worksheets are provided in the chapter to help students map their use of these resources.

Chapter 3 "Discovering How You Learn," includes the VARK Learning Styles Inventory, to help students identify their preferred learning styles, and discusses MBTI and multiple intelligences. The chapter also addresses learning disabilities that many students struggle with in college.

Chapter 4 "Getting the Most Out of Class," presents students with engagement strategies they can apply through listening, participating, and note-taking before class, in class, and after class.

Chapter 5 "Reading to Learn from College Textbooks," offers tips and tools for active reading, increasing comprehension, and understanding the differences in math, science, and social science textbooks. The chapter focuses on strategies for improving academic reading and vocabulary development.

Chapter 6 "Studying, Understanding, and Remembering," provides memory improvement techniques and study skills that promote deep learning. The chapter includes a new tool for students to use to consider changes they are willing to make so that study time is more efficient.

Chapter 7 "Taking Tests Successfully," is a chapter filled with strategies students can apply as they prepare for tests in various courses. In particular, the emotional aspect of test taking is discussed, and a test anxiety quiz is provided that allows students to evaluate how serious an issue this is for them and create a plan to overcome it. The chapter concludes with a discussion of academic honesty.

Chapter 8 "Information Literacy," covers topics such as effective use of the library; working with librarians; choosing, narrowing, and researching topics for writing assignments; using keywords; and finding and evaluating both traditional and electronic sources.

Chapter 9 "Writing and Speaking," guides students in using their research in writing and speaking. The chapter presents the writing process, includes an expanded coverage on plagiarism, and provides tips for successful speaking.

Chapter 10 "Thinking Critically," features a helpful visual guide to Bloom's Taxonomy, streamlined coverage of faulty reasoning and logical fallacies, and a scenario on vending machines in schools. Students can use this scenario to practice their critical thinking and argument skills.

Chapter 11 "Managing Your Health, Emotions, and Relationships in a Diverse World," discusses multiple aspects of college life to help students stay healthy physically and emotionally, and effectively function within their diverse college communities. The chapter offers suggestions for getting involved in campus life, manage relationships, and appreciate diversity.

Chapter 12 "Making the Right Career Choice," serves as a step-by-step guide to selecting a major and exploring careers and presents strategies for career planning, enhancing marketability; developing the right mindset for creating a strong future; conducting industry and company research; gaining experience while in college; and job searching.

EXTENSIVE RESOURCES FOR INSTRUCTORS

- **LaunchPad for *Your College Experience,* Two-Year College Edition.** LaunchPad combines an interactive e-book with high-quality multimedia content and ready-made assessment options, including LearningCurve adaptive quizzing. Pre-built units are easy to assign or adapt with your own material, such as readings, videos, quizzes, discussion groups, and more. LaunchPad also provides access to a grade book that provides a clear window on performance for your whole class, for individual students, and for individual assignments. The result is superior book specific content in a breakthrough user interface in which power and simplicity go hand in hand. To package LaunchPad for *Your College Experience* with the text, use ISBN 978-1-319-01296-0. To order LaunchPad standalone, use ISBN 978-1-4576-9024-2.

- ***LearningCurve for College Success*** is an online, adaptive, self-quizzing program that quickly learns what students already know and helps them practice what they don't yet understand. LearningCurve motivates students to engage with key concepts before they come to class so that they are ready to participate and offers reporting tools to help you discern your student's needs. To package *LearningCurve for College Success* for **free** with the text, use ISBN 978-1-319-01294-6. To order LearningCurve standalone, use ISBN 978-1-4576-7999-5.

- **Instructor's Annotated Edition.** A valuable tool for new and experienced instructors alike, the Instructor's Annotated Edition includes the full text of the student edition with abundant marginal annotations, chapter-specific exercises, and helpful suggestions for teaching, fully updated and revised by the authors. In this edition are numerous Retention Strategy tips and exercises to help you help your students succeed and stay in school.

- **Instructor's Manual and Test Bank.** The Instructor's Manual and Test Bank includes chapter objectives, teaching suggestions, a sample lesson plan for each chapter, sample syllabi, final projects for the end of the course, and various case studies that are relevant to the topics covered. It also includes test questions for each chapter, a midterm, and a final exam. The Instructor's Manual and Test Bank is available online.

- **Computerized Test Bank.** The Computerized Test Bank contains more than 600 multiple-choice, true/false, short-answer, and essay questions designed to assess students' understanding of key concepts. An answer key is included.

- ***French Fries Are Not Vegetables.*** This comprehensive instructional DVD features multiple resources for class and professional use. Also available online on Video Central: College Success. ISBN 978-0-312-65073-5.

- **Custom Solutions program.** Bedford/St. Martin's Custom Publishing offers the highest-quality books and media, created in consultation with publishing professionals who are committed to the discipline. Make *Your College Experience,* Two-Year College Edition fit your course and goals by integrating your own materials, including only the parts of the text you intend to use in your course, or both. Contact your local Macmillan Education sales representative for more information.

- **CS Select custom database.** The CS Select database allows you to create a textbook for your College Success course that reflects your course objectives and uses just the content you need. Start with one of our core texts, then rearrange chapters, delete chapters, and add additional content–including your own original content—to create just the book you're looking for. Get started by visiting **macmillanhighered .com/csSelect**.

- **TradeUp.** Bring more value and choice to your students' first-year experience by packaging *Your College Experience,* Two-Year College Edition with one of a thousand titles from Macmillan publishers at a 50 percent discount from the regular price. Contact your local Macmillan Education sales representative for more information.

STUDENT RESOURCES

- **LaunchPad for *Your College Experience,* Two-Year College Edition.** LaunchPad is an online course solution that offers our acclaimed content including eBook, videos, LearningCurve adaptive quizzes, and more. For more information, see the section under Extensive Resources for Instructors. To package LaunchPad for *Your College Experience* with this title, use ISBN 978-1-319-01296-0. To order LaunchPad standalone, use ISBN 978-1-4576-9024-2.

- *LearningCurve for College Success* is an online, adaptive, self-quizzing program that quickly learns what students already know and helps them practice what they don't yet understand. For more information, see the section under Extensive Resources for Instructors. To package *LearningCurve for College Success* for **free** with the text, use ISBN 978-1-319-01294-6. To order LearningCurve standalone, use ISBN 978-1-4576-7999-5.

- **College Success companion site: bedfordstmartins.com/collegesuccess /resources**. The College Success companion site offers a number of tools to use in class including videos with quizzing, downloadable podcasts, flashcards of key terms, and links to apps which students can use on their phones or computers to reinforce success strategies. From the companion Web site, you can also access instructor materials whenever you need them.

- *VideoCentral: College Success* is a premiere collection of videos for the college success classroom. The site features the 30-minute documentary *French Fries Are Not Vegetables and Other College Lessons: A Documentary of the First Year of College,* which follows five students through the life-changing transition of the first year of college. Learn more at **macmillanhighered.com/videosuccess/catalog**. *VideoCentral* also includes access to the following:

    Sixteen brief *Conversation Starters* that combine student and instructor interviews on the most important topics taught in first-year seminar courses.

Sixteen accompanying video glossary definitions with questions that bring these topics to life.

- **Bedford e-Book to Go for *Your College Experience*, Two-Year College Edition.** For roughly half the cost of a print book, **Bedford e-Book to Go** offers an affordable alternative for students. To learn more, visit **macmillanhighered.com/aboutebooks.**

- **Additional e-Book formats.** You can also find PDF versions of our books when you shop online at our publishing partners' sites: CourseSmart, Barnes & Noble NookStudy; Kno; CafeScribe; or Chegg.

- *The Bedford/St. Martin's Planner* includes everything that students need to plan and use their time effectively, with advice on preparing schedules and to-do lists, along with blank schedules and calendars (monthly and weekly) for planning. Integrated into the planner are tips and advice on fixing common grammar errors, taking notes, and succeeding on tests; an address book; and an annotated list of useful Web sites. The planner fits easily into a backpack or purse, so students can take it anywhere. To order *The Bedford/St. Martin's Planner* packaged **free** with the text, use ISBN 978-1-319-01293-9. To order the planner standalone, use ISBN 978-0-312-57447-5.

- *Bedford/St. Martin's Insider's Guides.* These concise and student-friendly booklets on topics that are critical to college success are a perfect complement to your textbook and course. One Insider Guide can be packaged with *any* Bedford/St. Martin's textbook at no additional cost. Additional Insider's Guides can also be packaged for additional cost. Topics include:
  - **New!** *Insider's Guide to College Etiquette*, 2e
  - **New!** *Insider's Guide for Returning Veterans*
  - **New!** *Insider's Guide to Transferring*
  - *Insider's Guide to Academic Planning*
  - *Insider's Guide to Beating Test Anxiety*
  - *Insider's Guide to Building Confidence*
  - *Insider's Guide to Career Services*
  - *Insider's Guide to College Ethics and Personal Responsibility*
  - *Insider's Guide to Community College*
  - *Insider's Guide to Credit Cards*, 2e
  - *Insider's Guide to Getting Involved on Campus*
  - *Insider's Guide to Global Citizenship*
  - *Insider's Guide to Time Management*, 2e

For more information on ordering one of these guides with the text, go to **macmillanhighered.com/collegesuccess.**

- *Journal Writing: A Beginning.* Designed to give students an opportunity to use writing as a way to explore their thoughts and feelings, this writing journal includes a generous supply of inspirational quotes placed throughout the pages, tips for journaling, and suggested journal topics. ISBN 978-0-312-59027-7.

ACKNOWLEDGMENTS

Special thanks to the reviewers who helped develop this Two-Year College Edition.

Torris Anderson, Jr., Ocean County College

Cynthia Armster, City Colleges of Chicago

Sherry Ash, San Jacinto College-Central

Diego Baez, Harry S. Truman College

Beverly Brucks, Illinois Central College

Richard Conway, Nassau Community College

David Ferreira, Broward College

Maria Galyon, Jefferson Community and Technical College

Jo Ann Jenkins, Moraine Valley Community College

Jill Loveless, Mohave Community College

Gail Malone, South Plains College

Patrick Peyer, Rock Valley College

Claudia Swicegood, Rowan-Cabarrus Community College

Susan Taylor, North Florida Community College

Kim Toby, Somerset Community College

As we look to the future, we are excited about the numerous improvements to this text that our creative Bedford/St. Martin's team has made and will continue to make. Special thanks to Edwin Hill, Vice President of Editorial, Humanities; Karen Henry, Editorial Director for English and Music; Simon Glick, Senior Executive Editor for College Success; Jennifer Jacobson, Development Editor of Ohlinger Publishing Services; Bethany Gordon, Associate Editor; Christina Shea, Senior Marketing Manager; and Kerri Cardone, Production Editor.

Most of all, we thank you, the users of our book, for you are the true inspirations for our work.

CONTRIBUTORS

Although this text speaks with the voices of its three authors, it represents contributions from many other people. We gratefully acknowledge those contributions and thank these individuals whose special expertise has made it possible to introduce new students to their college experience through the holistic approach we deeply believe in.

 Lea Susan Engle was an essential contributor to the chapter on information literacy. Lea is a former instructor and first-year experience librarian at Texas A&M University and current PhD student at The School of Information at The University of Texas at Austin. Lea earned a B.A. in Women's Studies from the University of Maryland, College Park and holds an M.S. in Information Studies and an M.A. in Women's and Gender Studies from the University of Texas at Austin.

Her professional interests include first-year experience, creative approaches to library outreach, feminist pedagogy, library service to GLBTQ users, formative assessment, taking risks, and fostering cross-campus collaborations. She works in libraries because they are important and empowering community spaces where all people are welcome to participate in free and equal access to information.

Casey Reid was a vital contributor to the chapter on time management for today's students. Casey graduated in 2002 from Missouri State University with a BA in Anthropology and Professional Writing and in 2004 with an MA in Writing. From 2004 through 2011, she worked as English faculty at Metropolitan Community College (MCC) in Kansas City. After taking on the time management challenge of grading papers for 16-17 English classes every year, she took on a new challenge as the College Orientation Coordinator at MCC. Now, she coordinates a mandatory first-year seminar class for MCC's 6,000–7,000 new students, which includes supervising over 100 instructors and managing the associated Peer Leader program. When she isn't working, volunteering, or helping with the various associations in which she holds positions (Midwest Regional Association for Developmental Education, Heartland College Reading and Learning Association, 49/63 Neighborhood Coalition), she adds balance to her life by running, biking, hiking, reading, spending time with her three rescued dogs, and hanging out with friends and family.

Chapter 12 has been shaped by Heather N. Maietta. Heather is Associate Vice President of Career and Corporate Engagement at Merrimack College. Heather has presented or co-presented more than thirty times nationally on topics related to career and professional preparation and is a Certified Career Development Facilitator Instructor through the National Career Development Association.

Heather has authored articles and research reports in several publications, including *About Campus; Career Convergence;* and *ESource.* Heather has also co-authored three textbooks for Kendall/Hunt Publishers. Most recently, she co-authored and edited *The Senior Year: Culminating Experiences and Transitions*, published by The National Resource Center on the First -Year Experience and Students in Transition.

Heather also serves on the Notre Dame Education Center Board of Directors, an organization that provides education and support services for adult learners in the Greater Lawrence Community.

Chris Gurrie is Assistant Professor of Speech at the University of Tampa. Dr. Gurrie is an active public speaker and participates in invited lectures, workshops, and conferences in the areas of faculty development, first-year life and leadership, communicating effectively with *PowerPoint*, and communication and immediacy. He contributed the first generation of Tech Tips that were adapted for this new text, and wrote the *Guide to Teaching with You-Tube*, available as part of the Instructor's Manual and Test Bank.

1 Making the Transition to College and Planning Your Academic Journey

PRE-READING ACTIVITY: Before you start reading, take a few minutes to look through this chapter. What do you think this chapter is going to be about? List three topics that you think will be helpful to you or three questions you have about the chapter.

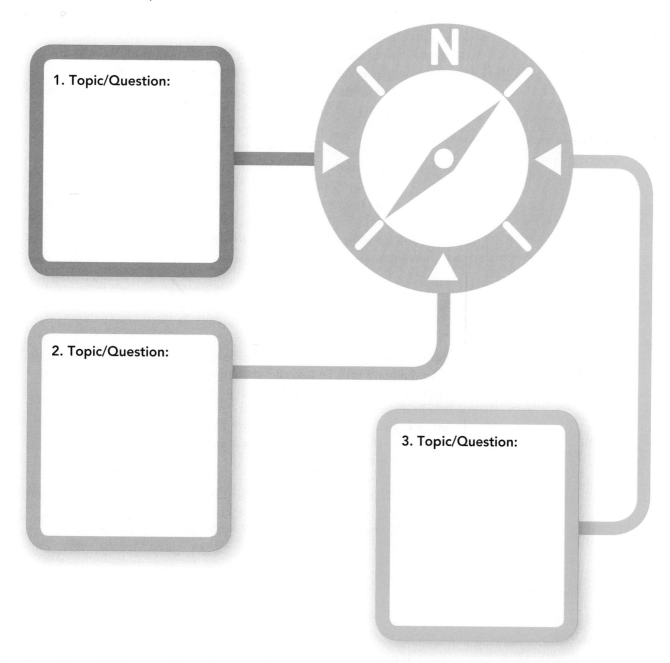

1. Topic/Question:

2. Topic/Question:

3. Topic/Question:

📁 PROFILE ⊗

Maria Lopez, 18
Early Childhood Education Major, *Lone Star College*

Source: arek_malang /Shutterstock

Maria Lopez always knew she was going to college even though no one else in her family had ever attended any college or university. For Maria, going to Lone Star College was an easy choice, and she is very happy that she chose to attend a two-year college. "It is close to home," she explains, "so I can still help my family, keep my part-time job, and continue my education with some of my high school friends."

Now that her first year is under way, Maria has learned there are some key differences between high school and college, specifically the amount of time she spends studying. "In high school, I studied maybe five hours a week," she explains. "Now I study many more hours, something I learned was important right away in my first-year-experience course. I also quickly learned the importance of organizing, managing my time, and staying on top of my assignments. Setting goals and finding a purpose for being in college have also led to my success."

> "In my first-year-experience course . . . I . . . quickly learned the importance of organizing, managing my time, and staying on top of my assignments."

Maria enjoys attending her college. "Here everyone guides you," she says. "You can ask for help from your instructors, other students, and a lot of other people like tutors or counselors. I think I would be lost at a university in my first year, not having anyone to teach me about the rules of the college and how it is different from high school."

Maria, like many other two-year college students, hopes to graduate and find a good job. Today, the workplace is changing so much that most people will need some education beyond high school to support themselves and their families properly. In the United States, more than 67 percent of high school graduates (approximately 21 million students) attend college. As the job market changes, even some students with four-year college degrees are attending two-year colleges to prepare themselves for a second career.

Because a college education is so important, this book will present you with a set of strategies to help you succeed in college. As you're settling into your new college routine, we want to welcome you to the world of higher education.

The fact that you are reading this textbook probably means that, like Maria, you are enrolled in a first-year seminar or "college success" course at a two-year college. Both the course (possibly the most important course you will take) and this textbook (possibly the most important textbook you will read) are all about improving your chances for success in college and beyond. Before you start reading, you probably have some questions.

Did I Make the Right Choice to Attend a Two-Year College?

You have joined about 7 million other students enrolled in more than 1,400 two-year colleges in the United States. These colleges have one single goal: to help their students graduate and become successful in their future career or studies. Two-year colleges are a great starting point because they provide affordable and supportive environments where students can understand their strengths, work on their weaknesses, and grow into their future roles. If your goal is to start a career or change the one you already have, you have made the right choice to be at a two-year college. If you want to transfer to a four-year college or university to get a higher degree, you too have made the right choice to start at a two-year college.

Why Am I Taking This Course?

Research shows that college success courses will help you and other first-year students avoid some of the mistakes—both academic and personal—that many beginning students make. This course will also help you achieve your goal of graduating from your college and offer skills and practical advice that can help you become successful not only in college but also later in life. Each chapter in this textbook includes activities that invite you to work on your own, discuss your ideas with a small group of students or the whole class, or try doing new things. All chapters introduce and define key words used in college and related to the topics covered in this course. In addition, every chapter offers a technology tip to help you use different tools and systems effectively.

What Am I Going to Get Out of This Course?

This course will provide a safe environment for sharing your successes and your challenges, getting to know other first-year students, beginning a lasting relationship with your instructor and some other students, developing your academic plan based on your strengths and interests, and thinking about your career after graduating from college or transferring to a four-year college or university.

As individuals with many years of experience working with first-year students, we're well aware that starting college can be challenging. But we also know that if you apply the ideas in this book to your everyday life, you are more likely to enjoy your time in college, graduate, and achieve your life goals.

To begin, in this first chapter, we'll discuss how you fit into the whole idea of college. We'll consider why the United States has more colleges and universities than any other country in the world. We'll also help you explore the purposes of college—many that your college might define for you—and set goals for your college experience. Even more important, we'll help you define your purposes for being here and offer many strategies to help you succeed.

1.2 THE COLLEGE EXPERIENCE

So what is the college experience? Depending on who you are, what your life situation is, and why you decided to enroll, college can mean different things. Some students attend two-year colleges to complete their first two years close to home and at a low cost; then they move on to a four-year college or university for a higher degree. Others want to be trained for specific careers and get a job after graduation. Still others may already have jobs but want to change their careers or improve their chances for a promotion. College is the main responsibility for some students; for others, it can be an additional major responsibility added to family or work obligations. Some students come to the United States from other countries just to study. College is really far more than any single image you might carry around in your head.

Basically, college is a process of formal education that will help prepare you to achieve success after you graduate. Because knowledge and information expand all the time, however, college classes won't teach you everything you will ever need to know. Perhaps the most important skill you will learn in college is how to keep learning throughout your life. Your college classes can give you the experience you will need in creating, managing, and using new information.

Why College Is Important to Our Society

American society values higher education, which explains why the United States has so many colleges and universities—more than 4,400. College is the primary way in which people can improve their lives. What you earn in the future will depend on what you learn now. As Figure 1.1 shows, the more education you have, the more likely you are to be employed and the higher your earnings will be.

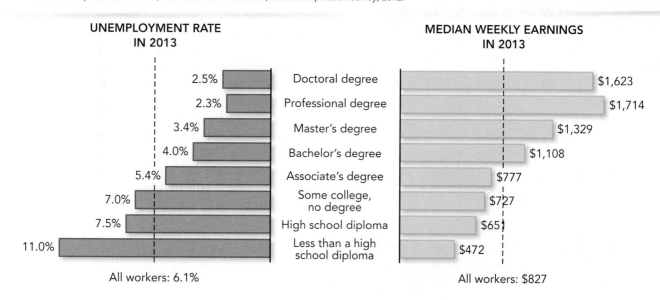

FIGURE 1.1 > Education Pays

Source: U.S. Department of Labor, Bureau of Labor Statistics, *Current Population Survey*, 2012.

In most countries today, receiving a college degree gives you the opportunity to achieve your goals and dreams regardless of your background, race, ethnicity, national origin, immigration status, family income level, family history, or personal connections. Two-year colleges, in particular, play an important role in providing diverse students with educational opportunities because they accept all students regardless of their past academic performance and help them achieve success. In addition, students can get a great education at a much lower cost than at a four-year college or university.

College is also important because it prepares citizens for leadership roles. Without a college degree, you would find it difficult to be a leader in your community, company, profession, or military unit.

In addition to increasing your earning power, college is about helping you become a better thinker—someone who doesn't believe everything he or she hears or reads but instead looks for evidence before forming an opinion. Developing such thinking skills will give you the ability to make sound decisions throughout your life.

Although college is often thought of as a time when high school students become young adults, we realize that many two-year college students are already adults, some with families of their own. Whatever your age, college can be a time when you

- Take some risks,
- Learn new things,
- Meet new and different people—all in a relatively safe environment.

It's OK to experiment in college, within limits, because that's what college is designed for.

Explore Your Options

College is a great place to connect with others, take some risks, and find a career: nursing, business, law enforcement, or perhaps culinary arts.
Source: © Nik Wheeler/Corbis.

College will provide you with numerous opportunities for developing a variety of social networks, both in person and online. These networks will help you make friends with instructors and fellow students who share your interests and goals. Social media (such as Facebook and Twitter) provide ways to expand your social networks in college; most colleges and on-campus organizations have their own Facebook pages where students share different kinds of information.

College definitely can and should be enjoyable, and we hope it will be for you. College provides the chance to

- Meet new people and make new friends.
- Explore student clubs.
- Take advantage of leadership opportunities.
- Join athletic teams.
- Participate in many exciting activities and events.

Getting involved in campus life improves your college experience and your chances for a good job, so make sure to take advantage of student activities on your campus. For example, some clubs are related to professions; an education club may include students who plan to become teachers, or a business club may give students an opportunity to learn more about companies in their area and to interact with business professionals and leaders.

In addition to being a pleasant experience, college is a lot of work. Being a college student means spending hours studying each week, staying up late at night or getting up early in the morning to study, taking exams, and possibly working harder than you ever have. For many students, college becomes like a job with defined duties, expectations, and obligations. If you already have a job, this will be your second one.

Most important, college will be a set of experiences that will help you to further define and achieve your own goals. You might feel that you know exactly what you want to do with your life—where you want to go from here. Or, like many students, you might be struggling to find where you fit in life and work. It is possible that as you discover more about yourself and your abilities, your purpose for coming to college will change. In fact, a majority of college students change their plans at least once during the college years, and some students find they need to transfer to another college or university to meet their academic goals.

Here are some additional questions to ask yourself as you continue thinking about why you're at your two-year college:

- Am I here to find out who I am and to study a subject that I am truly interested in, regardless of whether it leads to a career?

- Am I here to complete my first two years of college to transfer to a four-year college or university?
- Am I here to prepare myself for employment?
- Am I here to improve specific skills for a job I already have?

YOUR TURN › WORK TOGETHER

Ask a couple of your classmates why they decided to attend this two-year college and what they expect college to be like. Compare your reasons and expectations with theirs. Do you find similarities or differences?

SETTING GOALS FOR YOUR COLLEGE EXPERIENCE AND BEYOND

1.3

What is success? Is success about money, friendship, or power? Is it about achieving excellence in college and beyond or about finding a purpose in your life? For most people, success is a combination of all of these factors and more. While luck or "who you know" may play a role in success, first and foremost it will be the result of your planning and hard work.

To become successful, where do you begin? First, it is important to establish goals—goals for today, this week, this month, this term, this year, and beyond. While some students prefer to go with the flow and let life happen to them, those students are more likely to waste their time and less likely to achieve success in college or in a career. So instead of simply reacting to what college and life present, think about how you can take more control over the decisions and choices you make now to achieve your goals. While it is easy to make general plans, you need to determine which short-term steps are necessary if those plans are to become a reality.

As you plan your college experience and life goals, think about your personal strengths. For instance, are you interested in science? Do you like to help sick people? If your answers to these questions are yes, then you may want to consider a career in health care like nursing or physical therapy. Do you like to help people learn? Do you think you enjoy teaching? If so, you might want to think about education. Do you like to work with computers? Do you like to design games? If so, you may want to think about computer science or game design. Your campus advising and career centers can help you discover your strengths and weaknesses, which, combined with your interests, can help you explore career choices.

Savage Chickens   by Doug Savage

www.savagechickens.com

Score!

Do you have friends who are lucky or have a knack for getting what they want? What seems to be luck can often be a function of careful planning and setting short- and long-term goals.

Source: © Doug Savage

Getting Started

College is an ideal time for setting or resetting short- and long-term goals. A short-term goal might be to read a few pages from your history text twice a week for the first exam. A long-term goal might be to take college courses required for your program that would help you achieve your career goals.

Thinking about a career might seem unrelated to some of the general courses you are required to take in your first year. It may be hard to see the connection between a history or math course and what you want to do with the rest of your life. If you're open to learning, you may discover potential areas of interest that you have not considered before—areas of interest that may lead you to discover a new career path.

Follow these guidelines to set some short-term goals, and consider how they fall within the framework of setting goals that are *Specific*, *Measurable*, *Attainable*, *Relevant*, and achievable within a given *Time* (SMART):

1. Be specific about what you want to achieve and when.
2. State your goal in measurable terms.
3. Be sure that the goal is achievable. If you don't have the necessary skills, strengths, and resources to achieve your goal, change it. Be sure you really want to reach the goal. Don't set out to work toward something only because you want to please others.
4. Know how the goal is relevant to your life and why the goal matters. Be sure your goal helps your larger plan and can give you a sense of moving forward.
5. Consider whether the goal is achievable within the time frame you desire. Consider the difficulties you might have. Plan for ways you might deal with problems. Decide which goal comes next. How will you begin? Create steps and a time line for reaching your next goal.

For instance, let's assume that after you graduate you might want to get a job. What are some short-term goals that would help you reach this long-term objective? One goal might be to take courses that prepare you for the career of your choice. That goal isn't very specific, however, nor does it state a particular time period. A much more specific goal would be to decide which courses you should take in which term. An even more specific goal would be to review the college catalog, identify all the courses you want to take, and list them on a personal timeline. You could also look for courses that give you the opportunity to gain some experience and help you better understand what kind of work you might be doing after you graduate. You can see an academic counselor or adviser who can help you create a program plan, specifying which courses you need to take and in what order.

FIGURE 1.2 ❯ Practice Setting SMART Goals

Using this chart, try to set one goal in each of the areas listed: academic, career, personal, and financial. Follow the goal through time, from immediate to long term. An example is provided for you.

TYPES OF GOALS	IMMEDIATE (this week)	SHORT-TERM (this term)	LONG-TERM (this year)
Example: Academic	*I will list all of my tests and projects due dates on my academic calendar.*	*I will make a file folder to store my own test and exam grades in case there is a discrepancy with my final course grades.*	*I will search online for programs in my field at four-year colleges and universities of my choice to determine if I have the grades to be admitted.*
Academic			
Career			
Personal			
Financial			

It is always good to have some actual experience before making a final decision about your future work. Your goal for this week could be doing an online search or visiting your campus career counselor to find out about the knowledge and skills that your future job requires.

Before working toward any long-term goal, it's important for you to be realistic and honest with yourself. Is this your goal—one you yourself want—or is this a goal that a parent or friend said was right for you? Given your abilities and interests, is the goal realistic? Remember that dreaming up long-term goals is the easy part. To reach your goals, you need to be specific and systematic about the steps you will take today, this week, and throughout your college experience. Because attending college costs a great deal of money, you need to set goals and make decisions about your major and career early to avoid any unnecessary coursework and extra cost.

Academic Planning: Choosing a Major

Some students come to college with clear direction; they know what they want to study, what jobs and careers they would like to enter after college, or to which four-year colleges and universities they want to transfer after graduation. Others enter college as undecided, understanding that their experience with different academic subjects will help them make an academic choice. Still others start a program of study but are uncertain how that program can help them find a job later. Each of these situations is normal.

Even before you have figured out your own purpose for college, you might be required to select a program of study also referred to as a **major,** an area of study like psychology, engineering, education, or nursing. In every major, students take a variety of courses; some are directly related to the area of study, while others are general education and elective courses. For example, all students should take college-level math and English courses as part of general education, but they can choose electives depending on their interests.

Many students change majors as they better understand their strengths and weaknesses, learn more about career options, and become interested in different areas of study. Some two-year colleges allow you to be undecided for a while or to select liberal arts as your major until you make a decision about what to study. It's okay if you don't know immediately which major or career to choose. An academic adviser or counselor can provide you with proper information and guidance to make a decision about your major.

Choosing a major early allows you to better plan the courses you need to take and get connected with instructors and students within your program. Later, you might change the major you chose during your first year. Try a major you think you'll like, and see what develops. Your major may or may not match the title of your future job.

Even if you are ready to select a major, it's a good idea to keep an open mind and consider your options. You might learn that the career you always dreamed of isn't what you thought it would be at all. Working part-time or participating in co-curricular activities such as joining a club can help you make decisions and learn more about yourself in the process. Students who connect what they learn inside and outside the classroom have a better, more satisfying college experience than those who focus only on classwork.

If you are planning to transfer to a four-year college or university after graduating from your two-year college, it is beneficial for you to choose your major early, explore the available academic programs, and select your courses based on the requirements of the college or university of your choice. Completing courses that you can transfer will help you save both time and money. Most two-year colleges have a transfer center or, at the very least, a transfer counselor whose job is to provide academic advisement and prepare students for a successful transfer to a four-year college or university.

Your major and career ultimately have to fit your interests and your overall life goals. How you connect your classes with your extracurricular activities and work experience prepares you for a successful transition to your career.

Connecting Majors and Careers

At some point, you might ask yourself: Why am I in college? Although it sounds like an easy question to answer, it's not. Many students would immediately respond, "So I can get a good job or education for a specific career." Yet some majors do not lead to a specific career path or job. You actually can enter most career paths from any number of academic majors. Only a few technical or professional fields—such as accounting, nursing, and engineering—are tied to specific majors.

Exploring your interests is the best way to choose an academic major and a career. Here are some helpful strategies:

1. **Know your interests, skills, values, and personality.** Because today's college graduates face competition in entering the world of work, employers expect them to be fully prepared. The chapter on Discovering How You Learn, will guide you in assessing your unique style of learning, connecting that style with your academic success, interacting with the world, and making decisions about your future. Assessing your skills and personality is particularly important if you have no idea what you are interested in studying or what career paths are related to your choice of major.

2. **Pay attention to grades.** Employers and four-year colleges and universities want candidates with good grades. Good grades show that you have the necessary knowledge and skills and a strong work ethic, which are very important to all employers.

3. **Explore career paths.** Talking to or observing professionals in your areas of interest is an excellent way to try before you buy. Participation in "job shadowing" or "a-day-in-the-life" programs is time well spent. Many college graduates enjoy being career mentors for current students. This is also a great way to network with those working in your area of interest. Ask your career center about scheduling one of these opportunities.

4. **Create a digital footprint.** Have you Googled yourself lately? Do you like what you see? Would an employer? Your online image matters, and it can influence how others see you and what they think of you. If you do not like your online image, improve it. This may mean deleting some photos or removing the tags from comments or pictures online that others have posted.

5. **Discover leadership opportunities.** Companies want to hire leaders and look for leadership experience in college students when hiring for internships or employment. Being active in a campus club or organization helps develop your skills in leadership and teamwork. Volunteer to be a team leader when working with a group on classroom projects. Look for campus leadership employment opportunities, such as becoming an orientation leader. Active involvement in these opportunities will help you improve your leadership skills.

6. **Develop computer skills.** Most of today's college students are comfortable with technology; however, not all technology experience is equal. Holding the record for fastest text messaging or reaching the highest level on your favorite video game does not mean you are proficient in the *right* kinds of technology needed to be successful in college and

beyond. As you begin to make decisions about your career path, explore and become familiar with technologies used in your field. Take advantage of the computer courses and workshops your college offers, or learn by experimenting with different software programs on your own.

7. **Build communication skills.** The ability to communicate verbally with people inside and outside of an organization is one of the most important skills that employers look for in new graduates. Take every available opportunity to practice communicating, whether through classroom presentations, group work, leadership, and job opportunities. Also pay attention to nonverbal communication skills. Rolling your eyes, for example, may not be an appropriate response when your instructor is speaking with you.

8. **Take advantage of experiential learning. Experiential learning** is learning by doing and from experience. Internships and service learning courses are two common forms of experiential learning, but they are not the only ways to gain experience in your area of study. Find opportunities to apply what you learn in your courses to what you do outside the classroom.

YOUR TURN > WORK TOGETHER

With two or three other students, discuss how you imagine your first job after college. Will you be working in an office, a hospital, a studio, or a lab? Or will you be working outdoors? If any of your classmates already have careers, find out why and how they chose those careers.

1.4

MAKING THE TRANSITION

If you just graduated from high school, you will find some clear differences between high school and college. For instance, in college you are probably part of a more diverse student body, not just in terms of race but also in terms of age, religion, political opinions, and life experiences. You have more potential friends to choose from; they may or may not be from your neighborhood, place of worship, or high school.

Also, you can choose from many more types of courses, but managing your time is sure to be more difficult because your classes will meet on different days and times, and you will have additional commitments, including work, family, and community activities. In high school, you may have had frequent tests and quizzes, but tests in college are sometimes given only twice a term. You will most likely be required to do more writing in college than in high school, and you will be encouraged to do original research and examine different points of view on a topic. You will be expected to study outside of class, prepare assignments, read different materials, and be ready for in-class discussions.

Your instructors might rely far less on textbooks and far more on lectures than your high school teachers did. But they also might allow you more freedom to express views that are different from theirs. You may also have opportunities to share and use some of your personal and work experience. Some of your instructors may have private offices and keep regular **office hours**, the posted hours when they are in their office and available to students. It's up to you to take the initiative to visit your instructors during their office hours. Most instructors must keep office hours and must be available during that time, so don't feel like you are asking them for a special favor. Check with your instructors to find out if you need to make an appointment before coming to their offices. You might be able to ask your instructor a quick question before or after class. While you will be able to get far more help by actually visiting his or her office. You can ask the instructor for direct help with any questions or problems that you have. By taking advantage of office hours, you will also let the instructor know that you are serious about learning.

Instructors who teach part-time at your college are called **adjuncts**, and they may not have assigned offices. Adjuncts often meet with their students before or after class or by appointment. Many students develop close relationships with their instructors. All college instructors are available to help you with your coursework, and you may also find one or more to be lifelong mentors and friends. The best way to make a connection with your instructors is to schedule appointments early in the term.

Connecting with Your Instructors

One of the most important types of relationships you can develop in college is with your instructors. The primary responsibility of two-year college instructors is *to teach*, which is often not the case at four-year colleges and universities, where teaching is less important than research. Relationships with instructors are based on mutual respect. Instructors who respect students treat them fairly and are willing to help them both in and out of class. Students who respect instructors come to class regularly and take their work seriously.

Instructors may have expectations that are different from those of their students. All instructors expect students to come to class, do the assigned work in the best way they can, listen and participate in class, and not give up when they have to learn a difficult lesson. In college, it is your responsibility to meet the expectations of your instructors. In return, you should expect your instructors to be organized and prepared, to be knowledgeable about the subjects they are teaching, to provide comments on your papers and exams, and to grade your work fairly. You should be able to approach your instructors when you need academic help or if you have a personal problem that may make studying difficult.

Finding Your Place

In your first weeks in college you may feel alone. You may not immediately meet others who look, dress, or think like you, but your college will offer many ways for you to connect with other students. Soon you'll find new friends with whom you'll share a lot in common.

Source: © Will & Deni McIntyre /Corbis

Of all the relationships you experience in college, those you have with instructors may be among the most enjoyable and influential. But you must take the initiative to visit your instructors during their office hours. Instructors are available to help you with your coursework, and you may also find one or more to be lifelong mentors and friends.

If you ever have a problem with an instructor, ask for a meeting to discuss your problem and see if you can work things out. If the instructor refuses, go to a person in a higher position in the department or college. If the problem is a grade, remember that you cannot force the instructor to change a grade. However, you can always speak with your instructor about your grade, find out what mistakes you made, and see how you can improve your grade in the future. Most important, don't let a bad experience change your feelings about college. Each instructor will probably be out of your life by the end of the term, so if there are problems, just do your best, focus on your studies, and get through the course.

Challenges and Opportunities for Nontraditional Students

If you are a **nontraditional student**—someone who is not an eighteen-year-old recent high school graduate and may have a job and their own family—you might find that college presents both opportunities *and* challenges. While college can be an opportunity for a new beginning, working full-time and attending college at night, on weekends, or both can mean extra stress, especially with a family at home.

Nontraditional students often experience a lack of freedom because of many important competing responsibilities. Working, caring for a family, and having other responsibilities will compete for the time and attention it takes to do your best or even to simply stay in college. You might wonder how you will ever get through college and still manage to take care of your family or others who depend on you. You might worry that they won't understand your need to study many hours outside class—behind closed doors or in your campus library—to keep up with your coursework. As you walk around college, you might feel uncertain about your ability to keep up with academic work. You also might find it difficult to relate to younger students who sometimes don't seem to take academic work seriously.

In spite of your concerns, you should know that many college instructors value working with nontraditional students because your life experiences have shown you the importance of an education. Nontraditional students tend to be very motivated because of their level of maturity and experience that will make up for any initial difficulties they might have. As an experienced person, you will also bring a unique and rich point of view to what you're learning in your classes.

Attitude, Motivation, and Commitment

What attitudes and behaviors will help you to achieve your goals and be successful in college? If you are fresh out of high school, it will be important for you to learn to deal with more freedom. Your college instructors are not going to tell you what, how, or when to study. In almost every aspect of your life, you will have to have primary responsibility for your own attitudes and behaviors.

If you are a nontraditional student, you might find yourself with less freedom than others in your college: You might have a difficult daily commute, or you might have to arrange and pay for child care. You might have to manage work and school responsibilities and still find time for family and other duties. You may also need to let your family know that attending college means that you have to spend time studying, and that you may ask them for help or need their support more than ever.

The practical challenges you are facing may worry you. But what will motivate you to be successful? What about the enormous investment of time and money that getting a college degree requires? Are you convinced that the investment will pay off? Have you selected a major, or is this on your list of things to do? Do you know where to go when you need help with a personal or financial problem?

Thoughts like these are very common. Although your classmates might not say it out loud, many of them share your doubts and fears. This course will be a safe place for you to talk about all of these issues with people who care about you and your success in college.

YOUR TURN > TRY IT

Write some synonyms for the word *motivation*. Do these words describe the way you feel about college in general? Do they describe the way you feel about all of your classes? List what motivates you the most in attending college.

_____

_____

_____

Understanding College Terminology

In college, you will hear a lot of terms that may be new to you. It is important for you to learn these terms as quickly as possible. The following is a list of commonly used terms and their meanings:

Academic plan: An academic plan lists the courses you need to take and complete in every program of study to graduate with a degree.

Credit hours: Credit hours represent the number of clock hours you spend in each class every week during a term and the number of credits you will earn if you satisfactorily complete a course. A one-credit course generally meets for 50 to 60 minutes once a week.

Degree: The term *degree* refers to the type of diploma students receive after graduation. Two-year colleges have associate in arts (AA), associate in science (AS), and associate in applied science (AAS) degree programs. They all carry about sixty credits. AA and AS degrees, and some AAS degrees, allow students to transfer to four-year colleges or universities. However, the AAS degree has fewer transferable courses. Most courses in AAS programs focus on training students for a specific profession or career.

General education: General education courses are introductory courses—such as English, math, history, or psychology—that almost every student will have to take in order to earn a degree.

Grade point average (GPA): Your GPA is the average of points you receive based on your grades for each course. Generally, college GPAs range from 0 (F) to 4.0 (A or A+).

Grading criteria: Every syllabus includes grading criteria that show how assignments, tests, papers, exams, or presentations are graded and what percentage of the final grade they each carry. The criteria also show how letter grades (A, B, C, D, F) are calculated: A = 95–100, A– = 90–95, and so on.

Major: A major is an area of study like psychology, engineering, education, or nursing.

Syllabus: A syllabus is a contract between the students and the instructor in each course. Generally, instructors provide the syllabus to their students during the first class session. It includes basic information about the course, the instructor's expectations, grading criteria, the attendance policy, and a week-by-week plan for the course, and assignments, exams, papers, and projects. Make sure you review the syllabus for every course carefully at the beginning of the term and keep them in your course notebook with other course materials.

Transcript: Your transcript is your academic record; it shows your major, when you took particular courses, your grades for each course, and your overall GPA.

Transfer policies: Transfer policies are rules and regulations about which two-year college courses you can transfer to a four-year college or university. For example, some four-year institutions accept only those courses in which students have earned a grade of C or better.

EMAIL ETIQUETTE

THE PROBLEM *You need help with an assignment and have to send your instructor an email, but you've never sent an email to a teacher before.*

THE FIX *Take a few minutes to figure out what exactly you need to ask, jot down your main points, and then construct a clear and concise email.*

HOW TO DO IT

As you have been planning for college, you have probably heard how you'll use technology as a student. You need to activate your college email as soon as possible to receive information regarding class cancellations, weather-related closings, student events, and other types of college communication or what your instructors may be sending you. You should check your college email daily or at least every other day.

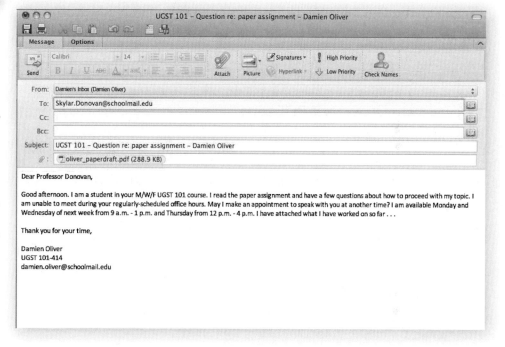

Whether your class is online or face-to-face, at some point you will need to communicate with your instructor via email. Although you may prefer to use Facebook, Twitter, or Instagram, be sure to use email to communicate with your instructors unless they tell you otherwise. Writing emails to your instructors is different from writing emails to your friends.

1. Look at the example shown here and follow its format. It's best to use your college email address, because it has your name and your college's email address helping your professor recognize you as a student. If you have to use another email address, use a professional, simple address that includes your name.

2. Make the subject line informative. Your instructor might receive hundreds of emails every day, and a relevant subject like the name of the course or the assignment helps them respond faster. A subject line like "Class" or "Question" isn't helpful; a blank subject line usually goes to the spam folder.

3. Address your instructor with respect. Think about how you address your instructor in class, or look at your syllabus to see their proper title. If an instructor uses *Doctor*, then you should use *Doctor*. If you don't know their title, you can never go wrong with *Dear Professor*, plus your instructor's last name.

4. Sign every email with your full name, course number, and email address.

5. When attaching files to your email (a skill you should have), use widely accepted file formats like .doc, .docx, or .pdf. Also, be sure your last name is included in the file name you use. See the example shown.

THINK
WRITE
APPLY

THINK

Think about what you have learned in this chapter about the benefits of college. List the reasons why college is important to you or what motivates you to do your best in college.

1. _____

   _____

2. _____

   _____

3. _____

   _____

WRITE

Take a few minutes to think about what you found most useful or meaningful in this chapter, and write a paragraph explaining it to a friend. Did anything that was covered in this chapter leave you with more questions than answers?

_____

_____

_____

_____

_____

APPLY

What are your goals for this term? Using the SMART goal-setting guide on pages 10–11, list five goals on the chart on page 21.

Goal	Timeline	Steps	Importance	Difficulties	How to Deal with Difficulties
Visiting my instructors during office hours	Visit each instructor at least once by the middle of the term.	1. Mark my calendar to meet with instructors. 2. Think of questions I need to ask each instructor.	High	I may not be available during an instructor's office hours.	Email the instructor and ask for an appointment.

AT YOUR COLLEGE

VISIT . . .	*IF YOU NEED HELP . . .*
Academic Advising Center	selecting courses, obtaining information on degree requirements, and deciding on a major.
Academic Learning/Skills Center	with memory skills and studying for exams.
Computer Center	using Word, Excel, PowerPoint, and email.
Counseling Center	dealing with personal problems and stress management.
Math Center	improving your math skills.
Writing Center	writing your first paper or revising a first draft.
Career Center	with career interest assessments, counseling, finding a major, job and internship listings, interviewing with prospective employers, and preparing résumés and interview skills.
Transfer Center	finding information about transfer policies, programs at four-year colleges and universities that you can transfer to, and meeting the requirements of transfer.
Adult Reentry Center	as a returning student, in making supportive contacts with other adult students and gathering information about services such as child care.
Veterans Office	as a veteran, in managing financial aid and paperwork.
International Student Services	as an international student, in making the transition to a new country and culture as well as to the college.

MY COLLEGE'S RESOURCES

2 Managing Time, Energy, and Money

PRE-READING ACTIVITY: This chapter is about managing your most valuable resources: time, energy, and money. Managing each of these is challenging for almost all college students. List two challenges you have in managing your time, energy, and money. Do you have control over how you spend your time and money? How about how you manage your energy?

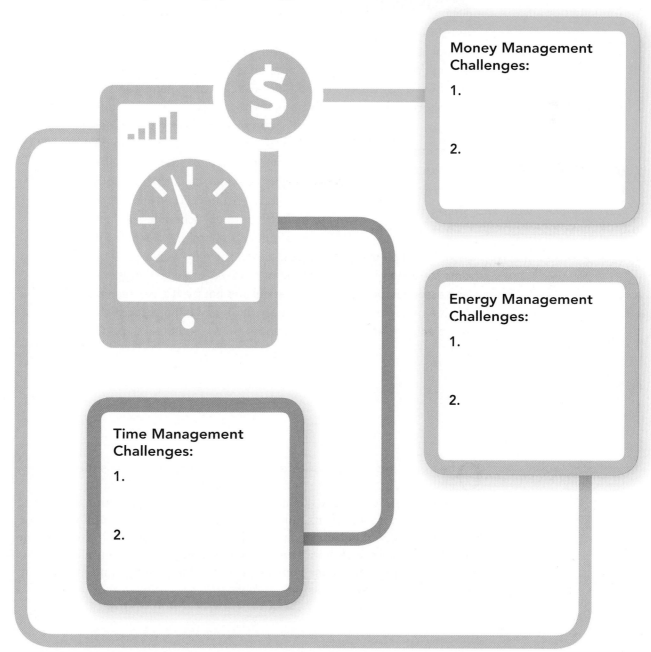

Money Management Challenges:

1.

2.

Energy Management Challenges:

1.

2.

Time Management Challenges:

1.

2.

📁 **PROFILE** ✖

Jasmine Williams, 25
Business Major, *Two-year college*

Source: Tyler Olson /Shutterstock

When Jasmine Williams started college, she knew that she would have many competing obligations: work, family, and studying for her courses. Holding a job as a nursing assistant and taking care of her family were already demanding, and Jasmine was determined to pursue her educational goal to become a registered nurse. In the middle of her first term, she felt pressure from her job responsibilities, family members who needed her time and attention, and school assignments that were getting more complex; she did not have enough energy to do it all. "Sometimes I just got overwhelmed with school and just wanted to work or take care of my family and would put my schoolwork on the back burner. This had some bad side effects," she explains. "Once I saw the drop in my grades, I knew that I had to reprioritize and get back on track."

Jasmine needed to work, but she realized if she put herself and her family on a strict budget, she could cut back on her work hours. Then she prioritized her time to maintain her busy schedule and her sanity.

"My main priorities are family, school, and work," she says. "I find places in my schedule to fit them in every week and also find time to reenergize myself a little bit, too. All of these things are important and essential for me to be successful and happy. It's like each part of my life is a puzzle piece. If I don't keep making sure that each piece fits, or if any piece is missing, the puzzle doesn't work and breaks apart."

> "It's like each part of my life is a puzzle piece. If I don't make sure each piece fits, or if any piece is missing, the puzzle doesn't work and breaks apart."

One of the keys to Jasmine's success is organization across the three main aspects of her life—family, work, and college. Because there is only so much time in a day, Jasmine focused on prioritizing and scheduling to make room for everything, including time for her to relax and enjoy her life. She prioritized her family and college over her work, and she was able to cut back on her work hours and stick to a budget. Getting organized involves learning how to use your resources—time, energy, and money—in the most effective ways possible.

Different people approach time differently based on their personality and background. Some people are always on time while others are almost always late. In every class, some students enter all due dates for assignments on a calendar as soon as they receive each syllabus. Other students take a more laid-back approach and prefer to go with the flow rather than follow a daily or weekly schedule. These students might deal well with the unexpected, but they also might leave everything to the last minute and not be as successful as they could be if they managed their time differently. Improving your organizational skills can help you do better at school, work, and life. Most two-year college students have a lot of responsibilities in addition to attending classes and studying; they often work and have families to take care of, especially if they are nontraditional students. For these students in particular, more organization almost always leads to more success, so the time and energy they spend to get organized will pay off hire. Think of it this way: If *you* were hiring someone for a job, wouldn't you an organized person who gets things done on time?

Taking Control of Your Time

The first step to effective time management is recognizing that you can be in control. The next time you find yourself saying, "I don't have time," stop and ask yourself whether it is actually true. Do you *really* not have time, or have you made a choice not to make time for a particular task or activity?

When we say we don't have time, we imply that we don't have a choice. We do have a choice because we have control over how we use our time and how many commitments and small decisions we choose to make. We have control over what time we get up in the morning; how much sleep we get; and how much time we spend studying, working, and exercising. All of these small decisions have a big impact on our success in college and in life.

Your Head Cannot Be Your Only Planner

How you manage your time reflects what you value—and what consequences you are willing to accept when you make certain choices. If you value time with friends above all, your academic work likely takes a backseat to social activities. How you manage your time corresponds to how successful you will be in college and life. Almost all successful people use some sort of calendar or planner to help them keep up with their appointments, assignments, tasks, and other important activities. Using your head as your only planner, trying to remember everything you have to do without recording it anywhere, means that you will probably forget important events and deadlines.

Plan Your Academic Term

Getting a bird's-eye view—or big picture—of each term will allow you to plan effectively. An **academic calendar** shows important dates that are specific to your campus: financial aid, registration, add/drop deadlines; midterm and final exam dates; holidays and graduation deadlines. You may have received an academic calendar when you registered for classes; you can also find the academic calendar posted on your college Web site.

Knowing your big-picture academic deadlines will be helpful as you add deadlines for specific assignments, papers, and exams into your calendar. It is also important to refer to your college's academic calendar to add important dates and deadlines such as when the registration starts and ends and when you need to pay for your courses or file your application for financial aid or scholarships. Remember that you have to keep track of important dates not only in your own life but also in the lives of those close to you—birthdays, doctors' appointments, work schedules, travel, your children's activities, visits from out-of-town guests, and so on. Different aspects of your life have different sorts of time requirements, and the goal is to stay on top of all of them.

You might prefer to use an electronic calendar on your phone, tablet, laptop, or other devices. (See the Tech Tip on p. 50 for different options.) Regardless of the format you prefer it's a good idea to begin the academic term by reviewing your syllabus for each course and then completing a preview (Figure 2.1), recording all of your commitments for each day, and using different colors for each category:

- Classes
- Study time for each class you're taking
- Tests and assignment due dates
- Personal obligations such as work, family, friends
- Scheduled social events (include phone numbers in case you need to cancel)

Recording your daily commitments allows you to examine your toughest weeks each month and during the term. If research paper deadlines and test dates fall during the same week, find time to finish some assignments

FIGURE 2.1 › Monthly Calendar

Using the course syllabi provided by your instructors, create your own monthly calendars for your entire term. Provide details such as the number of hours you anticipate spending on each assignment or task.

MONTH: SEPTEMBER

MONDAY	TUESDAY	WEDNESDAY	THURSDAY	FRIDAY	SATURDAY	SUNDAY
					1	2
3 9–12 Work	4 First Day of Classes 9–12 Psychology 2–5 Work *8–9 Psychology: Read Ch. 1*	5 9–12 Work 1–4 Math *8–10 Math HW1*	6 10-1 English 2-5 Work *8-10 English: Read Ch. 1*	7 10-12 Work Mom's doctor's appointment 2-4 *9-10 Psychology: Review Notes*	8 10-4 Work *8-9 Math HW 1* *9-10 English: Read Ch. 1*	9 *2-4 Review Math Notes* *6-10 Party at Susan's [235-523-6898]*
10 9-12 Work 1-5 Biology 6-8 Nina's Parent-Teacher Conference	11 9-12 Psychology 2-5 Work *8-10 Biology: Read Ch. 1*	12 9-12 Work 1-4 Math *8-10 Psychology: Read Ch. 2*	13 10-1 English 2-5 Work *7-8 Math HW 2* *9-11 Biology: Read Ch. 1*	14 10-12 Work 1-3 Lunch with Mary *6-7 Start English Summary Paper*	15 10-4 Work 4-6 Shopping *9-10 Finish English Summary Paper*	16 *10-1 Study for Psychology Test* *6-8 Review Math notes for Quiz 1*
17 9-12 Work 1-5 Biology *7-10 Study for Psychology Test*	18 9-12 Psychology Psychology Test 1 2-5 Work *8-9 Review Math notes for Quiz 1*	19 Work 9-12 Math 1-4 Math Quiz 1 *8-9 Revise English Summary Paper*	20 10-1 English English Summary Paper due 2-5 Work *8-10 Biology: Read Ch. 2*	21 10-12 Work 1-2 Attend student club meeting *6-9 Math HW 3*	22 10-4 Work *5-7 Psychology: Read Ch. 3* *9-10 English: Read Ch. 2*	23 *10-12 Biology: Read Ch. 2* *9-10 Biology: Lab Report 1*
24 9-12 Work 1-5 Biology *6-8 Math Tutoring* *10-11 Math HW 3*	25 9-12 Psychology 2-5 Work *8-10 Biology: Read Ch. 3* *10-11 Math HW 3*	26 9-12 Work 1-4 Math *8-9 Psychology: Read Ch. 4* *9-10 Prepare English Paper Outline*	27 10-1 English 2-5 Work *7-9 Math HW* *9-10 Review Biology Notes*	28 10-12 Work *1-3 Meet with Biology Study Group* *8-9 Biology: Lab report 2* *9-11 English: Read Ch. 3*	29 10-4 Work 4-6 Nina's Birthday Party Preparation *8-9 English: Read Ch. 3*	30 10-3 Nina's Birthday Party Preparation 4-8 Nina's Birthday

early to free up study time. If you use an electronic calendar, set reminders for these important deadlines and dates.

Overall, you should create monthly (Figure 2.1), weekly (Figure 2.2), and daily (Figure 2.3) views of your calendar. All three views are available in an electronic planner, but if you are using paper planners you can create monthly, weekly, and daily calendars, too.

Once you complete your monthly templates, you can put them together to preview your entire academic term. Remember to provide

FIGURE 2.2 › Weekly Timetable

Using your term calendar, create your own weekly timetable using a conventional template or one that uses an app such as LifeTopix. At the beginning of your term, track all of your activities for a full week by entering into your schedule everything you do and how much time each task requires. Use this record to help you estimate the time you will need for similar activities in the future.

SEPTEMBER

Time	MONDAY 3	TUESDAY 4 First Day of Classes	WEDNESDAY 5	THURSDAY 6	FRIDAY 7	SATURDAY 8	SUNDAY 9
5 am							
6 am							
7 am							
8 am							
9 am	Work	Psychology	Work				
10 am				English	Work	Work	
11 am							
12 pm							
1 pm			Math				
2 pm		Work		Work	Mom's doctor's appointment		Review Math Notes
3 pm							
4 pm							
5 pm							
6 pm							Party at Susan's [235-523-6898]
7 pm							
8 pm		Psychology: Read Ch. 1	Math HW 1	English: Read Ch. 1		Math HW 1	
9 pm					Psychology: Review Notes	English: Read Ch. 1	
10 pm							
11 pm							
12 pm							

details such as the number of hours you anticipate spending on each assignment or task.

As you create your schedule, try to reserve study time for each class and for each assignment. Not all assignments are equal. Estimate how much time you will need for each one, and begin your work well before the assignment is due. A good time manager frequently finishes assignments before actual due dates to allow for emergencies. If you are also working on or off campus, reconsider how many hours per week it will be reasonable for you to be employed above and beyond this commitment and whether you need to reduce your credit load. Remember that managing your time effectively requires practice. You may have to rearrange your schedule a few times, rethink some priorities, and try to use your time differently. The more you apply time management skills, the more time you can save.

Being a good student does not necessarily mean studying day and night and doing little else. Scheduling time for work and pleasure is important, too. After all, most students have to juggle a *lot* of responsibilities. You might have to work to help pay for school, and you probably want to spend time with family or friends to recharge your battery—you might even need to take care of loved ones. And most people also need time for themselves to relax and unwind; that time can include getting some exercise, reading a book for pleasure, or seeing a movie. Notice that the daily planner (Figure 2.3) includes time for other activities as well as time for classes and studying.

FIGURE 2.3 > Daily Planner

Notice how college, work, and personal activities are noted on this daily planner.

	FRIDAY, SEPTEMBER 14
5 am	
6 am	
7 am	
8 am	
9 am	
10 am	Work
11 am	
12 pm	
1 pm	Lunch with Mary
2 pm	
3 pm	
4 pm	
5 pm	
6 pm	Start English Summary Paper
7 pm	
8 pm	

When using an electronic calendar, it's a good idea to print a backup copy in case you lose your phone, cannot access the Internet, experience a computer crash, or leave your charger at home. Carry your calendar with you in a place where you're not likely to lose it. Checking your calendar regularly helps you keep track of commitments and maintain control of your schedule. This practice will become invaluable to you in your career. Check your calendar daily for the current week as well as the coming week. It takes just a moment to be certain that you aren't forgetting something important, and it helps relieve stress. Consider setting regular times to check your calendar every day, perhaps right after eating breakfast and in the evening to see what's coming in the days and weeks ahead.

Keep the following points in mind as you organize your day:

- **Set realistic goals for your study time.** Assess how long it takes to read a chapter in different types of textbooks and how long it takes you to review your notes from different courses.

- **Use waiting, commuting, and travel time to review.** Allow time to review your notes after each class and as soon as you can. You can review your notes if you have a break between classes or while you're waiting for the bus or riding the train. If you have a long bus or train ride, consider formally budgeting this time in your planner, and use it wisely. If you have a long drive, consider listening to recorded notes or asking those riding with you to quiz you. Make a habit of using waiting time, and soon you'll do it without even thinking—it becomes bonus study time to help compensate for unexpected events that might pop up in your day and throw off your schedule.

- **Limit distracting and time-consuming communications.** Check your phone, tablet, or computer for messages or updates at a set time, not whenever you think of it. Constant texting, browsing, or posting can keep you from achieving your academic goals. Remember that when time has passed, you cannot get it back.

- **Avoid multitasking. Multitasking,** or doing more than one thing at a time, requires that you divide your attention among the tasks. You might think that you are quite good at multitasking. However, the reality is (and research shows) that you can get tasks done faster and more accurately if you concentrate on one at a time.[1] But don't take our word for it: Try setting aside time in your schedule to focus on one important task at a time and you'll probably find you do a better job on your assignment, test, or project, and will remember more about the experience.

- **Be flexible.** You cannot anticipate every disruption to your plans. Build extra time into your schedule so that unexpected events do not prevent you from meeting your goals.

You need breaks in your schedule for relaxation, catching up with friends and family, or spending time in the cafeteria or campus center.

---

[1]E. Ophir, C. Nass, and A. Wagner. Cognitive Control in Media Multitaskers, *Proceedings of The National Academy of Sciences, Vol 106, No. 37, 2009.*

YOUR TURN ❯ ON YOUR OWN

Use this blank calendar to map your schedule and most important tasks for the current month. Later in the chapter you'll be asked to prioritize what you write down here.

MONTH:						
MONDAY	TUESDAY	WEDNESDAY	THURSDAY	FRIDAY	SATURDAY	SUNDAY

Completing Large Assignments

Many students think they can start and finish a large assignment, such as a major paper, in the two or three days just before the due date. Even if you set aside a couple of days to only work on a large project, you can hardly use the time efficiently to finish it without any preparation and planning. For instance, if you have to write a ten-page paper, you will find it almost impossible to choose a topic, research it to find relevant information, take notes, create an outline, write a first draft, proofread, and revise your paper all in two or three days. The processes of gathering information and writing about a topic not only take time but also require thinking about and understanding the information for proper use in the paper. (You'll learn more about this in the chapter on "Writing and Speaking.")

Break large assignments such as major papers into smaller steps with deadlines. For example, you can establish a deadline for yourself to choose a topic. Then you can spend time over the next few weeks to research your topic, take notes, and begin drafting your paper. Breaking a large project into smaller steps is something you will probably have to do for yourself. Most instructors won't provide this level of detailed assistance for writing assignments during class time, but you can still meet with your instructors before or after class or during office hours, seek help from the writing center tutors or your college librarians. Taking a step-by-step approach to your first few papers or projects will give you experience you can apply to your future coursework. It will also give you more control over how you are spending your time and energy and reduce your stress.

Overcoming Procrastination

Procrastination is the habit of delaying something that needs your immediate attention. Putting things off can become a serious problem for college students. Students procrastinate for many reasons:

- Lack of motivation. Some students who are uncertain about the value of college may not be willing to do assigned work, even if a failing grade is the result.
- Fear of failure is common even among students who are highly motivated. Some students do not want to start a task because they feel they may not be successful at completing it and disappoint themselves, their parents, teachers, or peers.
- Some assigned work may seem boring or irrelevant. Students who have been given busywork in the past may assume that completing assignments is useless.

Here are some strategies for beating procrastination:

- Remind yourself of the possible consequences if you do not get down to work, and then get started. Also, remind yourself that simply not enjoying an assignment is not a good reason to put it off; it's an *excuse*, not a valid *reason*.
- Create a to-do list. Check off items as you get them done. Use the list to focus on the things that aren't getting done. Move them to the top of the next day's list, and make up your mind to do them. Working from a list will give you a feeling of accomplishment.
- Break big jobs into smaller steps. Tackle short, easy-to-accomplish tasks first.
- Avoid doing other things that might seem more fun, and promise yourself a reward for finishing the task, such as watching your favorite TV show or going out with friends. For completing larger tasks and assignments, give yourself bigger and better rewards.
- Find a place to study that's comfortable and doesn't allow for distractions and interruptions.
- Say no to friends and family members who want your attention; agree to spend time with them later, and schedule that time.
- Shut off and put away all electronic devices during planned study sessions. If you *need* to use an electronic device for studying, turn off all social media and any other applications not part of your studying— and *keep* them off. Consider asking those living with you to help keep you on track. If they see that you are not studying when you should be, ask them to remind you to get back to the books. If you study in your room, close your door.

If you find that the above ideas and strategies to overcome procrastination don't motivate you to get to work, consider re-examining your purpose and priorities in terms of college. If you are not willing or able to stop procrastinating, maybe you are not ready to commit to academic priorities at this point in your life. Only you can decide, but a counselor or academic adviser can help you sort it out. And remember that succeeding in your academic pursuits is one of the surest paths to increased success in life.

YOUR TURN ❯ WORK TOGETHER

With two or three other students, discuss ways to avoid procrastination. What works for you? Share examples from your experiences.

Setting Priorities

To stop procrastinating, think about how to **prioritize,** which means putting your tasks, goals, and values in order of importance (In the section Managing Your Energy later in this chapter, we'll discuss strategies to avoid becoming overextended. This goes hand in hand with setting priorities). Ask yourself which goals are most important but also which ones are most urgent. For example, studying in order to get a good grade on tomorrow's test might have to take priority over attending a job fair today, or completing an assignment that is due tomorrow might have to take priority over driving your friend somewhere.

However, don't ignore long-term goals in order to meet short-term goals. With good time management, you can study during the week prior to the test so that you can attend the job fair the day before. Skilled time managers often establish priorities by maintaining a to-do list on which they rank the items to determine schedules and deadlines for each task.

Once you have entered your future commitments in a term planner and decided how your time will be spent each week, create your to-do list, which is especially handy for last-minute reminders. A to-do list helps you keep track of errands to run, appointments to make, and anything else you might forget. You can keep this list on your cell phone or tablet, in a notebook, or on your bulletin board. Use your to-do list to keep track of all the tasks you need to remember, not just academics. Consider developing a system for prioritizing the items on your list: using different colors of ink for different groups of tasks; highlighting the most important assignments; marking items with one, two, or three stars; or adding letters A, B, C, and so on to indicate what is most important (Figure 2.4). As you complete each task, cross it off your list. You might be surprised by how much you have accomplished and how good you feel about it.

FIGURE 2.4 > To-Do List

A to-do list can help you keep track of the tasks you need to complete, appointments you need to make, and anything else you might forget. You can keep this list on your cell phone or tablet, in your notebook, or on your bulletin board. Use your to-do list to keep track of all the tasks you need to remember, not just academics. Consider prioritizing items with colors, stars, or letters.

THIS WEEK	COLLEGE	WORK	PERSONAL
Monday	B: Schedule a math tutoring session		A: Nina's Parent-Teacher Conference 6–8
Tuesday	B: Make appointment with Professor Smith to discuss paper topic		C: Order birthday gift for dad
Thursday	A: Finish English Summary Paper		
Friday		A: Review report No. 1	C: Make eye appointment

Finding a Balance. Another aspect of setting priorities while in college is finding a way to balance your academic schedule with the rest of your life. Social and extracurricular activities (e.g., participating in a club, writing for the college newspaper, attending lectures) are important parts of the college experience. Time spent alone and time spent thinking are also essential to your overall well-being.

For many students, the greatest challenge of prioritizing will be balancing college with work and family obligations that are equally important and are not optional. Advance planning will help you meet these challenges. You

Set Priorities Like the Pros

Professional coaches help their teams thrive by setting effective priorities, whether it's making a plan for the next play, for the whole game, or for an entire season. In setting your own priorities, take a lesson from these coaches: Prioritize your long-term plans while making sensible play-by-play decisions every day.

Source: Jeff Gross/Getty Images

should also talk with your family members and your employer to make sure that they understand your academic responsibilities. For example, you may be able to take a day off from work to prepare yourself for the final exam of a challenging course. Most instructors will work with you when conflicts arise, but if you have problems that can't be resolved easily, be sure to seek support from your college's counseling center. The counselors will understand your challenges and help you prioritize your many responsibilities.

YOUR TURN ❯ DISCUSS IT

Review the calendar for this month that you mapped out on page 31 and use letters, numbers, or other symbols to prioritize your tasks (A through F, 1 to 5, or 1 star to 5 stars). What are your most important obligations, other than your studies, that will have to fit into your time-management plan? Are any of them more important to you than doing well in college? Why or why not?

Staying Focused. Many students of all ages question their decision to attend college and sometimes feel overwhelmed by the additional responsibilities it brings. Some first-year students, especially recent high school graduates, might temporarily forget their main purposes for coming to college and spend their first term of college engaging in a wide array of new experiences.

Allowing yourself a little time to adjust to college is OK within limits, but you don't want to spend the next four or five years trying to make up for poor decisions made early in your college career, such as skipping class and not taking your assignments seriously. Such decisions can lead to a low GPA and the threat of academic probation, or worse, academic dismissal. Keep in mind that your grades will forever remain on your college transcript. You must send your transcript with your transfer application to a four-year college or university, and some employers might ask for a copy when you apply for a job.

A great way to focus (and to keep your priorities on track) is to finish what *needs* to be done before you move from work to pleasure. From time to time, you might have competing responsibilities; for example, you might have to work additional hours when you have an exam. In cases like these, talk to the people involved, including your instructors, to see how you can manage the conflict.

Time Is Valuable

Think of the last time you made an appointment with someone who either forgot the appointment entirely or was very late. How did you feel? Were you upset or disappointed because the person wasted your time? Most of us have experienced the frustration of having someone else disrespect our

Getting from Here to There
Unless you have a limo at your disposal, you'll have to plan your transportation carefully to be on time.
Source: Alan Chapman/Film Magic/Getty Images

time. In college, if you repeatedly arrive late for class or leave early, you are breaking the basic rules of politeness and showing a lack of respect for your instructors and your classmates.

Punctuality or being on time is expected in college, work, and elsewhere in our society. Being strictly on time may be a difficult adjustment for you if you grew up in a home or culture that is more flexible in its approach to time, but it is important to recognize the value of punctuality. Although you should not have to alter your cultural identity to succeed in college, you must be aware of the expectations that instructors typically have for students.

Here are a few basic guidelines for respectful behavior in class and in other interactions with instructors:

- Be in class on time. This entails getting enough sleep at night and waking up at a time that allows you to arrive in class early enough to take off your coat, shuffle through your backpack, and have your completed assignments and notebooks ready to go.
- Be on time for all scheduled appointments.
- Avoid behaviors that show a lack of respect for both the instructor and other students, such as answering your cell phone during class, unless it is a legitimate emergency. Similarly, texting, doing homework for another class, falling asleep, or talking (even whispering) during a lecture are all considered rude.
- Make transportation plans in advance (and have a backup plan).

Not only is time management important for you, but it is also a way in which you show respect for your coworkers, friends, family, and college instructors, and yourself.

YOUR TURN > TRY IT

List your current priorities in order of importance. What does your list say about you and your values? Why do you consider some things more important? Less important? As you review your list, have you put any items in the wrong place? What should you change, and why?

Most Important	Important	Less Important	Not Important
1.	1.	1.	1.
2.	2.	2.	2.
3.	3.	3.	3.
4.	4.	4.	4.
5.	5.	5.	5.

MANAGING YOUR ENERGY

2.2

Our best plans will not work if we do not have the energy to make them happen. You may plan to spend a couple of hours on your math homework before you go to bed in the evening at the end of a busy day. However, you may find that you are too tired to concentrate and solve the math problems. While learning to manage your time effectively, you must also learn to manage your energy so that you have more control over your life and can achieve success in college.

Stay Awake

Like this student, you probably have a lot of demands on your time. Make sure to effectively manage your energy by getting enough rest, eating properly, and pacing yourself, or you might find yourself falling asleep while studying.

Source: Ocean Corbis

Along with time, energy is an essential resource, and we have a choice in how we use it. Although energy is renewable, each one of us has a limited amount of it in the twenty-four-hour day. Each person has a daily pattern of physical, emotional, and mental activity. For instance, some people are early risers and have a lot of energy in the morning to get things done; others feel the least energetic and productive in the morning and can accomplish tasks at the end of the day more effectively, especially those tasks that require mental energy and concentration.

You can better manage your energy by recognizing your daily pattern and establishing a routine around it. Use Table 2.1 to record your high and low energy level every day for one week. Also mark when you woke up, when you went to bed, and when you took naps (if any).

TABLE 2.1 ❯ Monitoring Your Energy Level

DAY:			
Time	High Energy Level	Average Energy Level	Low Energy Level
5:00 AM			
6:00 AM			
7:00 AM			
8:00 AM			
9:00 AM			
10:00 AM			
11:00 AM			
12:00 PM			
1:00 PM			
2:00 PM			
3:00 PM			
4:00 PM			
5:00 PM			
6:00 PM			
7:00 PM			
8:00 PM			
9:00 PM			
10:00 PM			
11:00 PM			
12:00 AM			
1:00 AM			
2:00 AM			
3:00 AM			
4:00 AM			

Considering your daily energy level, obligations, and potential distractions, decide whether you study more effectively in the morning, afternoon, evening, or some combination. Determine whether you are capable of getting up very early in the morning to study or how late you can stay up at night and still get to morning classes on time.

Your energy level also depends on your diet and other habits such as exercise or lack of it. If you are juggling many responsibilities across several locations, you can use some very simple strategies to take care of yourself:

- Carry healthy snacks with you, such as fruit, nuts, or yogurt. You'll save time and money by avoiding trips to snack bars and convenience stores, and you'll keep your energy up by eating better.
- Drink plenty of water.
- Take brief naps when possible. Research shows that naps are more effective than caffeine.[2]

YOUR TURN ❯ ON YOUR OWN

What are you learning about yourself by completing Table 2.1? What are the best and worst times for you to study? Why?

Establish a Routine

Establish a study routine that is based on your daily energy pattern. The more firmly you set a specific time to study, the more effective you will be at keeping up with your schedule. If you have more energy on the weekend, for example, take advantage of that time to review or catch up on major projects, such as term papers, that can't be completed effectively in short blocks of time. Break down large tasks and focus on one thing at a time to make progress toward your academic goals.

Schedule some downtime for yourself to regain your energy. Different activities help different people relax and get energized. For example, you may watch TV for an hour or take a nap before you start doing your homework. Just make sure that you do not go over the amount of time you set aside as your downtime.

Don't Overextend Yourself

Being **overextended,** or having too much to do given the resources available to you, is a primary source of stress for college students. Determine what a realistic workload is for you, but note that this can vary significantly from one person to another, and only you can determine what is

[2]S. Medrick, D. Cai, S. Kanady, S. Drummond, Comparing the benefits of caffeine, naps and placebo on verbal, motor and perceptual memory. *Behavioural Brain Research,* Vol 193. No. 1, 2008.

Find Your Balance

It's important to find a balance between your studies, work, family, exercise, and other responsibilities in order not to overextend yourself. Keep your goals and priorities in mind, and avoid an event like this one the day before an exam!
Source: Jessica Rinaldi/Reuters/Corbis

realistic. Although being involved in social and family life is very important, don't allow your academic work to take a backseat to other time commitments. Take on only what you can handle. Learn to say no, as this is an effective time-management strategy! Say no to requests that will prevent you from meeting your academic goals. Remember that even if you can find the time for extra tasks, you may not be able to find the energy. If you are feeling stressed, reassess your time commitments and let go of one or more. If you choose to drop a course, make sure you do so before the drop deadline so that you won't have a low grade on your permanent record. If you receive financial aid, keep in mind that you must be registered for a minimum number of credit hours to be considered a full-time student to receive your current level of financial aid. Read more about financial aid in the next section of this chapter.

YOUR TURN > WORK TOGETHER

Energy management often requires the use of the word *no*. Discuss with another student how saying no relates to the way you can manage your energy.

2.3

MANAGING YOUR MONEY

Lack of money—just like lack of time—can lead to stress, which will use up energy you need for studying and other commitments. Because college is expensive (even though two-year college is the least expensive of them all), and most students have limited financial resources, a budget for college is a must. As with time and energy, you have control over how you spend money. By using the tools and strategies in this section, your level of control over money will increase.

Let's begin by learning how to budget. A **budget** is a spending plan that tracks all sources of income (financial aid, wages, money from parents, etc.) and expenses (rent, tuition, books, etc.) during a set period of time (weekly, monthly, etc.). Creating and following a budget will allow you to pay bills on time, cut costs, put some money away for emergencies, and finish college with as little debt as possible.

Creating a Budget

A budget will help you to live within your means, put money into savings, and possibly invest down the road. Here are a few tips to help you get started:

- **Gather basic information.** First, determine how much money is coming in (from a job, your savings, gifts from relatives, student loans, scholarship dollars, or grants) and when. List all your income sources, making note of how often you receive each type of income (weekly paychecks, quarterly loan payments, one-time gifts) and how much money you can expect each time. **Determine where your money is going and when.** Track your spending for a week or two (or, even better, a full month) by recording every bill you pay and every purchase you make. The kinds of expenses you should consider, like rent/mortgage, utilities, gas, food, or child care, will vary depending on your situation. If you are a nontraditional student who is holding down a job and has a family of your own to support, you will calculate your expenses differently than if you are a full-time college student fresh out of high school. Whatever your situation, keeping track of your expenses and learning about your spending behaviors are important habits to develop.
- **Build a plan.** Knowing when your money is coming in will help you decide how to structure your budget. For example, if most of your income comes in monthly, you'll want to create a monthly budget. If you are paid every other week, a biweekly budget might work better. Several tools are available online to help you create a budget, such as easy-to-use spreadsheets or budget wizards that you can download for free. To sample what's available, visit CashCourse (www.cashcourse.org).
- **Identify fixed and variable expenses.** A **fixed expense** is one that will cost you the same amount every time you pay it (like your rent). A **variable expense** is one that may change (like textbooks, because the number and cost of them will be different each term). Although you will know, more or less, how much your fixed expenses will be during each budget period, you might need to estimate your variable expenses with expected costs. Use past bills, credit card statements, and previous receipts to make informed guesses. When you are in doubt, it is always better to overestimate your expenses to avoid shortfalls at the end of your budget period.
- **Do a test run and make adjustments.** Use your budget plan for a few weeks and see how things go, recording your actual costs as you pay them. Whatever you do, don't give up if your bottom line is less than you expected. Budgeting is a lot like dieting; you might slip up and eat a pizza (or spend too much buying one), but all is not lost. If you stay focused and flexible, your budget can lead you to financial stability and independence.

Use the following chart to begin planning your budget. Fill in blank lines for other expense categories that apply to you. Then find a good online budget calculator, plug in your numbers, and build your budget from there.

Budget Worksheet

Cost Category	Fixed or Variable Expense	Expected Cost	Actual Cost
Rent/Mortgage			
Utilities			
Electricity			
Heat			
Water			
Cable/Internet			
Cell phone			
Transportation (car expenses or bus/train fare)			
Medical expenses			
Food (groceries, meals at school, eating out)			
Tuition			
Books			
Child care			
Miscellaneous			
Total			

Cutting Costs

Once you have put together a working budget, tried it out, and adjusted it, you're likely to discover that your expenses may be more than your income. Don't panic. Simply begin to look for ways to reduce those expenses. Here are some tips for saving money in college:

- **Recognize the difference between your needs and your wants.** A *need* is something you must have (like tuition and textbooks). On the other hand, your *wants* are goods and services that you wish to purchase but could live without (like concert tickets). Your budget should always provide for your needs before your wants.
- **Use low-cost transportation.** If owning a car takes up too much of your budget, consider lower-cost options such as taking public transportation, biking to college, carpooling with other students, or participating in a ride-sharing program.

- **Seek out discount entertainment options.** Take advantage of discounted or free tickets to concerts, movie theaters, sporting events, or other special events through your college.
- **Buy secondhand goods.** Use online resources such as Craigslist or thrift stores such as Goodwill to save a lot of money.
- **Avoid unnecessary fees.** Making late payments on your bills can lead to expensive fees and can lower your credit score (which in turn will raise your interest rates). You might want to set up automatic online payments to avoid making this costly mistake.

Getting Financial Aid

Very few students can pay the costs of attending college without some kind of help. Luckily, several sources of **financial aid**—sources of money that support your education—are available, such as the following:

- **Student loans** are a form of financial aid that must be paid back with interest.
- **Grants** are funds provided by the government or private organizations to help students pay for college. Grants do not need to be repaid, but most of them are given to students based on their financial needs. Some grants are specific to certain areas of study.
- **Scholarships** are funds that support your education. Like grants, they do not have to be repaid; they are usually based on students' academic performance but may also be based on need.
- **Work-study** means that students enrolled in college and are receiving financial aid can also have part-time jobs to help cover their education expenses not covered by their aid amount.

Many students manage to enroll and succeed in college with little or no financial support from their families or employers because of the financial aid they receive. Most financial assistance requires some form of application. To receive federal aid, students must complete the U.S. Department of Education's Free Application for Federal Student Aid (FAFSA) every year. The financial aid staff at your college can help you find the way to get the largest amount of grant and scholarship money, the lowest interest rate on loans, and work-study possibilities that fit your academic program.

While scholarships and grants are the best forms of aid because they do not have to be repaid, the federal government, states, and colleges offer many other forms of assistance, such as loans and work-study opportunities.

Show Me the Money

Don't let the paperwork scare you away. If you're not already receiving financial aid, be sure to consider all the available options. And remember that your college may also offer scholarships or grants, which you don't have to repay. Talk to someone in your college's financial aid office to find out if you qualify for any type of aid.

Source: RizaLin/PSU Vanguard

You might also be able to obtain funds from your employer, a local or national organization, or a private foundation. In your search for support, however, beware of scams; your college's financial aid office is the best place to explore sources of college funding.

How to Avoid Losing Your Funding

Once you receive financial aid, make sure that you remain qualified. If you earn at least average grades, complete your courses each term, and finish your program or degree on time, you should have no trouble maintaining your financial aid. Make the grade to save your aid.

Dropping or failing a class might put all or part of your financial aid at risk. Talk with a financial aid counselor before dropping a course to be sure you meet the minimum requirements for credit hours with your other courses. If you do decide to drop a course, do so officially. Some students think that if they just stop attending a class, they have dropped it. Without the proper paperwork, however, you are still enrolled in the course and will receive a failing grade and a bill even if you do not attend.

Achieving a Balance between Working and Borrowing

After developing your budget, deciding what you can pay from savings (if any), and taking scholarships and grants into consideration, you might still need more income. Each academic term or year, you should decide how much you can work while maintaining good grades and how much you should borrow in the form of student loans.

Paid employment while you are in college can be important for reasons other than money. Having a job in a field related to your major can help make you more employable later because it shows you have the capability to manage several priorities at the same time.

Understanding and Managing Credit Wisely

Your **credit score** is a single number that comes from a report that has information about accounts in your name such as credit cards, student loans, utility bills, cell phones, car loans, and so on. This score can determine whether or not you will qualify for a loan (car, home, student, etc.), what interest rates you will pay, how much your car insurance will cost, and your chances of being hired by some organizations.

While using credit cards responsibly is a good way to build credit, acquiring a credit card has become much more difficult for college students. Since May 2009, college students under the age of twenty-one cannot get a credit card unless they can prove they are able to make the payments or unless the credit card application is cosigned by a parent or guardian.

Even if you prove you can repay credit card debt, it is important for you to fully understand how credit cards work and how they can both help and hurt you. (Table 2.2 on page 47 lists credit cards dos and don'ts.) A credit card allows you to buy something now and pay for it later. Each month you will receive a statement listing all purchases you made using your credit card during the previous thirty days. The statement will request a payment toward your balance and will set a payment due date. Your payment options will vary: You can pay your entire balance, pay a specified amount of the balance, or pay only a minimum payment, which may be as low as $10.

Be careful. If you make only a minimum payment, the remaining balance on your card will be charged a finance fee, or interest charge, causing your balance to increase before your next bill arrives even if you don't make any more purchases. Paying the minimum payment is almost never a good strategy and can add years to your repayment time. In fact, if you continue to pay only $10 per month toward a $500 credit card balance, it will take you more than five years to pay it off! If you have a 13 percent interest rate, you'll pay more than $200 in interest —increasing the amount you'll pay for your original purchase by nearly 50 percent.

If you decide to apply for a credit card while you're in college, remember that credit cards should be used to build credit and to handle emergencies. They should not be used to buy things that you want but do not need. However, if you use your credit card just once a month and pay the balance as soon as the bill arrives, you will be on your way to a strong credit score in just a few years.

YOUR TURN > DISCUSS IT

Do you have your own credit card or one that you own jointly with your parents or spouse? If not, what are your reasons for not getting one? If you do have a card, do you feel you're in control of the way you use it? Why or why not? If you don't have a card, do you think you are ready for one? Why or why not?

Debit Cards

Although you might wish to use a credit card for emergencies and to establish a good credit rating, you might also look into the possibility of applying for a debit card. The big advantage of a debit card is that you don't always have to carry cash and thus don't run the risk of losing it or having it stolen. A disadvantage is that a debit card provides direct access to your checking account, so it's important that you keep your card in a safe place and away from your personal identification number (PIN). The safest way to protect your account is to commit your PIN to memory. If you lose your debit card or credit card, notify your bank immediately.

Another advantage of a debit card is that, if you choose not to participate in your bank's overdraft protection program, the amount of your purchases will be limited to the funds in your bank account (Overdraft protection links your checking account to a savings account, credit card, or line of credit and uses that account to pay transactions that would have otherwise triggered an overdraft fee). In this case, using a debit card versus a credit card can help you limit your spending. Although the term *overdraft protection* may sound appealing, keep in mind that if you choose to enroll in such a program, your bank may charge a hefty fee if you spend even just a little more than what you have in your account. And speaking of fees, be aware that if you use your debit card to withdraw cash from an ATM outside your bank's network, you will likely be charged one or more transaction fees.

Identity Theft

If you have a credit or debit card, you should protect your personal information against **identity theft,** which is a crime that occurs when someone uses another person's personal information. Carefully guard your social security number, credit or debit card numbers and PINs, bank account numbers, passwords, and any other identifying information that might enable someone to pretend to be you.

Identity theft can result in financial loss, ruined credit, or a harmful reputation. In some cases, the person who takes over the victim's identity may use funds in his or her accounts, apply for a credit card and use it, get loans, and even commit a crime. It is very costly for a victim to get the money back and rebuild his or her reputation. Here are a few tips to avoid identity theft:

- Shred documents that have your personal information when discarding them.
- Change your passwords frequently, and do not use your date of birth, mother's maiden name, or the last four digits of your social security number as a password.
- Review your bank, debit, and credit card statements closely, and immediately report any charges you do not recognize to your bank or your credit card company.
- When viewing personal information online, make sure your Internet connection is secure. When checking your bank account, paying bills, or shopping online with a credit card, avoid open networks such as those often available at airports and coffee shops. Only secure networks are appropriate for tasks such as these.
- Use computer virus protection, and update it regularly.

TABLE 2.2 ❯ Credit Card Dos and Don'ts

Dos	Don'ts
Do have a credit card for emergencies if possible, even if a family member cosigns for it. And remember: Spring break is not an emergency!	**Don't** use your credit card to bridge the gap between the lifestyle you would like to have and the one you can actually afford.
Do use your credit card to build credit by making small charges and paying them off each month.	**Don't** use your credit card to make unnecessary purchases.
Do set up automatic online payments to avoid expensive late fees. Remember that the payment due date is the date the payment should be received by the credit card lender, not the date you send it.	**Don't** make late payments. Paying your bill even one day late can result in a finance charge and raise the interest rate on that card and your other credit accounts.
Do keep an eye on your credit report by visiting the free Web site AnnualCreditReport .com at least once a year.	**Don't** share your credit card number and information with anyone.

GET ORGANIZED—DIGITALLY

Mapping out your schedule needn't be a chore. Think of your calendar as a compass. It's a guide for navigating your current term and will also keep you pointed toward your long-term goals.

THE PROBLEM *You keep forgetting assignments and can't find the paper planner that your college provided.*

THE FIX *Replace the lost planner with a free electronic calendar or phone app.*

HOW TO DO IT

Pick one of the following:

Google calendar (google.com/calendar).

It's free, it syncs with every type of device, and it is connected with a free Gmail account that includes document creation and storage software. With this Web application, you can input assignment deadlines and reminders, sync with group members' calendars during group projects, and even manage your social life by loading Facebook events.

iStudiez Pro app for Mac, iPhone, and iPad (http://istudentpro.com).

Rated the Best College Student App for 2011, iStudiez allows you to sync the following information across devices: a daily schedule, your calendar by term, assignments, grades, and instructor information.

If you own an Android device and want to ditch your paper planner, try out Studious (**play.google.com/store/apps/details?id=com.young.studious**). It is an all-in-one app for tracking your schedule, including upcoming homework deadlines, and can also be used for taking and managing notes. Best of all, it's free.

Then, take these steps:

- Find out if your college sells a special planner in the campus bookstore with important dates or deadlines already marked. If not, then get the academic calendar from your school's Web site. If neither of the first two suggestions works for you, then grab a sheet of paper or download a blank calendar page from the Internet.
- Draw up a plan for the term, entering your commitments for each week: classes, work hours, assignment deadlines, study groups (including contact numbers), and exam and off dates. Enter this information into an electronic calendar or write it onto a blank calendar.

Studious App for Android Devices

- Transfer all the information into Outlook, iCal, or a similar ShareWare program. When you open Outlook or iCal, you can view by day, week, or month. Simply click on a date or time slot, follow instructions on the toolbar to create a new entry, and start typing.
- Highlight the most important deadlines and activities. As you type in each new entry, you'll have the option to color-code items by category (i.e., school, work, family). Set reminder alarms to keep yourself on track.
- Use the to-do list on the side of the screen to jot down and prioritize tasks. Start a new to-do list every day or once a week. Every time you complete a task, delete it from the list.

Back up everything by syncing your calendar and to-do list with other electronic devices. If you need help, visit your college's computer lab or information technology (IT) department. Alternately, turn to a organized friend for advice, or click to an Outlook tutorial on the Internet.

- As a backup, file your original paper calendar away in case you experience technical difficulties down the road.

THINK

This chapter provided several strategies to manage your time, energy, and money. Which one is the hardest for you to manage? Why? What did you learn in this chapter that you think can help you in dealing with the challenges? Jot down your thoughts here and expand on them in a journal, notebook, or on your favorite device.

WRITE

It can be frustrating to realize that you have to spend time organizing yourself in order to manage your time effectively. Jot down a Summary of the time-management tips in this chapter that appealed to you and why.

APPLY

1. Take control of distractions you know are difficult for you. When you allow distractions to take control of your life, you may feel anxiety about the areas of your life you have ignored. On the next page are some possible distractions. Choose Yes (a problem) or No (not a problem) for each one. Are the problems you identify controllable? If so, what solutions might help you take control of your time? Use this worksheet to increase your awareness of what distractions are tripping you up and how to overcome them.

Possible Distractions	Yes (Y) No (N)	Controllable (C) Uncontrollable (U)	Solutions?
Cell phone			
Internet/Facebook			
Gaming/videos/music			
Sports/hobbies			
Television			
Lack of sleep			
Relationship problems			
Meals/snacks			
Daydreaming			
Perfectionism			
Errands/shopping			
Lost items			
Worries/stress			
Socializing/friends			
Multitasking			
Illness (yours or someone else's)			
Work schedule			
Pleasure reading			
Family members			

2. Money is a difficult subject to talk about, and sometimes it seems easier not to worry about it. Ask yourself hard questions. Do you spend money without much thought? Do you have a lot of debt? Click around the resources available at cashcourse.org. What did you find that can help you? Go to the notebook or file where you have taken notes on this chapter, and reflect and write about your thoughts on these questions.

   Devote more time building and refining the budget that you began in the Your Turn: On Your Own on page 42. In the notebook or file where you have been taking notes on this chapter, write down some observations about what you have learned about your spending habits.

3. Using the templates for calendars provided in this chapter, set up a monthly calendar for all the months in this academic term. Include all of your classes. Set up a weekly calendar for the next two full weeks that are approaching, and include the due dates for all assignments during this time. Then create specific to-do lists for your first three assignments.

WHERE TO GO FOR HELP

AT YOUR COLLEGE

VISIT . . .

Academic Learning/Skills Center

Counseling Center

Financial Aid and Scholarship Office

Career Center

Fitness Center

IF YOU NEED HELP . . .

reading textbooks, taking notes, and studying for exams.

dealing with time management, stress management, or money problems related to compulsive shopping or gambling.

applying for scholarships, grants, and loans.

finding a job, preparing résumés, or developing interview skills.

keeping up an exercise routine.

ONLINE

GO TO . . .

Budget Wizard: cashcourse.org

Free Application for Federal Student Aid: fafsa.ed.gov

FastWeb: FastWeb.com

Bankrate: bankrate.com

IF YOU NEED HELP . . .

creating and managing your budget. The National Endowment for Financial Education (NEFE) offers this free, secure, budgeting tool.

applying for financial aid. The online form allows you to set up an account, complete the application electronically, save your work, and monitor the progress of your application.

looking for free scholarship and discovering sources of educational funding you never knew existed.

understanding credit card interest rates, fees, and penalties. This free Web site provides unbiased information about the interest rates, fees, and penalties associated with major credit cards and private loans. It also provides calculators that let you determine the long-term costs of different kinds of borrowing.

MY COLLEGE'S RESOURCES

3 Discovering How You Learn

PRE-READING ACTIVITY: Think about something new you have learned recently in college, and in the spaces provided, specify what you learned, who helped you learn it, and how you learned it.

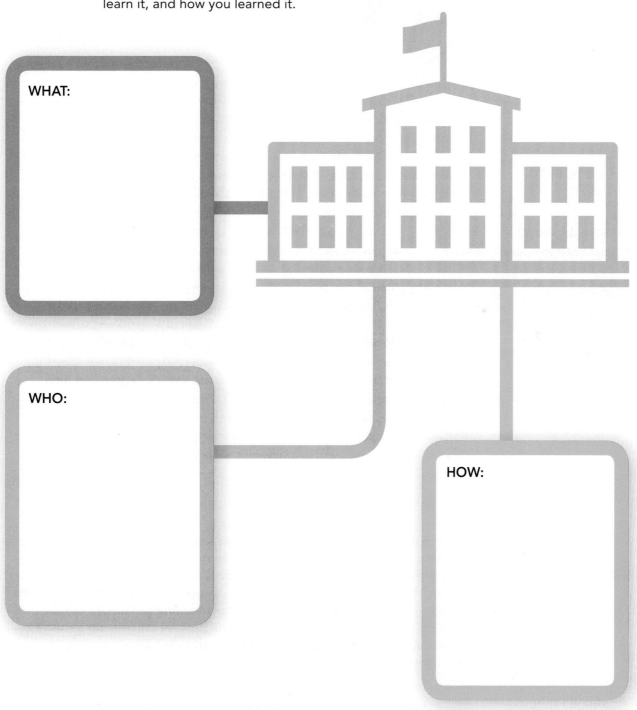

WHAT:

WHO:

HOW:

📁 **PROFILE**

Daniel Graham, 24
Computer Science Major, *Harold Washington College*

Source: eurobanks/ Shutterstock

Daniel Graham from Harold Washington College, a two-year college in the City College of Chicago system, didn't have much knowledge of how he learned before he started college. In his first term, he enrolled in a college success seminar, in which he discovered that people learn differently, and these ways of learning are referred to as learning styles. He also took a learning styles inventory and discovered that he learns best by doing and by reading and writing down material from class. In a recent interview, Daniel explained how he has successfully used several strategies that apply specifically to his form of learning: He rewrites terms and concepts in his own words so that he better understands what they mean, and he uses note cards to help him memorize. Daniel says, "Knowing how I learn has improved my performance. When I take notes, I read them silently on note cards and continue to return to them, so I can memorize the meaning."

"Knowing how I learn has improved my performance."

Daniel is not surprised that he learns by doing because, like many other two-year college students, he spends ten to fifteen hours a week working. Daniel's family owns a landscaping business and employs him part-time. "A hands-on approach has my name written all over it," he says. "I like being able to use my hands and express myself, and I like being able to figure things out just by playing with them for a bit." He adds that he uses this hands-on approach in college by doing things like taking practice exams until he feels ready for the real exam.

In the future, Daniel plans to finish his associate's degree and then explore job opportunities. In ten years, he hopes to be working in computer science, and he plans to continue to rely on his learning styles. He advises fellow students: "Apply your learning style to your everyday life. Eventually, you will learn in a different, smarter, and more efficient way."

Have you ever thought about how you learn? If not, it would probably help to think about this topic now that you are in college. People learn differently. This is hardly a new idea, but if you are to do well in college, it is important that you become aware of how you prefer to learn. Maybe you have trouble paying attention to a long lecture, or maybe listening is the way you learn best. You might love classroom discussion, or you might consider hearing what other students have to say in class a big waste of time.

Perhaps you have not thought about it, but college instructors have their own styles of teaching and communicating. Those different styles will be evident in the way that courses are organized and taught. Your preferred style of learning might not match up with the way some of your courses are taught. Many instructors just lecture; others use lots of visual aids, such as PowerPoint presentations, charts, graphs, and pictures. In science courses, you will conduct experiments or go on field trips where you can observe or touch what you are studying. In dance, theater, or physical education courses, learning takes place in both your body and your mind. And in almost all courses, you'll learn by reading textbooks and other materials. Some instructors are friendly and warm, particularly in two-year colleges with their focus on teaching; others seem to want little interaction with students.

This chapter will help you first to understand how you learn best and then to think of ways in which you can create a link between your style of learning and the expectations of each course and instructor. This chapter will also explore learning disabilities, which are common among college students. You will learn how to recognize them and what to do if you or someone you know has a learning disability.

THE VARK LEARNING STYLES INVENTORY

There are many ways of thinking about and describing learning styles. Some of these will make a lot of sense to you; others might seem confusing at first. Some learning style theories are very simple, and some are complex. You will notice at least a little overlap between the different theories and tools; using several of them might help you do a better job of discovering your *own* learning style. If you are interested in reading more about learning styles, the library and your campus learning center will have many resources.

There are also many ways to measure learning styles. The **VARK Inventory,** a sixteen-item questionnaire, focuses on how learners prefer to use their senses (hearing, seeing, writing and reading, or experiencing) to learn. The letters in VARK stand for *visual, aural, read/write,* and *kinesthetic.*

- **Visual learners** prefer to learn information through charts, graphs, symbols, and other visual means.
- **Aural learners** prefer to hear information.
- **Read/write learners** prefer to learn information that is displayed as words.
- **Kinesthetic learners** prefer to learn through experience and practice, whether simulated or real.

To determine your learning style according to the VARK Inventory, respond to the following questionnaire.

This questionnaire is designed to tell you about your preferences in working with information. Choose answers that explain your preference(s). Select *as many boxes as apply to you*. If none of the options applies to you, leave it blank. (You can also take the VARK online at **www.vark-learn.com/english /page.asp?p=questionnaire.**)

1. You are helping someone who wants to go to the airport, town center, or railway station. You would:
    - ☐ A. go with her.
    - ☐ B. tell her the directions.
    - ☐ C. write down the directions (without a map).
    - ☐ D. draw a map, or give her one.

2. You are not sure whether a word should be spelled "dependent" or "dependant." You would:
    - ☐ A. see the words in your mind and choose by the way they look.
    - ☐ B. think about how each word sounds and choose one.
    - ☐ C. find it in a dictionary.
    - ☐ D. write both words on paper and choose one.

3. You are planning a holiday for a group. You want some feedback from them about the plan. You would:
    - ☐ A. describe some of the highlights.
    - ☐ B. use a map or Web site to show them the places.
    - ☐ C. **give** them a copy of the printed itinerary.
    - ☐ D. phone, text, or e-mail them.

4. You are going to cook something as a special treat for your family. You would:
    - ☐ A. cook something you know without the need for instructions.
    - ☐ B. ask friends for suggestions.
    - ☐ C. look through a cookbook for ideas from the pictures.
    - ☐ D. use a cookbook where you know there is a good recipe.

5. A group of tourists want to learn about the parks or wildlife reserves in your area. You would:
    - ☐ A. talk about, or arrange a talk for them, about parks or wildlife reserves.
    - ☐ B. show them Internet pictures, photographs, or picture books.
    - ☐ C. take them to a park or wildlife reserve and walk with them.
    - ☐ D. give them a book or pamphlets about the parks or wildlife reserves.

6. You are about to purchase a digital camera or mobile phone. Other than price, what would most influence your decision?
    - ☐ A. trying or testing it
    - ☐ B. reading the details about its features
    - ☐ C. thinking that it is a modern design and looks good
    - ☐ D. hearing about its features from the salesperson

7. Remember a time when you learned how to do something new. Try to avoid choosing a physical skill (e.g., riding a bike). You learned best by:
    - ☐ A. watching a demonstration.
    - ☐ B. listening to somebody explaining it and asking questions.
    - ☐ C. diagrams and charts—visual clues.
    - ☐ D. written instructions—e.g., a manual or textbook.

8. You have a problem with your knee. You would prefer that the doctor:
    - ☐ A. give you an online source or written materials to read about your problem.
    - ☐ B. use a plastic model of a knee to show what was wrong.
    - ☐ C. describe what was wrong.
    - ☐ D. show you a diagram of what was wrong.

9. You want to learn a new program, skill, or game on a computer. You would:

☐ A. read the written instructions that came with the program.

☐ B. talk with people who know about the program.

☐ C. use the controls or keyboard.

☐ D. follow the diagrams in the book that came with it.

10. You like Web sites that have:

☐ A. things you can click on, shift, or try.

☐ B. interesting design and visual features.

☐ C. interesting written descriptions, lists, and explanations.

☐ D. audio channels where you can hear music, radio programs, or interviews.

11. Other than price, what would most influence your decision to buy a new nonfiction book?

☐ A. Thinking it looks appealing.

☐ B. Quickly reading parts of it.

☐ C. Hearing a friend talk about it and recommend it.

☐ D. Its real-life stories, experiences, and examples.

12. You are using a book, CD, or Web site to learn how to take photos with your new digital camera. You would like to have:

☐ A. a chance to ask questions and talk about the camera and its features.

☐ B. clear written instructions with lists and bullet points about what to do.

☐ C. diagrams showing the camera and what each part does.

☐ D. many examples of good and poor photos and how to improve them.

13. You prefer a teacher or a presenter who uses:

☐ A. demonstrations, models, or practical sessions.

☐ B. question and answer, talk, group discussion, or guest speakers.

☐ C. handouts, books, or readings.

☐ D. diagrams, charts, or graphs.

14. You have finished a competition or test and would like some feedback:

☐ A. using examples from what you have done.

☐ B. using a written description of your results.

☐ C. from somebody who talks it through with you.

☐ D. using graphs showing what you had achieved.

15. You are going to choose food at a restaurant or café. You would:

☐ A. choose something that you have had there before.

☐ B. listen to the waiter or ask friends to recommend choices.

☐ C. choose from the descriptions in the menu.

☐ D. look at what others are eating or look at pictures of each dish.

16. You have to make an important speech at a conference or special occasion. You would:

☐ A. make diagrams or get graphs to help explain things.

☐ B. write a few key words and practice saying your speech over and over.

☐ C. write out your speech and learn from reading it over several times.

☐ D. gather many examples and stories to make the talk real and practical.

Source: The VARK Questionnaire, Copyright Version 7.0 (2009) held by Neil D. Fleming, Christchurch, New Zealand and Charles C. Bonwell, Green Mountain Falls, Colorado 80819 U.S.A.

Scoring the VARK

Now you will match up each one of the boxes you selected with a category from the VARK Questionnaire using the following scoring chart. Circle the letter (V, A, R, or K) that corresponds to each one of your responses (A, B, C, or D). For example, if you marked both B and C for question 3, circle both the V and R in the 3rd row.

Responses to Question 3:	A	B	C	D
VARK letter	K	Ⓥ	Ⓡ	A

Count the number of each of the VARK letters you have circled to get your score for each VARK.

Scoring Chart

Question	A Category	B Category	C Category	D Category
1	K	A	R	V
2	V	A	R	K
3	K	V	R	A
4	K	A	V	R
5	A	V	K	R
6	K	R	V	A
7	K	A	V	R
8	R	K	A	V
9	R	A	K	V
10	K	V	R	A
11	V	R	A	K
12	A	R	V	K
13	K	A	R	V
14	K	R	A	V
15	K	A	R	V
16	V	A	R	K

Total number of Vs circled = _____   Total number of As circled = _____

Total number of Rs circled = _____   Total number of Ks circled = _____

Because you could choose more than one answer for each question, the scoring is not just a simple matter of counting. It is like four stepping-stones across some water. Enter your scores from highest to lowest on the stones in the figure, with their V, A, R, and K labels.

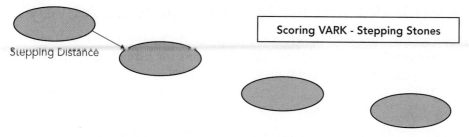

Stepping Distance

Scoring VARK - Stepping Stones

Your stepping distance comes from this table:

The total of my four VARK scores is	My stepping distance is
16–21	1
22–27	2
28–32	3
More than 32	4

Follow these steps to establish your preferences:

1. Your first preference is always your highest score. Check that first stone as one of your preferences.

2. Subtract your second-highest score from your first. If that figure is larger than your stepping distance, you have a single preference. Otherwise, check this stone as another preference and continue with step 3.

3. Subtract your third score from your second one. If that figure is larger than your stepping distance, you have a strong preference for two learning styles (bimodal). If not, check your third stone as a preference and continue with step 4.

4. Subtract your fourth score from your third one. If that figure is larger than your stepping distance, you have a strong preference for three learning styles (trimodal). You may also find that you prefer the four learning styles equally. Otherwise, check your fourth stone as a preference, and you have all four modes as your preferences!

Note: If you are bimodal or trimodal or you have checked all four modes as your preferences, you can be described as multimodal in your VARK preferences.

YOUR TURN › DISCUSS IT

Did your VARK score surprise you at all? Did you know what type of learner you were before using this tool? If so, when did you discover this? How do you use your learning style to your benefit? Be prepared to discuss your results and reflections with the class.

Using VARK Results to Study More Effectively

How can knowing your VARK score help you do better in your college classes? The following table offers suggestions for using learning styles to develop your own study strategies.

Study Strategies by Learning Style

Visual	Aural	Read/Write	Kinesthetic
Underline or highlight your notes.	Talk with others to make sure your lecture notes are accurate.	Write and rewrite your notes.	Use all your senses in learning: sight, touch, taste, smell, and hearing.
Use symbols, charts, or graphs to display your notes.	Record lectures (with permission) or record yourself reading your notes aloud and listen to either or both.	Read your notes silently.	Add to your notes with real-world examples.

3.2

THE MYERS-BRIGGS TYPE INDICATOR

One of the best-known and most widely used personality inventories that can also be used to describe learning styles is the **Myers-Briggs Type Indicator (MBTI)**.[1] While the VARK Inventory measures your preferences for using your senses to learn, the MBTI examines basic personality characteristics and how those relate to human interaction and learning. The MBTI was created by Isabel Briggs Myers and her mother, Katharine Cook Briggs. The inventory identifies and measures psychological types and is given to several million people around the world each year. Employers often give this inventory to employees to get a better understanding of how they perceive the world, make decisions, and get along with other people.

All the psychological types described by the MBTI are normal and healthy. There is no good or bad or right or wrong; people are simply different. When you complete the MBTI, your score represents your "psychological type" or the combination of your preferences on four different scales. These scales measure how you take in information and how you then make decisions or come to conclusions about that information. Based on these scales, you can be one of these types:

---

[1] Isabel Briggs Myers, *Introduction to Type*, 6th ed. (Palo Alto, CA: CPP, 1998).

Extravert	OR	Introvert
directing your energy and attention toward the outer world of people, events, and things.		directing your energy and attention toward the inner world of thoughts, feelings, and reflections.
Sensing Type	OR	**Intuitive Type**
perceiving the world and taking in information directly, through your five senses.		perceiving the world and taking in information indirectly, by using your intuition.
Thinking Type	OR	**Feeling Type**
making your decisions through logical, rational analysis.		making your decisions through your personal values, likes, and dislikes.
Judging Type	OR	**Perceiving Type.**
approaching the outside world by making decisions and judgments.		approaching the outside world by observing and perceiving.

To learn more about these personality types and to access a questionnaire to find out more about your type, visit the Myers & Briggs Foundation at **myersbriggs.org/my-mbti-personality-type/take-the-mbti-instrument/**.

Because each of the four different preferences has two possible choices, sixteen psychological types are possible. No matter what your Myers-Briggs type is, all components of personality have value in the learning process. The key to success, therefore, is to use all the attitudes and functions in their most positive sense. As you go about your studies, we recommend the following:

1. *Extraversion:* Take action. Now that you have a plan, act on it. Do whatever it takes. Create note cards, study outlines, study groups, and so on. If you are working on a paper, now is the time to start writing.
2. *Introversion:* Think it through. Before you take any action, carefully review everything you have encountered so far.
3. *Sensing:* Get the facts. Use sensing to find and learn the facts. How do we know facts when we see them? What is the evidence for what is being said?
4. *Intuition:* Get the ideas. Now use intuition to consider what those facts mean. Why are those facts being presented? What concepts and ideas are being supported by those facts? What are the implications? What is the big picture?
5. *Thinking:* Critically analyze. Use thinking to analyze the pros and cons of what is being presented. Are there gaps in the evidence? What more

Take a Time-out

Do you find that you need some occasional time by yourself? Although introverts are more likely to enjoy time alone, even extraverts can benefit from private time to relax or escape from the hustle and bustle of daily life.

do we need to know? Do the facts really support the conclusions? Are there alternative explanations? How well does what is presented hang together logically? How could our knowledge of it be improved?

6. *Feeling:* Make informed value judgments. Why is this material important? What does it contribute to people's good? Why might it be important to you personally? What is your personal opinion about it?

7. *Judging:* Organize and plan. Don't just dive in! Now is the time to organize and plan your studying so that you will learn and remember everything you need to know. Don't just plan in your head, either; write your plan down, in detail.

8. *Perceiving:* Change your plan as needed. Be flexible enough to change something that isn't working. Expect the unexpected and deal with the unforeseen. Don't give up the whole effort the minute your original plan stops working. Figure out what's wrong, come up with another, better plan, and start following that.[2]

3.3

MULTIPLE INTELLIGENCES

Another way of measuring how we learn is the theory of **multiple intelligences,** which suggests that all human beings have at least eight different types of intelligence. This theory was developed in 1983 by Dr. Howard Gardner, a professor of education at Harvard University. Gardner's theory is based on the idea that the traditional definition of human intelligence is very limited. Gardner argues that students should be encouraged to develop the abilities they have and that evaluation should measure all forms of intelligence.

Gardner's work is controversial because it questions our traditional definitions of intelligence. According to Gardner's theory, all human beings have at least eight different types of intelligence, as follows:

1. A **verbal/linguistic learner** likes to read, write, and tell stories and is good at memorizing information.
2. A **logical/mathematical** learner likes to work with numbers and is good at problem-solving and logical processes.
3. A **visual/spatial** learner likes to draw and play with machines and is good at puzzles and reading maps and charts.
4. A **bodily/kinesthetic** learner likes to move around and is good at sports, dance, and acting.
5. A **musical/rhythmic** learner likes to sing and play an instrument and is good at remembering melodies and noticing pitches and rhythms.
6. An **interpersonal** learner likes to have many friends and is good at understanding people, leading others, and mediating conflicts.
7. **An intrapersonal** learner likes to work alone, understands himself or herself well, and is an original thinker.
8. A **naturalistic** learner likes to be outside and is good at preservation, conservation, and organizing a living area.

---

[2]Ibid.

YOUR TURN > DISCUSS IT

What is the meaning of the term *intelligence*? Name some people you consider to be intelligent.

MULTIPLE INTELLIGENCES INVENTORY

Put a check mark next to all the items within each intelligence that apply to you.

Verbal/Linguistic Intelligence

____ I enjoy telling stories and jokes.

____ I enjoy word games (for example, Scrabble and puzzles).

____ I am a good speller (most of the time).

____ I like talking and writing about my ideas.

____ If something breaks and won't work, I read the instruction book before I try to fix it.

____ When I work with others in a group presentation, I prefer to do the writing and library research.

Logical/Mathematical Intelligence

____ I really enjoy my math class.

____ I like to find out how things work.

____ I enjoy computer and math games.

____ I love playing chess, checkers, or Monopoly.

____ If something breaks and won't work, I look at the pieces and try to figure out how it works.

Visual/Spatial Intelligence

____ I prefer a map to written directions.

____ I enjoy hobbies such as photography.

____ I like to doodle on paper whenever I can.

____ In a magazine, I prefer looking at the pictures rather than reading the text.

____ If something breaks and won't work, I tend to study the diagram of how it works.

Bodily/Kinesthetic Intelligence

____ My favorite class is gym because I like sports.

____ When looking at things, I like touching them.

____ I use a lot of body movements when talking.

____ I tend to tap my fingers or play with my pencil during class.

____ If something breaks and won't work, I tend to play with the pieces to try to fit them together.

Musical/Rhythmic Intelligence

____ I enjoy listening to CDs and the radio.

____ I like to sing.

____ I like to have music playing when doing homework or studying.

____ I can remember the melodies of many songs.

____ If something breaks and won't work, I tend to tap my fingers to a beat while I figure it out.

Interpersonal Intelligence

____ I get along well with others.

____ I have several very close friends.

____ I like working with others in groups.

____ Friends ask my advice because I seem to be a natural leader.

____ If something breaks and won't work, I try to find someone who can help me.

(continued)

Intrapersonal Intelligence

___ I like to work alone without anyone bothering me.

___ I don't like crowds.

___ I know my own strengths and weaknesses.

___ I find that I am strong-willed, independent, and don't follow the crowd.

___ If something breaks and won't work, I wonder whether it's worth fixing.

Naturalist Intelligence

___ I am keenly aware of my surroundings and of what goes on around me.

___ I like to collect things like rocks, sports cards, and stamps.

___ I like to get away from the city and enjoy nature.

___ I enjoy learning the names of living things in the environment, such as flowers and trees.

___ If something breaks down, I look around me to try and see what I can find to fix the problem.

Now, count up the checkmarks for each intelligence, and write each total for each intelligence here. Your score for each intelligence will be a number between 1 and 6:

TOTAL SCORE

___ Verbal/Linguistic

___ Logical/Mathematical

___ Visual/Spatial

___ Bodily/Kinesthetic

___ Musical/Rhythmic

___ Interpersonal

___ Intrapersonal

___ Naturalist

Your high scores of 3 or more will help you to get a sense of your own multiple intelligences. Depending on your background and age, some intelligences are likely to be more developed than others.

Now that you know where your intelligences are, you can work to strengthen the other intelligences that you do not use as often. How do your college courses measure ways in which you are intelligent? Where do they fall short? Looking to the future, you can use your intelligences to help you make decisions about a major, choose activities, and explore career options. It is important for you to be aware of your intelligences and share them with your academic adviser who can help you make sound future educational and career plans. This information will help you appreciate your own unique abilities and also those of others.

Source: Greg Gay and Gary Hams, "The Multiple Intelligences Inventory." From atsp.atutorspaces.com. Reprinted by permission of Greg Gay.

YOUR TURN > ON YOUR OWN

Pick a challenge you are facing right now. How many of the eight intelligences could help you deal with this challenge? List those here.

_____

_____

_____

_____

WHEN LEARNING STYLES AND TEACHING STYLES CONFLICT

This may not be surprising, but instructors tend to teach in ways that fit their *own* particular styles of learning. So an instructor who learns best in a read/write mode or aural mode will probably just lecture and give the class little opportunity for either interaction or visual and kinesthetic learning. But an instructor who prefers a more interactive, hands-on environment will likely involve students in discussion and learning through experience.

Which learning situations work best for you? Think about the following questions:

- Do you enjoy listening to lectures, or do you find yourself bored?
- When your instructor assigns a group discussion, what is your immediate reaction?
- Do you dislike talking with other students, or is that the way you learn best?
- How do you react to lab sessions when you have to conduct an actual experiment? Is this an activity you look forward to or one that you do not like?

Each of these learning situations is more interesting for some students than for others, but each is certainly going to be part of your college experience. Your college has intentionally designed courses that give you opportunities to listen to instructors who are well educated and trained in their fields, to interact with other students in structured groups, and to learn by doing. A true advantage of attending a two-year college is that your instructors' main job is to teach students like you, but they will do so with different styles. Because these are all essential components of your college education, it's important for you to make the most of each situation, learn the content of each course and in general learn how to learn better.

YOUR TURN ＞ ON YOUR OWN

Below, list the classes you are taking this term in order from most favorite to least favorite. Then add the instructor's teaching style for each class on your list. Do you think that your preferences have anything to do with the way the classes are taught? Why or why not?

"As we start a new school year, Mr. Smith, I just want you to know that I'm an Abstract-Sequential learner and trust that you'll conduct yourself accordingly!"

Source: William G. Browning, Minneapolis, MN

Learn to Adapt

Do you know your personal learning style? In college you will find that some instructors may have teaching styles that are challenging for you. Seek out the kinds of classes that conform to the way you like to learn, but also develop your adaptive strategies to make the most of any classroom setting.

When you recognize a mismatch between how you best learn and how you are being taught, you need to take control of your learning process and develop some strategies to learn the material the way you prefer. For instance, if you don't like listening to a lecture, you will want to sit close to the front of the classroom to reduce distractions. You might also want to record the lecture (with the instructor's permission) so that you can listen to it again. Don't depend on the instructor or the classroom environment to give you everything you need to make the most of your learning. Use your own preferences, talents, and abilities to develop many different ways to study and retain information. Look back through this chapter to remind yourself of the ways that you can use your own learning style to be more successful in any class you take.

3.5

LEARNING WITH A LEARNING DISABILITY

While everyone has a learning style, some people have a **learning disability**, a general term which covers a wide variety of specific learning problems resulting from neurological disorders that can make it difficult to acquire certain academic and social skills. A learning disability is a very common challenge to learning for students of any age. Learning disabilities are usually recognized and diagnosed in grade school, but some students can enter college without having been properly diagnosed or assisted.

Learning disabilities can show up as specific difficulties with spoken and written language, coordination, self-control, or attention. Such difficulties can impede learning to read, write, or do math. The term *learning disability* covers a broad range of symptoms and outcomes. Because of this, it is sometimes difficult to diagnose a learning disability or pinpoint the causes. The types of learning disabilities that most commonly affect college students are attention disorders *attention disorders*, which affect the ability to focus and concentrate, and *cognitive disorders*, which affect the development of academic skills, including reading, writing, and mathematics.

You might know someone who has been diagnosed with a learning disability, such as dyslexia, a reading disability that occurs when the brain does not properly recognize and process certain symbols, or attention deficit disorder that affects concentration and focus. It is also possible that you have a special learning need and are not aware of it. This section seeks to increase your self-awareness and your knowledge about such challenges to learning. You will learn more about common types of learning disabilities, how to recognize them, and what to do if you or someone you know has a learning disability.

Attention Disorders

Attention disorders are common in children, adolescents, and adults. Some students who have attention disorders appear to daydream a lot; even if you do get their attention, they can be easily distracted. Individuals with attention deficit disorder (ADD) or attention deficit/hyperactivity disorder (ADHD) often have trouble organizing tasks or completing their work. They don't seem to listen to or follow directions, and their work might be messy or appear careless. Although in legal and medical terms they are not strictly classified as learning disabilities, ADD and ADHD can seriously interfere with academic performance, leading some educators to classify them along with other learning disabilities.[3]

If you have trouble paying attention or getting organized, you won't really know whether you have ADD or ADHD until you are evaluated. Check out resources at your college or in your community. After you have been evaluated, follow the medical advice you get, which may or may not mean taking medication. If you do receive a prescription for medication, be sure to take it according to the doctor's directions. In the meantime, if you're having trouble getting and staying organized, whether or not you have an attention disorder, you can improve your focus through your own behavioral choices. The National Institute of Mental Health offers the following suggestions for adults with attention disorders:

> Adults with ADD or ADHD can learn how to organize their lives by using "props," such as a large calendar posted where it will be seen in the morning, date books, lists, and reminder notes. They can have a special place for keys, bills, and the paperwork of everyday life. Tasks can be organized into sections so that completion of each part can give a sense of accomplishment. Above all, adults who have ADD or ADHD should learn as much as they can about their disorder. (www.nimh.nih.gov/health/publications/attention -deficit-hyperactivity-disorder/can-adults-have-adhd.shtml).

[3]Adapted and reprinted from the public domain source by Sharyn Neuwirth, *Learning Disabilities* (Darby, PA: National Institute of Mental Health, 1993), 9-10.

Cognitive Learning Disabilities

Cognitive learning disabilities are related to mental tasks and processing. Dyslexia, for example, is a developmental reading disorder classified as a cognitive learning disability. A person can have problems with any of the tasks involved in reading. However, scientists have found that a significant number of people with dyslexia are not able to distinguish or separate the sounds in spoken words. For instance, dyslexic individuals sometimes have difficulty assigning the right sounds to letters, either individually or when letters combine to form words.

There is, of course, more to reading than recognizing words. If the brain is unable to form images or relate new ideas to those stored in memory, the reader can't understand or remember the new concepts. So other types of reading disabilities can appear when the focus of reading shifts from identifying words to comprehending a written passage.[4]

Writing, too, involves several brain areas and functions. The networks of the brain that control vocabulary, grammar, hand movement, and memory must all be in good working order. So a developmental writing disorder might result from problems in any of these areas. Someone who can't distinguish the sequence of sounds in a word will often have problems with spelling. People with writing disabilities, particularly expressive language disorders (the inability to express oneself using accurate language or sentence structure), are often unable to write complete, grammatical sentences.[5]

A student with a developmental arithmetic disorder will have difficulty recognizing numbers and symbols, memorizing facts such as the multiplication table, and understanding abstract concepts such as place value and fractions.[6]

Exploring Resources

If you have a documented learning disability, make sure to notify the office of disabled students services at your school to receive reasonable accommodations as required by law. Reasonable accommodations might include use of a computer during some exams, readers for tests, in-class note-takers, extra time for assignments and tests, and use of audio textbooks, depending on need and the type of disability.

Anyone who is diagnosed with a learning disability is in good company. Pop star Jewel, Olympic gold medal swimmer Michael Phelps, actor Patrick Dempsey, and CNN news anchor Anderson Cooper are just a few of the famous and successful people who have diagnosed learning disabilities. Here is a final important message: A learning disability is a learning difference but is in no way related to intelligence. Having a learning disability is not a sign that you are stupid. In fact, some of the most intelligent individuals in human history have had a learning disability.

---

4 Ibid., 7.

5 Ibid., 7–8.

6 Ibid., 8.

BRANCH OUT

If you enjoy long lectures, chances are you're an auditory learner. What if you're a visual learner who needs charts, graphs, and videos — and these are missing from the lecture? Or what if you're a hands-on learner who performs best when you are involved in a project and can work with others? Your two-year college may have a course management system (CMS) or a learning management system (LMS). A CMS or LMS is a Web site that boosts your ability to connect with your instructors, classmates, and the material you're studying both in class and out.

THE PROBLEM *You don't understand what a CMS/LMS is, or have no clue how to use one, and you're skeptical.*

THE FIX *With an open mind and patience, this technology can work for you. Figure out your learning style, for classes that complement your strengths and find ways to adapt to teaching techniques that lie outside your comfort zone.*

HOW TO DO IT

Think of all the advantages that a CMS/LMS offers like ways to help you connect with your instructors, your classmates, and the material. It lets you keep track of your grades and assignments. It offers a digital drop box for safely submitting your work. It also makes a lot of fun things possible, like online discussion forums and interactive group projects. These will allow you to do things like sketching ideas on whiteboards that other students can view or even collaborating on written assignments in real time. Some CMSs/LMSs make videos, recorded lectures, or even your instructor's lecture notes available. The basic ingredients of a CMS/LMS — video, audio, and text — appeal to different learning styles.

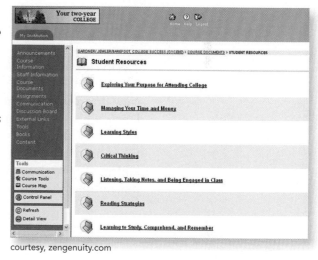

courtesy, zengenuity.com

1. **If you're an auditory learner, you'll love CMS/LMS audio recordings.** *To get the most from texts*, read your notes and textbook passages aloud as you study. (You can even record them to play back to yourself.) While you're at it, listen to audiobooks and join a study group for discussions. *To get the most from video clips*, listen to them once, and then again with your eyes closed.

2. **If you're a visual learner, you'll love CMS/LMS videos, pictures, maps, and graphs.** *To get the most from audio recordings and text*, take notes and illustrate them, playing up key points with colored highlighters, pictures, or symbols. Or create a graph or chart to display important concepts.

3. **If you're a hands-on learner, you'll enjoy CMS/LMS labs and group projects.** *To get the most from audio, video, and text*, sit in the front row in class take notes, and read things aloud as you study. Build models or spreadsheets. Take field trips to gather experience. Get creative!

KNOW THIS

Once you learn how to log into the system, do it often. CMS/LMS use varies from one instructor to another. If you're having trouble logging in or figuring out your username and password, ask your instructor for help.

Figure how much online activity you can handle. If you sign up for face-to-face classes, you might only use a CMS/LMS for a few things, like submitting assignments or swapping essays for peer review. If you enroll in a **hybrid** course, a course that uses both face-to-face and online instruction, your instructor may post outside reading material or create online discussions on your CMS. In a fully online course, you might do everything on the CMS/LMS, including taking exams. Before you register, think about which type of course suits your schedule and learning style. Not every student can be successful in an online course. You need to have the required technological knowledge, systems, and tools. Taking an online course demands time management and discipline as online courses have no scheduled meeting times.

THINK

Recognizing that people learn in different ways can be a relief. After reading this chapter, do you have a better understanding of your own learning style? What did you find to be the most interesting point in this chapter? What would you like to learn more about? Jot your ideas on the lines below.

WRITE

Now that you know more about your learning style and how you prefer to learn, what do you consider your strengths to be? What do you learn well and easily, and how can you apply these positive experiences to other learning situations? What are some of your weaknesses, and how can you address them? Jot down some thoughts here and expand on them in a journal, notebook, or on your favorite device.

APPLY

1. It is important to understand various learning styles for education purposes, but it is also important to understand how learning preferences affect career choices. Considering your preferred learning style, what might be the best careers for you? Why?

2. Use the following table to list all the classes you are taking this term. Based on the VARK Inventory, try to figure out the instructor's teaching style in each class. Then add your learning style. Does the teaching style in each class match your learning style? If not, list a strategy you can use to adapt.

My Classes	Teaching Style	My Learning Style	Match: Yes or No?	Strategy
Psychology	PowerPoint slides with lecture: Visual and Auditory	Read/Write	No	Read the chapter before the lecture, take notes during the lecture, and review notes after class

WHERE TO GO FOR HELP

AT YOUR COLLEGE

VISIT . . .

Counseling Center

Career Center

Disabled Student Services/ Counselor

IF YOU NEED HELP . . .

understanding learning styles.

learning how the Myers-Briggs Type Indicator can be used in career planning or how to align your Myers-Briggs type with your interests and career development options on campus.

getting advice on learning disability testing and diagnosis and in receiving accommodations if you have a learning disability.

ONLINE

GO TO . . .

LD Pride:
ldpride.net/learningstyles.MI.htm

National Center for Learning Disabilities:
www.ncld.org

Facebook:
facebook.com

National Institute of Mental Health:
nimh.nih.gov/health/publications
/attention-deficit-hyperactivity
-disorder/can-adults-have-adhd.shtml

IF YOU NEED HELP . . .

obtaining general information about learning styles and learning disabilities and using an interactive diagnostic tool to determine your learning style.

locating resources on diagnosing and understanding learning disabilities.

finding groups on Facebook created by students who have learning disabilities or ADHD. These groups are a great way to connect with other students with learning disabilities at your college or other colleges. If you have been diagnosed with a disability, the members of these groups can offer support and help you seek out appropriate resources in order to be successful in college.

getting information about how adults who have ADD or ADHD can get diagnosed and treated.

MY COLLEGE'S RESOURCES

PART TWO

STUDY STRATEGIES

 GETTING THE MOST OUT OF CLASS

STUDENT GOALS

- Become engaged in learning *75*
- Prepare for learning before class *77*
- Participate in class by listening critically and speaking up *78*
- Assess and improve your note-taking skills *81*
- Review your notes and textbook materials soon after class *81*

 READING TO LEARN FROM COLLEGE TEXTBOOKS

STUDENT GOALS

- Apply the four steps in active reading: previewing, marking, reading with concentration, and reviewing *97*
- Use strategies for reading textbooks across different subject areas *106*
- Improve and monitor your reading and develop your vocabulary *109*

 STUDYING, UNDERSTANDING, AND REMEMBERING

STUDENT GOALS

- Learn how to make good choices for better concentration and efficient studying *119*
- Understand how memory works and become familiar with myths about memory *121*
- Learn skills to improve your ability to remember *123*

7 TAKING TESTS SUCCESSFULLY

STUDENT GOALS

8 INFORMATION LITERACY

STUDENT GOALS

9 WRITING AND SPEAKING

STUDENT GOALS

4 Getting the Most Out of Class

PRE-READING ACTIVITY: In this chapter, you will learn different ways to be engaged in class to get the most out of being there. What do you think you can do before, during, and after class to be fully engaged in learning?

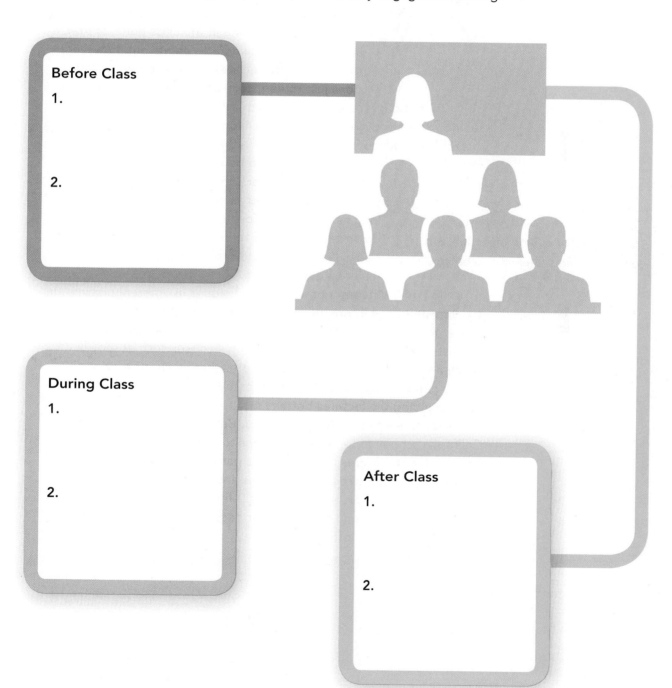

Before Class

1.

2.

During Class

1.

2.

After Class

1.

2.

PROFILE

Dillon Watts, 19
History Major, *San Bernardino Valley College*

Source: Monkey Business Images/Shutterstock

Dillon Watts grew up in San Bernardino, California. He left high school after his junior year and obtained his GED. The benefits of participating in class and being engaged in learning are obvious to Dillon. "Most of the time the questions you have are questions that will help the whole class," Dillon says. "Everyone in the class benefits from an instructor's answer." He points out, however, that no one appreciates a student asking questions just to earn participation points or to show off. "I try to be direct and simple when asking questions, so the class can get direct and simple answers," Dillon says.

This same attitude is also present in the way Dillon prepares for class. He explains: "I just make sure to be there on time, every time, and to try to stay until the class is over. I'm not a great note-taker. I find myself distracted as much as the next guy. But as long as I make an effort to pay attention and write down key points and read the chapter sections in books I'm supposed to read, I find it pretty easy to maintain good grades."

> "Taking notes should never be a substitute for paying attention and understanding the lectures better."

Dillon uses different note-taking techniques in different classes. "In a class with lots of information, I take notes really well. It makes it harder to actually pay attention to concepts, but it certainly pays off for tests and such," he says. "In less formal classes such as speech, which are full of ideas, I do not take notes that much, or even at all. Taking notes should never be a substitute for paying attention and understanding the lectures better."

Dillon plans to transfer to Stanford, Berkeley, or another four-year California school. In ten years he hopes to be a journalist or history teacher. He also hopes to put his class participation skills to good use. "It is my dream to take part in debates and public speeches," he says. His advice to other first-year students: "Try to get as much as you can out of your classes, and try to do your best, whether or not you feel like it. It always pays off in the end."

Dillon's advice is sound when you consider that to earn high grades in college, you'll need to take an active role in your classes by listening carefully, taking notes, asking questions, contributing to discussions, and providing answers. These active learning behaviors will improve your ability to understand complex ideas, find new possibilities, organize those ideas, and better remember the material once the class is over.

Many of the questions on college exams will be drawn from class lectures and discussions. Therefore, you need to attend each class and be actively involved. In addition to taking notes, you might consider recording the lecture and discussion, if you have the instructor's permission. If you don't understand some points, take the time to meet with the instructor after class or during office hours. Another strategy to increase your learning is to meet with a study group to compare your understanding of course material with that of your classmates.

This chapter reviews several note-taking methods. Choose the one that works best for you. Because writing down everything the instructor says is probably not possible, and you might not be sure what is most important, ask questions in class. This will ensure that you clearly understand your notes. Reviewing your notes with a tutor, someone from your campus learning center, or a friend from class can also help you clarify your understanding of the most important points.

Most of all, be sure to speak up. When you have a question to ask or a comment to share, don't let embarrassment or shyness stop you. You will be more likely to remember what happens in class if you are an active participant.

YOUR TURN > ON YOUR OWN

If you have saved any of your high school notebooks, look at the way you took notes and think about whether this method works for you now. If not, try taking notes while watching the news on TV or reading news online and see how you do.

BECOME ENGAGED IN LEARNING

4.1

Engaged students are those who are fully involved with the college experience and spend the time and the energy necessary to learn, both in and out of class. Engaged learners who have good listening and note-taking skills get the most out of college.

You can learn by listening to a lecture, and you can better understand that information by considering what the information means to you. Practice the techniques of **active learning** which means learning through participation—talking with others, asking questions in class, studying in groups, and going beyond the lecture material and required reading. Explore other information sources in the library or on the Internet. Think about how the material relates to your own life or experience. For instance, a psychology class might help you recognize patterns of behavior in your own family, or a sociology class may shed light on a team or group to which you belong. When you are actively engaged in learning, you will not only learn the material in your notes and textbooks, but you will also be practicing valuable skills that you can apply to college, work, and your personal life such as the following:

- **Working with others.** Learning to work with others is one of the most important skills you can develop for success in college and in your career.
- **Improving your thinking, listening, writing, and speaking skills.** These are the primary skills that define a college-educated person.
- **Functioning independently and teaching yourself.** Your first year of college will help you become an independent learner. Such learners do not always wait for an instructor to point them in the right direction.
- **Managing your time.** Time management sounds easy, but it is a challenge for almost all students, regardless of their academic ability.
- **Gaining sensitivity to cultural differences.** The world we live in requires all of us to develop our own knowledge about, and respect for, cultures that are different from our own.

Engagement in learning requires your full and active participation in the learning process. Your instructors will set the stage and provide valuable information, but it's up to you to do the rest. For instance, if you disagree with what your instructor says, politely share your opinion. Most instructors will listen. They might still disagree with you, but they might also appreciate your independent thinking efforts.

Stay Engaged
Students of all kinds will benefit from active learning strategies, whether in arts and science courses or professional training situations such as the one in which these military cadets are engaged.
Source: *The Washington Post*/Getty Images

Not all instructors teach in a way that includes active learning. Ask your friends for recommendations on instructors who encourage students to participate in class, work in groups, explore materials independently, and otherwise engage fully in learning.

ENGAGE BEFORE CLASS

4.2

Have you ever noticed how easy it is to learn the words of a song? It's easier to remember song lyrics than other kinds of information because songs follow a tune, have a beat, and often relate to things in our personal lives. It is easier to remember new information if you can connect it to what you already know. In your first-year classes, you'll be listening to and reading material that might seem hard to understand. Beginning on the first day of class, you will be more likely to remember what you hear and read if you try to link it to something you have already learned or experienced.

A very important first step toward success is to prepare before class. You should begin listening, learning, and remembering before each class session. Here are some strategies:

1. **Do the assigned reading.** Doing the assigned reading before class will help you understand new terms, listen better, and pick out the most important information when taking notes in class. Some instructors assign readings during class; others expect you to follow the **syllabus** (course outline) to keep up with the assigned readings. As you read, take good notes (more on note taking later in this chapter). In books you own, **annotate** (add explanatory notes in the margins), highlight, or underline key points. In books you do not own, such as library books, paraphrase the content and then annotate or highlight.

2. **Pay careful attention to your course syllabus.** The syllabus you receive at the start of each course will include the course requirements, your instructor's expectations, and the course grading breakdown. Instructors expect students to understand and follow the syllabus with few or no reminders. You might find that this is a key difference between college and high school.

3. **Make use of additional materials provided by the instructors.** Many instructors post lecture outlines or notes in the course management system (CMS) before class. Download and print these materials for easy use during class. CMS materials often provide hints about the topics that the instructor considers most important; they also can create an organizational structure for taking notes.

4. **Warm up for class.** Review chapter introductions and summaries that refer to related sections in your text, and quickly review your notes from the previous class period. This prepares you to pay attention, understand, and remember.

5. **Get organized.** Decide how you want to take notes. If you handwrite your notes, using three-ring binders can help you organize them; as you can punch holes in syllabi and other course handouts, and keep them with class notes. You might want to buy notebook paper with a large left-hand margin so that you can annotate your lecture notes (more on this later in the chapter). You can also download and print blank notebook paper from several free Web sites.

   If you take notes on a laptop or tablet, keep your files organized in separate folders for each of your classes, and make sure that the file name of each document includes the date and topic of the class. See the Tech Tip at the end of this chapter for more information on taking effective notes on electronic devices.

4.3

PARTICIPATE IN CLASS

Learning is not like watching sports. To really learn, you must listen carefully, talk about what you are learning, write about it, connect it to past experiences, and make what you learn part of yourself. To play a sport—and not just watch it—you have to participate. Participation is the heart of active learning. When you say something in class, whether in answer to a question or as part of a question you are asking, you are more likely to remember it than when you just listen to someone else saying it.

Listen Actively and with an Open Mind

Listening in class is different from listening to a TV show, listening to a friend, or even listening during a meeting. In such everyday activities, you might not be required to remember later or use the information you hear. Knowing how to listen in class can help you get more out of what you hear, understand better what you have heard, and save time. Here are some suggestions:

1. **Be ready for the message.** Prepare yourself to hear, to listen, and to receive the message. If you have done the assigned reading, you will already know details from the text, so you can focus your notes on key concepts during the lecture. You will also notice information that the text does not cover and will be prepared to pay closer attention when the instructor presents new material.
2. **Listen to the main concepts and central ideas, not just to facts and figures.** Although facts are important, they will be easier to remember and will make more sense when you can place them within concepts, themes, and ideas.

3. **Listen for new ideas.** Even if you are an expert on a topic, you can still learn something new. Do not assume that college instructors will present the same information you learned in a similar course in high school. Even if you're listening to a similar lecture, you will pick out and learn new information. As an engaged student, make a note of questions in your mind as you listen, but save the judgments for later.

4. **Repeat mentally.** Words can go in one ear and out the other unless you make an effort to remember them. Think about what you hear, and say it silently in your own words. If you cannot translate the information into your own words, ask the instructor for more explanation.

5. **Decide whether what you have heard is not important, somewhat important, or very important.** While most of what your instructors say and do in class is important, occasionally they may make comments or tell stories that are only somewhat related to the class material or may not be related at all. If an instructor's comment is really unrelated to the focus of the class, you don't need to write it down. If it's very important, make it a major point in your notes by highlighting or underlining it, or use it as a major topic in your outline if that's the method you use for taking notes. If it's somewhat important, try to relate it to a very important topic by writing it down as a part of that topic.

6. **Keep an open mind.** Every class holds the promise of letting you discover new ideas and uncover different opinions. Some instructors might present information that challenges your ideas and values on purpose. College is supposed to teach you to think in new ways and train you to provide support for your own beliefs. Instructors want you to think for yourself; they don't necessarily expect you to agree with everything they or your classmates say. However, if you want people to respect your values and ideas, you must show respect for theirs as well by listening to what they have to say with an open mind.

7. **Ask questions.** Early in the term, determine whether your instructor wants you to ask questions during the lecture. Some instructors prefer that students ask their questions after the lecture, during separate discussion sections, labs, or office hours. If your instructor answers questions when students ask them, speak up if you did not hear or understand what was said. Ask for explanations immediately, if possible; other students are likely to have the same questions. If you can't hear another student's question or response, ask him or her to repeat the question.

8. **Sort, organize, and categorize.** When you listen, try to match what you are hearing with what you already know. Take an active role in deciding how best to remember what you are learning. If you find yourself daydreaming during a lecture, quickly refocus your thoughts on the topic and actively take notes. After class or during your instructor's next office hours, ask him or her to help you fill in any gaps in your notes.

Previewing information before class is important as it creates an organized mental outline for the lecture ahead of time. Take a moment to preview the material you're studying now by writing down the four major headings of this chapter below.

_____

_____

_____

_____

Hands Up!

Participating in class not only helps you learn but also shows your instructor that you're interested and engaged. Like anything else, you may be anxious the first time you raise your hand. But after that first time, you'll probably find that participating in class raises your interest and enjoyment.

Speak Up

Naturally, you will be more likely to participate in a class in which the instructor emphasizes class discussion, calls on students by name, shows signs of approval and interest, and avoids criticizing students for an incorrect answer. Often, answers you and other students offer may not be quite correct, but they can lead to new perspectives on a topic.

Whether you are in a large or a small class, you might be nervous about asking a question, fearing you will make a fool of yourself. However, it is likely that other students have the same question but were too nervous to ask. If so, they may thank you silently or even aloud! Many instructors set time aside to answer questions in class, so to take full advantage of these opportunities, try using the following techniques:

1. **Take a seat as close to the front as possible and keep your eyes on the instructor.** Sitting close to the front can help you concentrate better and not get distracted by other students. It will also make it easier to maintain eye contact with your instructors.
2. **Focus on the lecture and class discussions.** Avoid distractions. Sit away from friends who can distract you, do not engage in side conversations, and turn off all electronic devices that you are not using for class.
3. **Raise your hand when you don't understand something.** If you don't understand something, you have the right to ask for an explanation. Never worry that you're asking a stupid question. The instructor might answer you immediately, ask you to wait until later in the class, or throw your question to the rest of the class. In each case, you benefit in several ways. The instructor

will get to know you, other students will get to know you, and you will learn from both the instructor and your classmates. But don't overdo it, or you'll risk disrupting class. Office hours provide the perfect opportunity for following up.

4. **Speak up in class.** Ask a question or volunteer to answer a question or make a comment. This becomes easier every time you do it.

5. **When the instructor calls on you to answer a question, don't bluff.** If you know the answer, give it. If you're not certain, begin with, "I think . . . , but I'm not sure I have it all correct." If you don't know, just say so.

6. **If you have recently read a book or article that is relevant to the class topic, bring it in.** Use it either to ask questions about the topic or to provide information that was not covered in class.

YOUR TURN ❯ WORK TOGETHER

Think about the number of times during the past week you have raised your hand in class to ask a question. How many times has it been? Do you ask questions frequently, or is this something you avoid? Make a list of the reasons you either do or don't ask questions in class. Would asking more questions help you earn better grades? Be prepared to share your reflections with a small group.

TAKE EFFECTIVE NOTES

What are effective notes? They are notes that cover all the important points of the lecture or reading material without being too detailed or too limited. Most important, effective notes prepare you to do well on quizzes or exams. They also help you understand and remember concepts and facts. Becoming an effective note-taker takes time and practice, but this skill will help you improve your learning and your grades in the first year and beyond.

Note-Taking Formats

You can make class time more productive by using your listening skills to take effective notes, but first you have to decide on one of the following four commonly used formats: Cornell, outline, paragraph, and list formats. Any format can work as long as you use it consistently.

Cornell Format. Using the **Cornell format,** one of the best-known methods for organizing notes, you create a "recall" column on each page of your notebook or your Word document by drawing a vertical line about two to three inches from the left border (see Figure 4.1). As you take notes during class—whether writing down or typing ideas, making lists, or using an outline or paragraph format—write only in the wider column on the right; leave the recall column on the left blank. The recall column is the place where you write down or type the main ideas and important details for tests and examinations as you go through your notes, which you should do as soon after class as possible, preferably within an hour or two. Many students have found the recall column to be an important part of note taking, one that becomes an effective study tool for tests and exams.

FIGURE 4.1 ❯ Note Taking in the Cornell Format

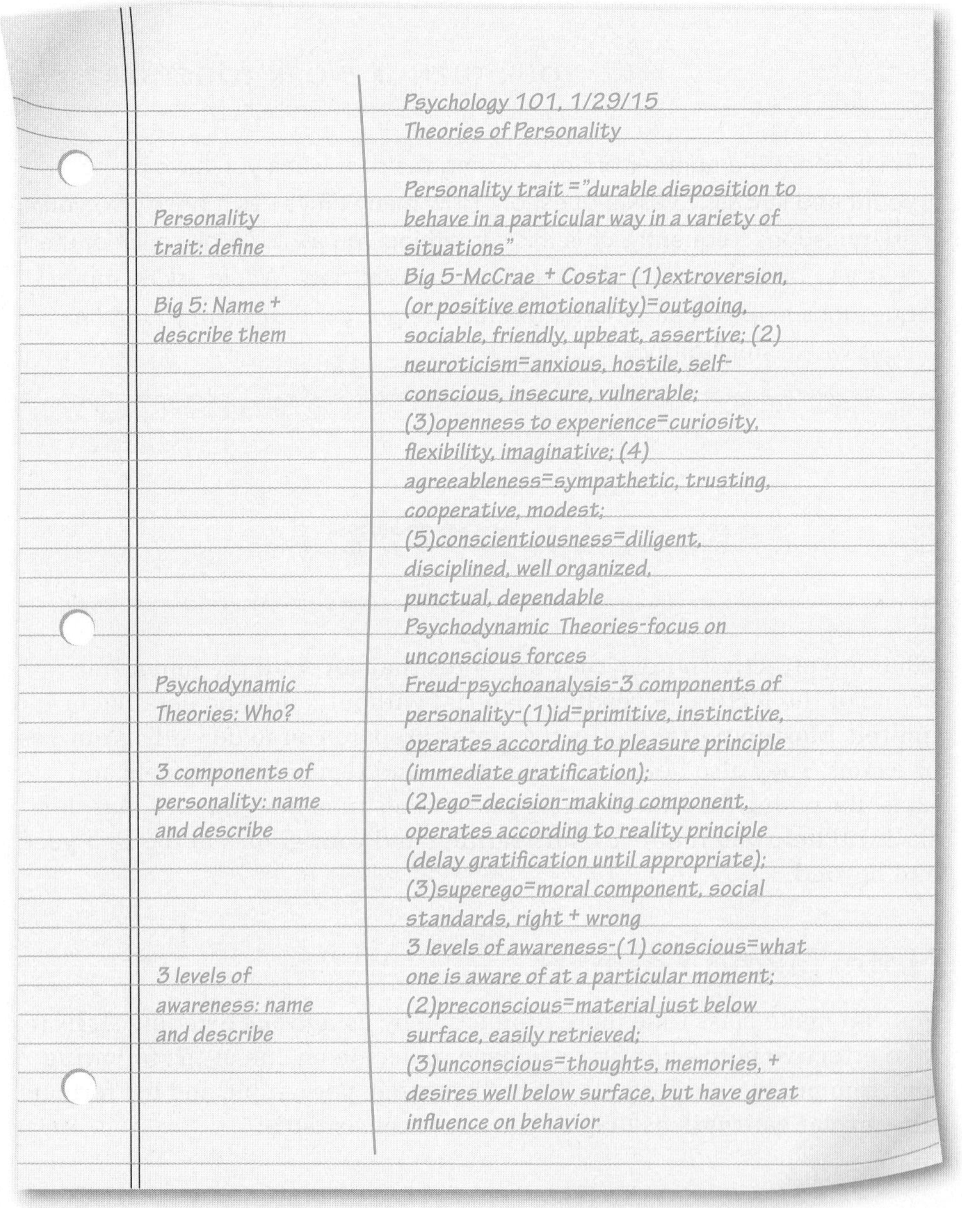

Psychology 101, 1/29/15
Theories of Personality

Personality trait: define	Personality trait ="durable disposition to behave in a particular way in a variety of situations"
Big 5: Name + describe them	Big 5-McCrae + Costa- (1)extroversion, (or positive emotionality)=outgoing, sociable, friendly, upbeat, assertive; (2) neuroticism=anxious, hostile, self-conscious, insecure, vulnerable; (3)openness to experience=curiosity, flexibility, imaginative; (4) agreeableness=sympathetic, trusting, cooperative, modest; (5)conscientiousness=diligent, disciplined, well organized, punctual, dependable
Psychodynamic Theories: Who?	Psychodynamic Theories-focus on unconscious forces
	Freud-psychoanalysis-3 components of personality-(1)id=primitive, instinctive, operates according to pleasure principle
3 components of personality: name and describe	(immediate gratification); (2)ego=decision-making component, operates according to reality principle (delay gratification until appropriate); (3)superego=moral component, social standards, right + wrong
3 levels of awareness: name and describe	3 levels of awareness-(1) conscious=what one is aware of at a particular moment; (2)preconscious=material just below surface, easily retrieved; (3)unconscious=thoughts, memories, + desires well below surface, but have great influence on behavior

Outline Format. Some students find that an **outline** is the best way for them to organize their notes. In a formal outline, Roman numerals (I, II, III, etc.) mark the main ideas. Other ideas relating to each key idea are marked by uppercase letters (A, B, C, etc.), numbers (1, 2, 3, etc.), and lowercase letters (a, b, c, etc.) in descending order of importance or detail. Using the outline format allows you to add details, definitions, examples, applications, and explanations (see Figure 4.2).

FIGURE 4.2 ❯ Note Taking in the Outline Format

Psychology 101, 1/29/15: Theories of Personality

I. Personality trait = "durable disposition to behave in a particular way in a variety of situations"
II. Big 5-McCrae + Costa
   A. Extroversion (or positive emotionality)=outgoing, sociable, friendly, upbeat, assertive
   B. Neuroticism=anxious, hostile, self-conscious, insecure, vulnerable
   C. Openness to experience=curiosity, flexibility, imaginative
   D. Agreeableness=sympathetic, trusting, cooperative, modest
   E. Conscientiousness=diligent, disciplined, well organized, punctual, dependable
III. Psychodynamic Theories-focus on unconscious forces-- Freud—psychoanalysis
   A. 3 components of personality
      1. Id=primitive, instinctive, operates according to pleasure principle (immediate gratification)
      2. Ego=decision-making component, operates according to reality principle (delay gratification until appropriate)
      3. Superego=moral component, social standards, right + wrong
   B. 3 levels of awareness
      1. Conscious=what one is aware of at a particular moment
      2. Preconscious=material just below surface, easily retrieved
      3. Unconscious=thoughts, memories, + desires well below surface, but have great influence on behavior

YOUR TURN ❯ TRY IT

During the next week, try using the Cornell format in one class and the outline format in another class. Then compare your notes and decide which format helps you the most when you are studying and preparing for tests.

Paragraph Format. When you are taking notes on what you are reading, you might decide to write **summary paragraphs**—a note-taking format in which you write two or three sentences that sum up a larger section of material (see Figure 4.3). This method might not work well for class notes because it's difficult to summarize a topic until your instructor has covered it completely. By the end of the lecture, you might have forgotten critical information.

FIGURE 4.3 › Note Taking in the Paragraph Format

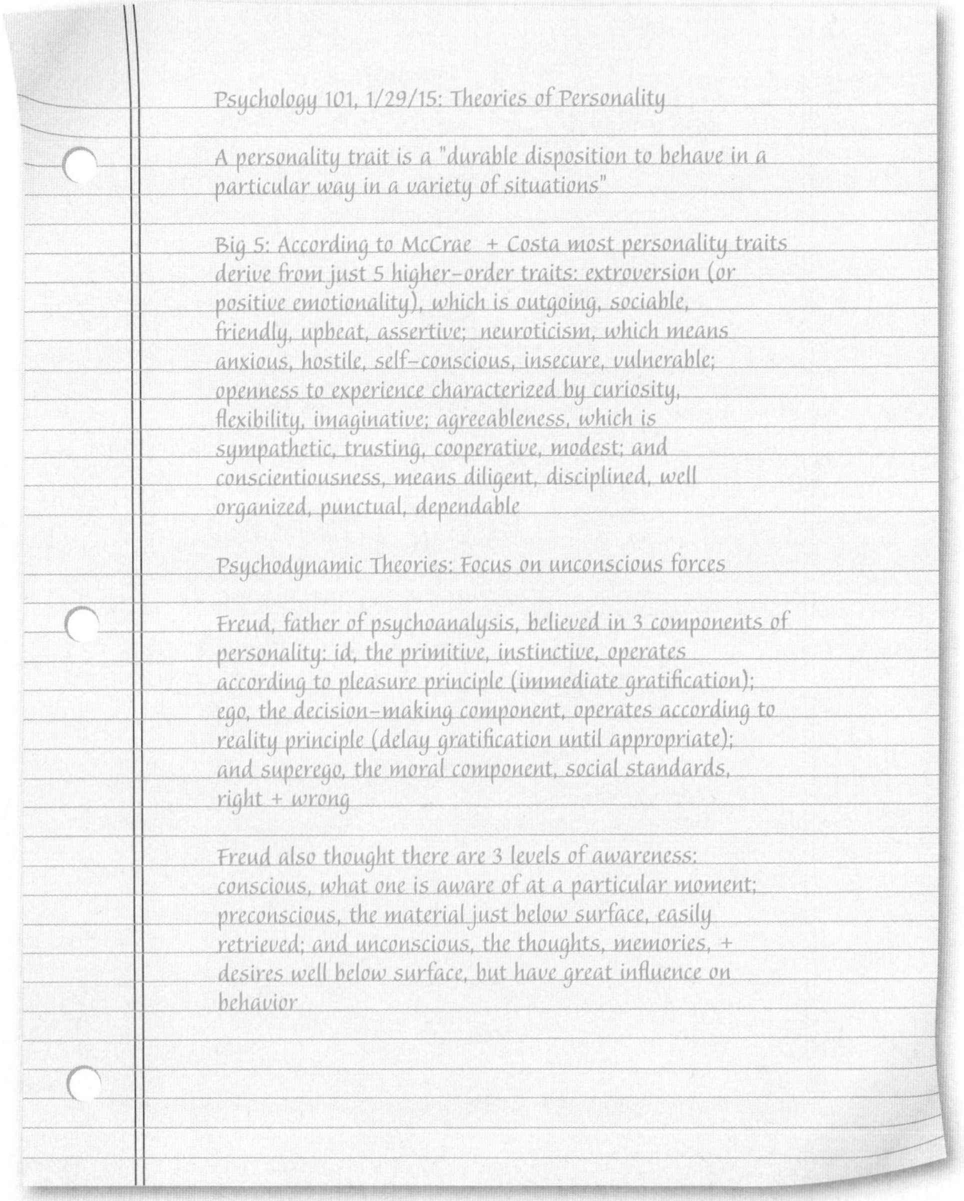

Psychology 101, 1/29/15: Theories of Personality

A personality trait is a "durable disposition to behave in a particular way in a variety of situations"

Big 5: According to McCrae + Costa most personality traits derive from just 5 higher-order traits: extroversion (or positive emotionality), which is outgoing, sociable, friendly, upbeat, assertive; neuroticism, which means anxious, hostile, self-conscious, insecure, vulnerable; openness to experience characterized by curiosity, flexibility, imaginative; agreeableness, which is sympathetic, trusting, cooperative, modest; and conscientiousness, means diligent, disciplined, well organized, punctual, dependable

Psychodynamic Theories: Focus on unconscious forces

Freud, father of psychoanalysis, believed in 3 components of personality: id, the primitive, instinctive, operates according to pleasure principle (immediate gratification); ego, the decision-making component, operates according to reality principle (delay gratification until appropriate); and superego, the moral component, social standards, right + wrong

Freud also thought there are 3 levels of awareness: conscious, what one is aware of at a particular moment; preconscious, the material just below surface, easily retrieved; and unconscious, the thoughts, memories, + desires well below surface, but have great influence on behavior

List Format. The list format can be effective in taking notes on terms and definitions, facts, or sequences such as personality types. It is easy to use lists in combination with the Cornell format, with key terms on the left and their definitions and explanations on the right (see Figure 4.4).

FIGURE 4.4 ❯ Note Taking in the List Format

> Psychology 101, 1/29/15: Theories of Personality
>
> - A personality trait is a "durable disposition to behave in a particular way in a variety of situations"
> - Big 5: According to McCrae + Costa most personality traits derive from just 5 higher-order traits
>   - extroversion, (or positive emotionality)=outgoing, sociable, friendly, upbeat, assertive
>   - neuroticism=anxious, hostile, self-conscious, insecure, vulnerable
>   - openness to experience=curiosity, flexibility, imaginative
>   - agreeableness=sympathetic, trusting, cooperative, modest
>   - conscientiousness=diligent, disciplined, well organized, punctual, dependable
> - Psychodynamic Theories: Focus on unconscious forces
> - Freud, father of psychoanalysis, believed in 3 components of personality
>   - id=primitive, instinctive, operates according to pleasure principle (immediate gratification)
>   - ego=decision-making component, operates according to reality principle (delay gratification until appropriate)
>   - superego=moral component, social standards, right + wrong
> - Freud also thought there are 3 levels of awareness
>   - conscious=what one is aware of at a particular moment
>   - preconscious=material just below surface, easily retrieved
>   - unconscious=thoughts, memories, + desires well below surface, but have great influence on behavior

YOUR TURN ❯ ON YOUR OWN

Using the list format, review this chapter and list the key ideas in your class notebook or on a digital device. Add definitions, examples, and other explanations related to each key idea.

Note-Taking Techniques

Whatever note-taking format you choose, follow these important steps:

1. **Identify the main ideas.** The first principle of effective note taking is to identify and write down the most important ideas around which the lecture is built. Although supporting details are important as well, focus your note taking on the main ideas. Such ideas can be buried in details, statistics, examples, or problems, but you will need to identify and record them for further study. Some instructors announce the purpose of a lecture or offer an outline of main ideas, followed by details. Other instructors develop presentation slides. If your instructor makes such materials available on a CMS beforehand, you can print them out and take notes on the outline or next to the slides during the lecture. Some instructors change their tone of voice or repeat themselves for each key idea. Some ask questions or provide an opportunity for discussion. If an instructor says something more than once, chances are it is important. Ask yourself, "What does my instructor want me to know at the end of today's class?"

2. **Don't try to write down everything.** Some first-year students try to do just that. They stop being thinkers and become just note takers. As you take notes, leave spaces so that you can fill in additional details that you might have missed during class but remember or read about later. Take the time to review and complete your notes as soon after class as possible. Once you have decided on a format for taking notes, you might also want to develop your own system of abbreviations. For example, you might write "inst" instead of "institution" or "eval" instead of "evaluation." Just make sure you will be able to understand your abbreviations when it's time to review.

3. **Don't be thrown by a disorganized lecturer.** When a lecture is disorganized, it's your job to try to organize what is said into general and specific points. When information is missing, you will need to indicate in your notes where the gaps are. After the lecture, review the reading material or ask your classmates to fill in these gaps, or ask your instructor. Some instructors have regular office hours for student appointments while others are willing to spend time after each class session to answer students' questions. However, it is amazing how few students use these opportunities for one-on-one instruction. The questions you ask might help your instructor realize which parts of the lecture need more attention or repetition.

4. **Keep your notes and supplementary materials for each course separate.** Whether you use folders, binders, or some combination, label your materials with the course number and name. Before class, label and date the paper you will be using for taking notes; after class, organize your notes chronologically. In your folder or binder, create separate tabbed sections for homework, lab assignments, graded and returned tests, and other materials. If you take notes electronically, you should create separate files and folders with specific names and dates. You can create a course folder and add subfolders for notes, assignments, and projects within each folder for that course.

5. **Download online notes, outlines or diagrams, charts, and graphs from the course management system (CMS) site and bring them to class.** You might be able to save yourself a lot of time during class if you do not have to try to copy graphs and diagrams while the instructor is talking. Instead, you can focus on the ideas being presented while adding your own labels and notes.

6. **If handouts are distributed in class, label them and place them near your notes.** Add handouts to your binder or folder as you review your notes each day.

Taking Notes in Nonlecture Courses. Always be ready to change your note-taking methods based on the situation. Group discussion is a popular way to teach in college because it engages students in active participation. On your campus you might also have courses with **Supplemental Instruction (SI)**, opportunities outside class to discuss the information covered in class.

How do you keep a record of what's happening in such classes? Assume you are taking notes in a problem-solving group assignment. You would begin your notes by asking yourself, "What is the problem?" and writing down the answer. As the discussion continues, you would list the solutions that are offered. These would be your main ideas. The important details might include the positive and negative aspects of each view or solution. The important thing to remember when taking notes in nonlecture courses is that you need to record the information presented by your classmates as well as by the instructor and to consider all reasonable ideas, even those that differ from your own.

When a course has separate lecture and discussion sessions, you will need to understand how the discussion sessions relate to and add to the lectures. If the material covered in the discussion session is different from what was covered in the lecture, you might need to ask for help in organizing your notes. When similar topics are covered, you can combine your notes so that you have full coverage of each topic.

How to organize the notes you take in a class discussion depends on the purpose or form of the discussion. It usually makes good sense to begin with the list of issues or topics of the discussion. Another approach is to list the questions raised for discussion. If the discussion explores reasons for and against a particular argument, divide your notes into columns or sections for each set of reasons. When different views are presented in discussion, record all the ideas. Your instructor might ask you to compare your own opinions to those of other students and explain why and how you formed those opinions.

Taking Notes in Mathematics and Science Courses. Many mathematics and science courses build on one another from term to term and from year to year. When you take notes in these courses, you will likely need to go back to the notes in the future. For example, when taking organic chemistry, you might need to review the notes you took in earlier chemistry courses. This can be particularly important if some time has passed since you completed your last related course, such as after a summer or a winter break.

Taking notes in math and science courses can be different from taking notes in other classes. The following tips can help:

- Write down any equations, formulas, diagrams, charts, graphs, and definitions that the instructor puts on the board or screen.
- Write the instructor's words as precisely as possible. Technical terms often have exact meanings and cannot be changed.
- Use standard symbols, abbreviations, and scientific notation.
- Write down all worked problems and examples step by step. The steps are often necessary in answering exam questions. Actively engage in solving the problem yourself as it is being solved at the front of the class. Be sure that you can follow the logic and understand the sequence of steps. If you have questions you cannot ask during lecture, write them down in your notes so that you can ask them in discussion, in the lab, or during the instructor's office hours.
- Consider taking your notes in pencil or erasable pen. You might need to make changes if you are copying long equations while also trying to pay attention to the instructor. You want to keep your notes as neat as possible. Later, you can use colored ink to add other details.
- Listen carefully to other students' questions and the instructor's answers. Take notes on the discussion and during question-and-answer periods.
- Use asterisks, exclamation points, question marks, or symbols of your own to highlight important points in your notes or questions that you need to come back to when you review.
- Refer back to the textbook after class; the text might contain better diagrams and other visual representations than you can draw while taking notes in class. If they are not provided in handouts or on the CMS, you might even want to scan or photocopy diagrams from the text and include them with your notes in your binder.
- Keep your binders for math and science courses until you graduate (or even longer if you are planning to transfer to a four-year college or university). They will serve as good review materials for later classes in math and science. In some cases, these notes can also be helpful in the workplace.

Using Technology to Take Notes. While some students use laptops, tablets, or other mobile devices for note taking (see the Tech Tip on p. 92), others prefer taking notes by hand so that they can easily circle important items or copy equations or diagrams while these are being presented. If you handwrite your notes, entering them on a computer after class for review purposes might be helpful, especially if you are a kinesthetic learner, preferring to learn through experience and practice. After class you can also cut and paste diagrams and other visuals into your notes and print a copy that might be easier to read than notes you wrote by hand.

Some students—especially aural learners, who prefer to hear information—find it is advantageous to record lectures. But if you record, don't become passive; listen actively. Students with specific types of learning disabilities might be urged to record lectures or use the services of note takers, who type on a laptop while the student views the notes on a separate screen.

YOUR TURN ❯ DISCUSS IN CLASS

Using the following table, list the advantages and disadvantages of taking notes electronically and by hand, and be prepared to discuss your ideas in class.

Electronic Notes		Handwritten Notes	
Advantages	Disadvantages	Advantages	Disadvantages

Review Your Notes

Unless we take steps to remember it, we forget much of the information we receive within the first twenty-four hours; in fact, the decline of memory over time is known as the **forgetting curve.** So if you do not review your notes almost immediately after class, it can be difficult to remember the material later. In two weeks, you will have forgotten up to 70 percent of it! Forgetting can be a serious problem when you are expected to learn and remember many different facts, figures, concepts, and relationships for a number of classes.

Immediate reviewing will help your overall understanding as well as your ability to remember important details during exams. Use the following three strategies:

1. **Write down the main ideas.** For five or ten minutes, quickly review your notes and select key words or phrases. Fill in the details you still remember but missed writing down. You might also want to ask your instructor or a classmate to quickly look at your notes to see if you have covered the major ideas.
2. **Repeat your ideas out loud.** Repeat a brief version of what you learned from the class either to yourself or to someone else. For many, the best way to learn something is to teach it to others. You will understand something better and remember it longer if you try to explain it. This helps you discover your own reactions and find the gaps in your understanding of the material. Asking and answering questions in class can also provide you with the feedback you need to make certain your understanding is accurate.

3. **Review your notes from the previous class just before the next class session.** As you sit in class the next time it meets, waiting for the instructor to begin, use the time to quickly review your notes from the previous class session. This will prepare you for the lecture that is about to begin and help you to ask questions about material from the earlier lecture that might not have been clear to you.

What if you have three classes in a row and no time for studying between them? Repeat the information as soon after class as possible. Review the most recent class first. Never delay doing this; if you do, it will take you longer to review, select main ideas, and repeat the ideas. With practice, you can complete the review of your main ideas from your notes quickly, perhaps between classes, during lunch, or while waiting for or riding the bus.

Compare Notes

Comparing notes with other students in a study group, SI session, or learning community has a number of benefits: You will probably take better notes when you know that

- someone else will see them,
- you can tell whether your notes are as clear and organized as those of other students,
- you can use your comparisons to see whether you agree on the most important points.

Take turns testing each other on what you have learned. This will help you predict exam questions and find out if you can answer them. In addition to sharing specific information from the class, you can also share with one another how you take and organize your notes. You might get new ideas that will help your overall learning.

Be aware, however, that merely copying another student's notes, no matter how good those notes are, does not benefit you as much as comparing notes does. If you had to be absent from a class because of illness or a family emergency, it's fine to look at another student's notes to see what you missed, but just rewriting those notes might not help you learn the material. Instead, summarize the other student's notes in your own words so that you know you understand the important points.

Class Notes and Homework

Once you have reviewed your notes, you can use them to complete homework assignments. Follow these steps:

1. **Do a warm-up for your homework.** Before doing the assignment, look through your notes again. Use a separate sheet of paper to rework examples, problems, or exercises. If there is related assigned material in the textbook, review it. Go back to the examples. Cover any answers or solutions, and try to respond to the questions or complete the problems without looking. Keep in mind that it can help to go back

through your course notes, reorganize them, highlight the important items, and create new notes that let you connect with the material.

2. **Do any assigned problems, and answer any assigned questions.** When you start doing your homework, read each question or problem and ask: What am I supposed to find or find out? What is most important? What is not all that important? Read each problem several times, and state it in your own words. Work the problem without referring to your notes or the text, as though you were taking a test. In this way, you will test your knowledge and know when you are prepared for exams.

3. **Don't give up too soon.** Start your homework with the hardest subject first while you are most energetic. When you face a problem or question that you cannot easily solve or answer, move on only after you have tried long enough. After you have completed the whole assignment, come back to any problems or questions that you could not solve or answer. Try once more, and then take a break. You might need to think about a particularly difficult problem for several hours or even days. Inspiration might come when you are waiting at a stoplight or just before you fall asleep.

4. **Complete your work.** When you finish an assignment, talk to yourself about what you learned from it. Think about how the problems and questions were different from one another, which strategies were successful, and what form the answers took. Be sure to review any material you have not mastered. Ask for help from the instructor, a classmate, a study group, the campus learning center, or a tutor to learn how to answer questions that stumped you.

YOUR TURN > ON YOUR OWN

Now that you've read suggestions about taking notes and studying for class, and practiced using different note-taking formats, which ideas will you use in your own note taking? List the ideas and formats that you like the most and explain your reasons.

TAKE NOTES LIKE A ROCK STAR

People remember only half of what they hear, which is a major reason you need to take lecture notes. Good note taking will also help you learn and remember key concepts and make it easier to study for tests. So why not improve your note-taking skills?

THE PROBLEM · *You don't know how to use your digital lecture notes to help you remember class material.*

THE FIX · *Use basic programs like Word, Excel, and PowerPoint to make your notes more organized and effective. Also check out apps like Evernote and OneNote.*

HOW TO DO IT

1. **Word** is great for taking notes in most classes. To emphasize main ideas, you can use boldface or underlining, font size or color, use highlights of different colors, or insert text boxes or charts. You can make bullet points or outlines and insert comment bubbles for emphasis. You can cut and paste material as you review your notes to make things organized and clear. You can also create different folders for each of your classes so that you can find everything you need with one click. (Note: Play around on the toolbars until you learn how the various tools work.)

2. **Excel** is especially good for economics and accounting courses, or any class that involves making calculations or financial statements. You can insert messages inside the cells of a spreadsheet to explain calculations. The notes will appear whenever you place your cursor over that cell.

3. **PowerPoint** can be a valuable tool for visual learners. Instead of keeping your notes in one long Word document, you can open up a Power-Point slideshow and type right into it. That way, every time your instructor introduces a new term or concept, you can open a new slide. It's a nice way to break up the material. Good to know: Some instructors post the PowerPoint slides that they plan to use in class a few hours in advance. Print them out and take them with you as note-taking tools; you can even write notes on the slides themselves. More and more, instructors are using the dynamic presentation tool, Prezi, described as a "virtual whiteboard." Prezi allows you to convert slides to pdf format.

CLEVER TRICKS

Date your notes. Focus on writing down the main points, using phrases or key words instead of long sentences. Keep your notes in order and in one place. Back up *everything*. If you're not a tech whiz, keep a pen and paper handy for sketching graphs and diagrams. Label your notes clearly. And if you find yourself struggling to keep up, practice your listening and typing skills.

THINK

Reflect on what you have learned in this chapter about being engaged in learning and getting the most out of class. List some of the ways you can fully participate in your classes and increase your engagement in and out of your classes based on what you have learned.

WRITE

This chapter explores multiple strategies for being an active listener and being engaged in class. What new strategies did you learn that you had never thought about or used before? What questions about effective note taking do you still have? Jot down some thoughts here and expand on them in a journal, in a notebook, or on your favorite digital device.

APPLY

1. Use the Cornell format to take notes on this chapter.
2. Create a PowerPoint presentation on the main points of this chapter.

WHERE TO GO FOR HELP

AT YOUR COLLEGE

VISIT . . .	IF YOU NEED HELP . . .
Academic Learning/Skills Center	preparing for class, taking notes, organizing your notes, and reviewing your notes with a tutor. Most centers offer note-taking tips and workshops for first-year students.
Computer Center	using Word, Excel, PowerPoint, OneNote, or Evernote to organize your notes.
Math Center	improving the notes you take in your math classes.
Disabled Student Services	arranging for a note-taker if you cannot take notes due to your documented disability.
Fellow college students	finding a tutor or joining a study group. Often, the best help we can get comes from those who are closest to us: fellow students. Keep an eye out in your classes for the most serious students. Those are the ones to seek out. It does not diminish you in any way to seek assistance from your peers.

ONLINE

GO TO . . .	IF YOU NEED HELP . . .
Toastmasters International: toastmasters.org	finding public speaking tips.
School for Champions: school-for-champions.com /grades/speaking.htm	locating guidelines for speaking in class.
Knowledge NoteBook: knowledgenotebook.com /review/best-note-taking-tips -from-10-colleges.html	finding note-taking tips.

MY COLLEGE'S RESOURCES

5 Reading to Learn from College Textbooks

PRE-READING ACTIVITY: This chapter offers strategies for learning from college textbooks. What are some of the challenges you are facing in reading and understanding your textbooks this term?

2. Challenge:

1. Challenge:

3. Challenge:

PROFILE

Irene Ramirez, 25

Early Childhood Education Major, *Community College of Rhode Island*

Irene Ramirez was born in New York City and spent most of her childhood in the Dominican Republic where she also went to high school. After graduating, she attended another community college but left at the end of her first term when she got married. Recently, she decided to re-enroll in school and again chose a community college because of smaller class sizes and more personal instruction, which she values highly, both as a student and as a mother raising two small children.

"It isn't easy being a mom, a wife, and also a full-time student," Irene explains. "Time is the hardest thing to find when you have toddlers, but they are my motivation." Irene uses a number of strategies to maximize her time and do the amount of reading expected in college. "I take small chunks of time and get the work done. I use my children's nap time as study time. I know nap time gives me at least two hours to go over an assignment." She uses those small blocks of time to learn. "If I don't have a lot of time, I look over the material. When I have more time, I highlight the things that stuck in my head and identify main ideas." Irene also types her notes. "That way," she explains, "my mind focuses on the material more so than when I just read it. Even if I don't remember something after reading it, I'll probably remember it after writing it down." Most important, though, Irene is careful to give herself enough time to learn the way that works best for her. "It took me a long time to figure out how it was easiest for me to learn," she says, "but I finally did, and I use the strategies that work for me."

> **"Time is the hardest thing to find when you have toddlers, but they are my motivation."**

Irene's one piece of advice to other first-year students is: "Always read before you go to class, even if it's just before going in. Material will make a lot more sense when you have seen it once before. You will be able to better understand concepts, and you won't forget main ideas."

After graduating from the Community College of Rhode Island, Irene plans to work as an early childhood teacher. She has also set a long-term goal of managing a daycare. Irene isn't afraid of dreaming big. "If I set out to do something, I have to give it my all," she says. "That's my expectation for myself."

As Irene suggested, reading college textbooks is more challenging than reading high school texts or reading for pleasure. College texts are full of concepts, terms, and complex information that you are expected to learn on your own in a short period of time. To accomplish this, you will find it helpful to use the active reading strategies presented in this chapter. They can help you get the most out of your college reading.

Depending on how much reading you did before coming to college—reading for pleasure, for your classes, or for work—you might find that reading is your favorite or least favorite way to learn. Even if reading *isn't* your favorite thing to do, it is absolutely essential to doing well in college and at work—no matter what your major or profession might be.

A PLAN FOR ACTIVE READING

Active reading involves participating in reading by using strategies, such as highlighting and taking notes, that help you stay focused. Active reading is different from reading novels or magazines for pleasure, which doesn't require you to do anything while you are reading. Active reading will increase your focus and concentration, promote greater understanding of what you read, and prepare you to study for tests and exams. These are the four steps in active reading designed to help you read college textbooks:

1. Previewing
2. Marking
3. Reading with concentration
4. Reviewing

YOUR TURN > WORK TOGETHER

With a group of your classmates, discuss which of these four steps you always, sometimes, or never do. Have one member of the group keep a tally and report results to the class. Which steps, if any, do your classmates think are necessary, and why?

Previewing

Previewing is the step in active reading when you take a first look at assigned reading before you really tackle the content. Think of previewing as browsing in a newly remodeled store. You locate the pharmacy and grocery areas. You get a feel for the locations of the men's, women's, and children's clothing departments; housewares; and electronics. You pinpoint the restrooms and checkout areas. You get a sense for where things are in relation to each other and compared to where they used to be. You identify where to find the items that you buy most often, whether they are diapers, milk, school supplies, or prescriptions. You get oriented.

Previewing a chapter in your textbook or other assigned reading is similar: the purpose is to get the big picture, to understand the main ideas in the reading and how those ideas connect with what you already know and to the material the instructor covers in class. Here's how you do it:

- Begin by reading the title of the chapter. Ask yourself: What do I already know about this subject?
- Next, quickly read through the learning objectives, if the chapter has them, or the introductory paragraphs. **Learning objectives** are what the main ideas or skills students are expected to learn from reading the chapter.
- Then turn to the end of the chapter and read the summary if there is one. A **summary** provides the most important ideas in the chapter.
- Finally, take a few minutes to skim the chapter, looking at the headings, subheadings, key terms, and tables and figures. Look for study exercises at the end of the chapter.

As part of your preview, note how many pages the chapter contains. It's a good idea to decide in advance how many pages you can reasonably expect to cover in your first study period. This can help build your concentration as you work toward your goal of reading a specific number of pages. Before long, you'll know how many pages are practical for you to read at one sitting.

Previewing might require some time up front, but it will save you time later. As you preview the text material, look for connections between the text and the related lecture material. Remember the related terms and concepts in your notes from the lecture. Use these strategies to warm up. Ask yourself: Why am I reading this? What do I want to know?

Keep in mind that different types of textbooks can require more or less time to read. For example, depending on your interests and previous knowledge, you might be able to read a psychology text more quickly than a biology text that includes many unfamiliar scientific words. Ask for help from your instructor, another student, or a tutor at the academic learning center.

Mapping. **Mapping** is a preview strategy in which you draw a wheel or branching structure to show relationships between main ideas and secondary ideas and how different concepts and terms fit together; it also helps you make connections to what you already know about the subject (see Figure 5.1). Mapping the chapter as you preview it provides a visual guide for how different chapter ideas work together. Because many students identify themselves as visual learners, visual mapping is an excellent learning tool not only for reading but also for test preparation.

In the wheel structure, place the central idea of the chapter in the circle. The central idea should be in the introduction to the chapter and might be even in the chapter title. Place secondary ideas on the lines connected to the circle, and place offshoots of those ideas on the lines attached to the main lines. In the branching map, the main idea goes at the top, followed by supporting ideas on the second tier, and so forth. Fill in the title first. Then, as you skim the chapter, use the headings and subheadings to fill in the key ideas.

FIGURE 5.1 > Wheel and Branching Maps

Wheel Map

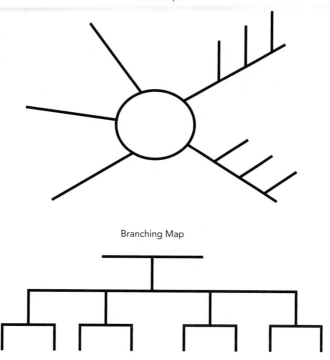

Branching Map

YOUR TURN > ON YOUR OWN

Sketch either the wheel map or the branching map on a piece of notebook paper and map this chapter.

Outlining or Listing. Perhaps you are more of a read/write learner than a visual learner and prefer a more step-by-step visual image. If so, consider making an outline of the headings and subheadings in the chapter (see Figure 5.2 on the next page). You can usually identify main topics, subtopics, and specific terms under each subtopic in your text by the size of the print. Notice, also, that the different levels of headings in a textbook look different. They are designed to show relationships among topics and subtopics covered within a section. Flip through this textbook to see how the headings are designed. (Review the chapter on Getting the Most Out of Class for more on outlining.)

To save time when you are outlining, don't write full sentences. Rather, include clear explanations of new technical terms and symbols. Pay special attention to topics that the instructor covered in class. If you aren't sure whether your outlines contain too much or too little detail, compare them with the outlines your classmates or members of your study group have made. Check with your instructor during office hours. In preparing for a test, review your chapter outlines to see how everything fits together.

FIGURE 5.2 › Sample Outline

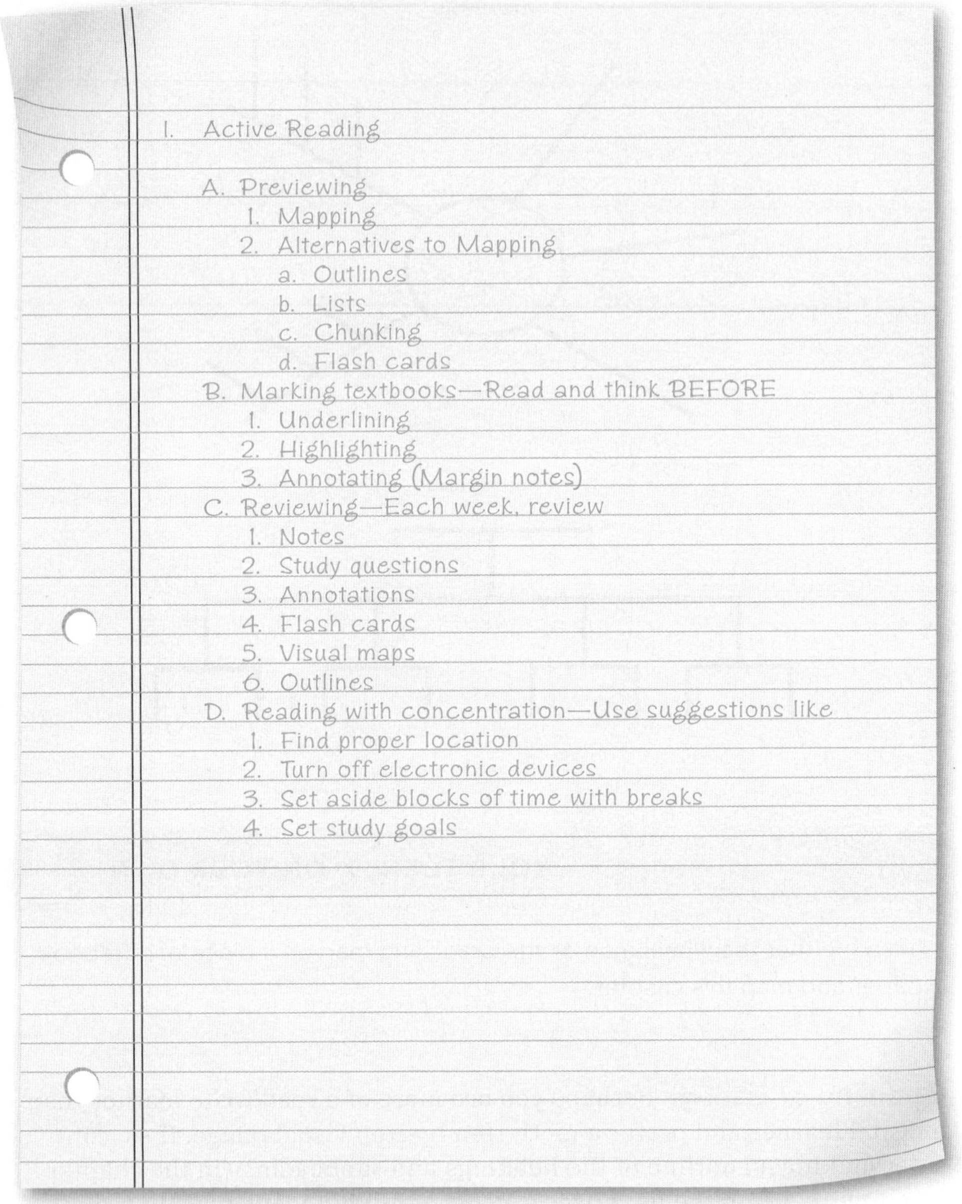

I. Active Reading

   A. Previewing
      1. Mapping
      2. Alternatives to Mapping
         a. Outlines
         b. Lists
         c. Chunking
         d. Flash cards
   B. Marking textbooks—Read and think BEFORE
      1. Underlining
      2. Highlighting
      3. Annotating (Margin notes)
   C. Reviewing—Each week, review
      1. Notes
      2. Study questions
      3. Annotations
      4. Flash cards
      5. Visual maps
      6. Outlines
   D. Reading with concentration—Use suggestions like
      1. Find proper location
      2. Turn off electronic devices
      3. Set aside blocks of time with breaks
      4. Set study goals

Another previewing technique is listing. A list can be effective when you are dealing with a text that introduces many new terms and their definitions. Set up the list with the terms in the left column, and fill in definitions, descriptions, and examples on the right as you read or reread. Divide the terms on your list into groups of five, seven, or nine, and leave white space between the clusters so that you can visualize each group in your mind. This practice is known as **chunking**. We learn material best when it is in chunks of five, seven, or nine.

Creating Flash Cards. **Flash cards** are like portable test questions—you write a question or term on the front of a small card and the answer or definition on the back. Or in a course that requires you to memorize dates,

FIGURE 5.3 › Examples of Flash Cards

like American history, you might write a key date on one side of the card and the event on the other. To study chemistry, you would write a chemical formula on one side and the ionic compound on the other. You might use flash cards to learn vocabulary words or practice simple sentences for a language course as shown in Figure 5.3. Creating the cards from your readings and using them to prepare for exams are great ways to retain information and are especially helpful for visual and kinesthetic learners. Some apps, such as Flashcardlet and Chegg Flashcards, enable you to create flash cards on your mobile devices.

YOUR TURN › ON YOUR OWN

Prepare flash cards for the key terms that appear in this chapter. Key terms are defined where they appear in the text.

Strategies for Reading and Marking Your Textbook

After completing your preview, you are ready to read the text actively. With your map, outline, list, or flash cards to guide you, mark the sections that are most important. To avoid marking too much or marking the wrong information, first read without using your pencil or highlighter. This means you should read the text *at least* twice.

FIGURE 5.4 > Examples of Marking

Using a combination of highlighting, lines, and margin notes, the reader has made the content of this page easy for review. Without reading the text, note the highlighted words and phrases and the margin notes, and see how much information you can gather from them. Then read the text itself. Does the markup serve as a study aid? Does it cover the essential points? Would you have marked this page any differently? Why or why not?

CULTURE AND HUMAN BEHAVIOR

The Stress of Adapting to a New Culture

differences affecting cultural stress

Refugees, immigrants, and even international students are often unprepared for the dramatically different values, language, food, customs, and climate that await them in their new land. The process of changing one's values and customs as a result of contact with another culture is referred to as *acculturation*. **Acculturative stress** is the stress that results from the pressure of adapting to a new culture (Sam & Berry, 2010).

acceptance of new culture reduces stress also speaking new language, education, & social support

Many factors can influence the degree of acculturative stress that a person experiences. For example, when the new society accepts ethnic and cultural diversity, acculturative stress is reduced (Mana & others, 2009). The transition is also eased when the person has some familiarity with the new language and customs, advanced education, and social support from friends, family members, and cultural associations (Schwartz & others, 2010). Acculturative stress is also lower if the new culture is similar to the culture of origin.

how attitudes affect stress

Cross-cultural psychologist John Berry (2003, 2006) has found that a person's attitudes are important in determining how much acculturative stress is experienced (Sam & Berry, 2010). When people encounter a new cultural environment, they are faced with two questions: (1) Should I seek positive relations with the dominant society? (2) Is my original cultural identity of value to me, and should I try to maintain it?

4 patterns of acculturation

The answers produce one of four possible patterns of acculturation: integration, assimilation, separation, or marginalization (see the diagram). Each pattern represents a different way of coping with the stress of adapting to a new culture (Berry, 1994, 2003). 1*Integrated* individuals continue to value their original cultural customs but also seek to become part of the dominant society. They embrace a *bicultural* identity (Hunyh & others, 2011). Biculturalism is associated with higher self-esteem and lower levels of depression, anxiety, and stress, suggesting that the bicultural identity may be the most adaptive acculturation pattern (Schwartz & others, 2010). The successfully integrated individual's level of acculturative stress will be low (Lee, 2010). 2*Assimilated* individuals give up their old cultural identity and try to become part of the new society. They adopt the customs and social values of the new environment, and abandon their original cultural traditions.

possible rejection by both cultures

Assimilation usually involves a moderate level of stress, partly because it involves a psychological loss—one's previous cultural identity. People who follow this pattern also face the possibility of being rejected either by members of the majority culture or by members of their original culture (Schwartz & others, 2010). The

Acculturative Stress Acculturative stress can be reduced when immigrants learn the language and customs of their newly adopted home. Here, two friends, one from China, one from Cuba, help each other in an English class in Miami, Florida.

process of learning new behaviors and suppressing old behaviors can also be moderately stressful.

3*Individuals who follow the pattern of *separation* maintain their cultural identity and avoid contact with the new culture. They may refuse to learn the new language, live in a neighborhood that is primarily populated by others of the same ethnic background, and socialize only with members of their own ethnic group.

In some cases, separation is not voluntary, but is due to the dominant society's unwillingness to accept the new immigrants. Thus, it can be the result of discrimination. Whether voluntary or involuntary, the level of acculturative stress associated with separation tends to be high.

4*Finally, the *marginalized* person lacks cultural and psychological contact with *both* his traditional cultural group and the culture of his new society. By taking the path of marginalization, he lost the important features of his traditional culture but has not replaced them with a new cultural identity.

Although rare, the path of marginalization is associated with the greatest degree of acculturative stress. Marginalized individuals are stuck in an unresolved conflict between their traditional culture and the new society, and may feel as if they don't really belong anywhere. Fortunately, only a small percentage of immigrants fall into this category (Schwartz & others, 2010).

*separation may be self-imposed or discriminating

higher stress with separation

*marginalized = higher level of stress

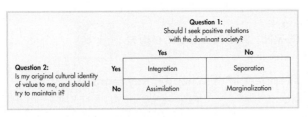

Question 1:
Should I seek positive relations with the dominant society?

Question 2: Is my original cultural identity of value to me, and should I try to maintain it?		Yes	No
	Yes	Integration	Separation
	No	Assimilation	Marginalization

Patterns of Adapting to a New Culture According to cross-cultural psychologist John Berry, there are four basic patterns of adapting to a new culture (Sam & Berry, 2010). Which pattern is followed depends on how the person responds to the two key questions shown.

Source: "The Stress of Adapting to a New Culture," Adapted from *Discovering Psychology*, 6th ed., p. 534, by D. H. Hockenbury and S. E. Hockenbury. Copyright © 2013 by Worth Publishers. Used with permission.

Marking is an active reading strategy that helps you focus and concentrate as you read. When you mark your textbook, you underline, highlight, or make margin notes or annotations. (**Annotations** are notes or remarks about a piece of writing.) Figure 5.4 provides an example of each method. No matter what method you prefer, remember these two important guidelines:

1. **Read before you mark.** Finish reading a section before you decide which are the most important ideas and concepts.
2. **Think before you mark.** When you read a text for the first time, everything can seem important. After you complete a section, reflect on it to identify the key ideas. Ask yourself: What are the most important ideas? What terms has the instructor emphasized in class? What will I see on the test? This can help you avoid marking too much material. On a practical note, if you find that you have made mistakes in how you have highlighted or that your textbooks were already highlighted by another student, select a completely different color highlighter to use.

Here are two additional guidelines about textbook marking:

- **Take notes along with marking.** If you only make notes or underline in your textbook, you will have to read all the pages again. Rather than relying on marking alone, consider taking notes as you read. You can add your notes to the map, outline, list, or flash cards you created while you previewed the text. These methods are also more practical if you intend to review with a friend or study group.
- **Do more than just highlighting or underlining.** Highlights and underlines are intended to pull your eye only to key words and important facts. If highlighting or underlining is actually a form of procrastination for you (you are reading through the material but planning to learn it at a later date) or if you are highlighting or underlining nearly everything you read, you might be doing yourself more harm than good. You won't be able to identify important concepts quickly if they're lost in a sea of color or lines. Ask yourself whether your highlighting or underlining is helping you be more active in your learning process. If not, you might want to try a different technique such as making margin notes or annotations. If you find that you have made mistakes in how you have highlighted or that your textbooks were already highlighted by another student, select a completely different color highlighter to use. Just noting what's most important doesn't mean you learn the material, and it can give you a false sense of security. When you force yourself to put something in your own words while taking notes, you are not only predicting exam questions but also evaluating whether you can answer them. Although these active reading strategies take more time at the beginning, they save you time in the long run because they help you focus on the reading and make it easy to review.

Reviewing

The final step in active textbook reading is reviewing. **Reviewing** means to look through your assigned

Mark and Review

Among the best approaches to getting more from your reading are marking the text and reviewing carefully. These strategies are good enough for George Clooney. Are they good enough for you?

Source: Michael Buckner/ Getty Images for American Foundation for Equal Rights

reading again. Many students expect to read through their text material once and be able to remember the ideas four, six, or even twelve weeks later at test time. More realistically, you will need to include regular reviews in your study process. Here is where your notes, study questions, margin notes and annotations, flash cards, visual maps, or outlines will be most useful. Your study goal should be to review the material from each chapter every week. Here are some strategies:

- Consider ways to use your senses to review.
- Recite aloud.
- Tick off each item on a list on your fingertips.
- Post diagrams, maps, or outlines around your living space to see them often and visualize them while taking the test.

Reading with Concentration

Students often have trouble concentrating or understanding the content when they read textbooks. This is normal, and many factors contribute to this problem: the time of day, your energy level, your interest in the material, and your study location.

Consider these suggestions, and decide which would help you improve your reading ability:

- **Find a quiet study place.** Choose a room or location away from traffic and distracting noises such as the campus information commons. Avoid studying in your bed because your body is conditioned to go to sleep there.
- **Mute or power off your electronic devices.** Store your cell phone in your book bag or some other place where you aren't tempted to check it. If you are reading on a device like a laptop or tablet, download what you need and disconnect from Wi-Fi to not to be tempted to email, chat, or check social media sites.
- **Read in blocks of time, with short breaks in between.** Some students can read for 50 minutes; others find that a 50-minute reading period is too long. By reading for small blocks of time throughout the day instead of cramming in all your reading at the end of the day, you should be able to process material more easily.
- **Set goals for your study period.** A realistic goal might be "I will read twenty pages of my psychology text in the next 50 minutes." Reward yourself with a 10-minute break after each 50-minute study period.
- **Engage in physical activity during breaks.** If you have trouble concentrating or staying awake, take a quick walk around the library or down the hall. Stretch or take some deep breaths, and think positively about your study goals. Then go back to studying.
- **Actively engage with the material.** Write study questions in the margins, take notes, or recite key ideas. Reread confusing parts of the text, and make a note to ask your instructor for clarification.
- **Focus on the important portions of the text.** Pay attention to the first and last sentences of paragraphs and to words in italics or bold type.
- **Understand the words.** Use the glossary in the text or a dictionary to define unfamiliar terms.

- **Use organizers as you read.** Keep the maps, outlines, lists, or flash cards you created during your preview as you read, and add to them as you go. For example, you can use the following table to organize the information while you are reading:

Date:	Title:
Textbook:	**Chapter:**
What is the overall idea of the reading?	
What is the **main idea** of each major section of the reading?	Section 1: Section 2: Section 3:
What are the **supporting ideas** presented in the reading? Examples? Statistics? Any reference to research?	1. 4. 2. 5. 3.
What are the key terms and what do they mean?	
What are the conclusions from the reading?	
What are two or three things that I remember after reading?	1. 2. 3.

YOUR TURN > TRY IT

The next time you are reading a textbook, monitor your ability to concentrate. Check your watch when you begin, and check it again when your mind begins to wander. How many minutes did you concentrate on your reading? What can you do to keep your mind from wandering?

STRATEGIES FOR READING TEXTBOOKS

As you begin reading, be sure to learn more about the textbook and its author by reading sections at the beginning of the book, such as the preface, foreword, introduction, and author's biographical sketch. The **preface,** a brief overview near the beginning of a book, is usually written by the author (or authors) and will tell you why they wrote the book and what material the book covers; it will also explain the book's organization and give insight into the author's viewpoint—all of which will likely help you see the relationships among the facts presented and comprehend the ideas presented across the book. Reading the preface can come in handy if you are feeling a little lost at different points in the term. The preface often lays out the tools available in each chapter to guide you through the content so if you find yourself struggling with the reading, be sure you are taking advantage of these tools.

The **foreword** is often an endorsement of the book written by someone other than the author. Some books have an additional **introduction** that reviews the book's overall organization and its contents, often chapter by chapter. Some textbooks include study questions at the end of each chapter. Take time to read and respond to these questions, whether or not your instructor requires you to do so.

YOUR TURN **>** DISCUSS IT

How do you usually read a textbook chapter? Do you just read it? Do you highlight or take notes as you go?

Textbooks Are Not Created Equal

Textbooks in the major **disciplines**—areas of academic study—are different in their organizations and styles of writing. Some may be easier to understand than others, but don't give up if the reading level is challenging.

Math and science texts are filled with graphs and figures that you will need to understand in order to grasp the content and the classroom presentations. They are also likely to have less text and more practice exercises than other textbooks do. If you have trouble reading and understanding any of your textbooks, get help from your instructor or your college's academic learning center.

Textbooks must try to cover a lot of material in a limited space, and they won't necessarily provide all the things you want to know about a topic. If you find yourself interested in a particular topic, go to the **primary sources**—the original research or documents on a topic. You'll find those referenced in almost all textbooks, either at the end of the chapters or in the back of the book.

You might also go to other related sources that make the text more interesting and easier to understand. Your instructors might use the textbook only to supplement the lectures. Some instructors expect you to read the textbook carefully while others are much more concerned that you can understand broad concepts that come primarily from lectures. Ask your instructors what the tests will cover and what types of questions will be used.

Finally, not all textbooks are written in the same way. Some are better designed and written than others. If your textbook seems disorganized or hard to understand, let your instructor know your opinion. Other students likely feel the same way. Your instructor might spend some class time explaining the text, and he or she can meet with you during office hours to help you with the material.

Math Texts

While the previous suggestions about textbook reading apply across the board, mathematics textbooks present some special challenges because they usually have lots of symbols and few words. Each statement and every line in the solution of a problem needs to be considered and processed slowly. Typically, the author presents the material through definitions, theorems, and sample problems. As you read, pay special attention to definitions. Learning all the terms that relate to a new topic is the first step toward understanding.

Math texts usually include derivations of formulas and proofs of theorems. You must understand and be able to apply the formulas and theorems, but unless your course has a particularly theoretical emphasis, you are less likely to be responsible for all the proofs. So if you get lost in the proof of a theorem, go on to the next item in the section. When you come to a sample problem, it's time to get busy. Pick up pencil and paper, and work through the problem in the book. Then cover the solution and think through the problem on your own.

Of course, the exercises in each section are the most important part of any math textbook. A large portion of the time you devote to the course will be spent completing assigned exercises. It is absolutely necessary to do this homework before the next class, whether or not your instructor collects it. Success in mathematics requires regular practice, and students who keep up with math homework, either alone or in groups, perform better than students who don't, particularly when they include in their study groups other students who are more advanced in the study of math.

After you complete the assignment, skim through the other exercises in the problem set. Reading the unassigned problems will help you understand more about the topic. Finally, talk the material through to yourself, and be sure your focus is on understanding the problem and its solution, not on memorization. Memorizing something might help you remember how to work through one problem, but it does not help you learn the steps involved so that you can use them for solving other similar problems.

Getting the Most Out of Your Textbooks

Math and science texts are filled with graphs and figures that you will need to understand to learn the content and the classroom presentations. If you have trouble reading and understanding any of your textbooks, get help from your instructor or your classmates.

YOUR TURN > DISCUSS IT

Discuss with classmates two or three of your challenges in learning from your math textbooks. Share some strategies that you use to study math.

Science Texts

Your approach to your science textbook will depend somewhat on whether you are studying a math-based science, such as physics, or a text-based science, such as biology. In either case, you need to become familiar with the overall format of the book. Review the table of contents and the **glossary** (a list of key words and their definitions), and check the material in the **appendixes** (supplemental materials at the end of the book). There you will find lists of physical constants, unit conversions, and various charts and tables. Many physics and chemistry books also include a mini-review of the math you will need in science courses.

Notice the organization of each chapter, and pay special attention to graphs, charts, and boxes. The amount of technical detail might seem overwhelming. Remember that textbook authors take great care in presenting material in a logical format, and they include tools to guide you through the material. Learning objectives at the start and summaries at the end of each chapter can be useful to study both before and after reading the chapter. You will usually find answers to selected problems in the back of the book. Use the answer key or the student solutions manual to increase your understanding of the chapters.

As you begin an assigned section in a science text, skim the material quickly to gain a general idea of the topic and to begin becoming familiar with the new vocabulary and technical symbols. Then look over the end-of-chapter problems so that you'll know what to look for in your detailed reading of the chapter. State a specific goal: "I'm going to learn about recent developments in plate tectonics," or "I'm going to distinguish between mitosis and meiosis," or "Tonight I'm going to focus on the topics in this chapter that were stressed in class."

Should you underline and highlight, or should you outline the material in your science textbooks? You might decide to underline or highlight for a subject such as anatomy, which involves a lot of memorization. In most sciences, however, it is best to outline the text chapters.

Social Science and Humanities Texts

Many of the suggestions that apply to science textbooks also apply to reading in the **social sciences** (academic disciplines that examine human aspects of the world, such as sociology, psychology, anthropology, economics, political science, and history). Social science textbooks are filled with special terms specific to the particular field of study. These texts also describe research and theory building and contain references to many primary sources. Your social science texts might also describe differences in opinions or perspectives. Social scientists do not all agree on any one issue, and you might be introduced to a number of ongoing debates about particular issues. In fact, your reading can become more interesting if you seek out different opinions about the same issue. You might have to go beyond your course textbook, but your library will be a good source of various viewpoints about ongoing controversies.

Textbooks in the **humanities** (branches of knowledge that investigate human beings, their culture, and their self-expression, such as philosophy, religion, literature, music, and art) provide facts, examples, opinions, and original material such as stories or essays. You will often be asked to react to your reading by identifying central themes or characters.

YOUR TURN › WORK TOGETHER

In a small group, discuss how important you think textbooks are in your courses. What are some other ways to access the information you want and need in order to learn?

Supplementary Material

Whether your instructor requires you to read material in addition to the textbook, you will learn more about the topic if you go to some of the primary and supplementary sources that are referenced in each chapter of your text. These sources can be journal articles, research papers, or original essays, and they can be found online or in your library. Reading the original source material will give you more detail than most textbooks do.

Many of these sources were originally written for other instructors or researchers. Therefore, they often refer to concepts that are familiar to other scholars but not necessarily to first-year college students. If you are reading a journal article that describes a theory or research study, one technique for easier understanding is to read from the end to the beginning. That is, read the article's conclusion and discussion sections. Then go back to see how the author performed the experiment or formed the ideas. In almost all scholarly journals, articles are introduced by an **abstract**, a paragraph-length summary of the methods and major findings. Reading the abstract is a quick way to get the main points of a research article before you start reading it. As you're reading research articles, always ask yourself: So what? Was the research important to what we know about the topic, or, in your opinion, was it unnecessary?

5.3

IMPROVING YOUR READING

With effort, you *can* improve your reading. Remember to be flexible and to adjust *how* you read depending on *what* you are reading. Here are a few suggestions:

- Evaluate the importance and difficulty of the assigned readings, and adjust your reading style and the time you set aside to do the reading.

How you read your math textbook is different from how you read your psychology textbook. When reading your math textbook, you should have a notebook to record your solutions to the problems. When you read your psychology textbook, you should be highlighting the important ideas or making margin notes.

- Connect one important idea to another by asking yourself: Why am I reading this? Where does this fit in? Writing summaries and preparing notes and outlines can help you connect ideas across the chapters.
- When the textbook material is exactly the same as the lecture material, you can save time by concentrating mainly on one or the other.

It takes a planned approach to read and understand textbook materials and other assigned readings and to remember what you have read.

Monitoring Your Reading

You can monitor your comprehension while reading textbooks by asking yourself: Do I understand this? If not, stop and reread the material. Look up words that are not clear. Try to clarify the main points and how they relate to one another.

Another way to check that you understand what you are reading is to try to recite the material aloud, either to yourself or to your study partner. Using a study group to monitor your comprehension gives you immediate feedback and is highly motivating. After you have read with concentration from the first section of the chapter, proceed to each subsequent section until you have finished the chapter.

After you have completed each section and before you move on to the next section, ask again: What are the key ideas? What will I see on the test? At the end of each section, try to guess what information the author will present in the next section.

Developing Your Vocabulary

Textbooks are full of new words and terms. A **vocabulary** is a set of words in a particular language or field of knowledge. As you become familiar with the vocabulary of an academic field, reading the texts related to that field becomes easier.

If words are such a basic and essential component of our knowledge, what is the best way to learn them? The following are some basic vocabulary-building strategies:

- **Notice and write down unfamiliar terms during your preview of a text.** Consider making a flash card for each term or making a list of terms.
- **Think about the context when you come across challenging words.** See whether you can guess the meaning of an unfamiliar term by using the words around it.
- **Consider a word's parts.** If context by itself is not enough to help you guess the meaning of an unfamiliar word, try analyzing the term to discover its root (or base part) and any prefixes (parts that come before the root) or suffixes (parts that follow the root). For example, *transport* has the root *port*, which means "carry," and the prefix *trans*, which means "across." Together the word means "carrying across" or "carrying from

one place to another." Knowing the meaning of prefixes and suffixes can be very helpful. For example, *anti* means "against," and *pro* means "for."

- **Use the glossary of the text or a dictionary.** Textbook publishers carefully compile glossaries to help students learn the vocabulary of a given discipline. If the text has no glossary, have a dictionary on hand. If a given word has more than one definition, search for the meaning that fits your text. The online Merriam-Webster Dictionary (**merriam-webster.com**) is especially helpful for college students.
- **Use new words in your writing and speaking.** If you use a new word a few times, you'll soon know it. In addition, flash cards can be handy at exam time for reviewing the definitions of new words.

YOUR TURN > TRY IT

Choose a chapter in this or another textbook. As you read it, list the words that are new to you or that you're not sure you understand. Look up a few of these words in a dictionary. Set a goal to add at least one new word a week to your personal vocabulary. Note these words and their definitions here.

_____

_____

_____

_____

What to Do When You Fall Behind on Your Reading

From time to time, life might get in the way of doing your assigned readings on time. You may get sick or have to take care of a sick family member, you may have to work extra hours, or you may have a personal problem that prevents you from concentrating on your courses for a short time. Unfortunately, some students procrastinate and think they can catch up. That is a myth. The less you read and do your assignments, the harder you will have to work to make up for the lost time.

A Marathon, Not a Sprint
If you fall behind in your reading, you're not alone — many students do. Remember that your studies are more like a marathon than a sprint; you should take time to catch up, but do so at a steady pace. Do your assigned readings, study with others, get help, and do not give up!
Source: © Jerome Prevost/TempSport/Corbis

If you try to follow the schedule for your assigned readings but fall behind, do not panic. Here are some suggestions for getting back on track:

- **Add one or two hours a day to your study time to go back and read the parts that you missed.** In particular, take advantage of every spare moment to read; for example, read during lunch hour at work or while you are waiting for public transportation or at the doctor's office.
- **Join a study group.** If everyone in the group reads a section of the assigned chapter and shares and discusses his or her notes, summaries, or outlines with the group, you can all cover the content more quickly.
- **Ask for help.** Visit your college's learning center to work with a tutor who can help you with difficult concepts in the textbook.
- **Talk to your instructor.** Ask for extra time to make up your assignments if you have fallen behind because of a valid reason such as sickness or dealing with a personal problem. Most instructors are willing to make a one-time exception to help students catch up.
- **Do not give up.** You may have to work harder for a short period of time, but you will soon get caught up.

If English Is Not Your First Language

The English language is one of the most difficult languages to learn. Words are often spelled differently from the way they sound, and the language is full of **idioms**—phrases that cannot be understood from the individual meanings of the words. If for example, you instructor tells you to "hit the books," she does not mean for you to physically pound your texts with your fist but rather to study hard.

If you are learning English and are having trouble reading your texts, don't give up. Reading slowly and reading more than once can help you improve your comprehension. Make sure that you have two good dictionaries—one in English and one that links English with your primary language—and look up every key word you don't know. Be sure to practice thinking, writing, and speaking in English, and take advantage of your college's services. Your campus might have English as a second language (ESL) tutoring and workshops. Ask your adviser or your first-year seminar instructor to help you find where those services are offered on your campus.

EMBRACE THE E-BOOK

THE PROBLEM *Your back hurts from carrying around heavy textbooks, and you're aware that you can buy them as e-books.*

THE FIX *Discover how a digital reader differs from (and can even be better than) printed books.*

HOW TO DO IT

THE PROS

- Digital reading devices (e-readers) are portable—most weigh about a pound—and can hold thousands of books.
- With most e-readers, you can buy books online from anywhere or you can download them from the public library and start reading them within minutes.
- You can type notes in an e-book, highlight passages, or copy and paste sections.
- You can print out pages simply by connecting your device to your printer.
- Many e-readers even accept audiobooks and can read to you aloud.
- You can adjust the size of an e-book's text, making it easier to read.
- Some e-readers link directly to a built-in dictionary. Just highlight a word, and the device will look it up. Others will also link to reference Web sites like Google or Wikipedia when a Wi-Fi or 4G connection is available.
- E-books are searchable and even sharable.

THE CONS

- Digital reading devices are expensive.
- Unlike books, they can break if you drop them.
- It's harder to flip through pages of an e-book than of a printed book.

GOOD TO KNOW

The most popular e-readers are the iPad, the Kindle, the Nook, and the Kobo Touch. Each comes in several different versions. Basic models are designed to replicate the experience of reading a paper book. More expensive models offer touch color screens, Web browsers, video, music, and thousands of free and for-purchase apps.

THINK

This chapter is full of strategies for effectively reading your college textbooks. What strategies did you find the most useful? What do you think is your biggest challenge in using these strategies to improve your reading habits?

Strategies I learned and will use:

1. _____

2. _____

3. _____

Challenges in using the strategies:

1. _____

2. _____

3. _____

WRITE

It is easy to say that there is not enough time in the day to get everything done, especially when you have a long reading assignment. Challenge yourself to avoid using this excuse. How can you modify your daily activities to make time for reading? What have you learned in this chapter that can help you with that? Jot down a few thoughts here, and then expand on them in a journal, in a notebook, or on your favorite digital device.

_____

_____

_____

_____

APPLY

1. Look through your course syllabi, and identify a chapter that you need to read in the next couple of weeks. Preview the chapter and prepare an outline in your notebook or on a digital device, using the following format, based on the headings and subheadings:

Title:

I.

    A.

    B.

        1.

        2.

            a.

                (1)

                (2)

            b.

(Continue outlining.)

2. As you read a chapter of this or another textbook, complete the following table:

Date:	Title:
Textbook:	**Chapter:**
What is the overall idea of the reading?	
What is the **main idea** of each major section of the reading?	Section 1: Section 2: Section 3:
What are the **supporting ideas** presented in the reading? Examples? Statistics? Any reference to research?	1. 2. 3. 4. 5.
What are the **key terms** and what do they mean?	
What are the conclusions from the reading?	
What are two or three things that **you remember** after reading?	1. 2. 3.

WHERE TO GO FOR HELP

AT YOUR COLLEGE

VISIT . . .

Academic Learning/Skills Center

Fellow Students

Disabled Student Services

IF YOU NEED HELP . . .

reading textbooks, taking notes, and studying for exams.

joining a study group or finding a study partner. You are much more likely to be successful if you study with other students.

arranging for accommodations because you have a reading disability.

ONLINE

GO TO . . .

Bucks County Community College:
http://faculty.bucks.edu/specpop/annotate.htm

Niagara University's Office for Academic Support:
niagara.edu/oas-21-tips

IF YOU NEED HELP . . .

finding a guide for annotating your textbooks.

discovering tips for better textbook reading.

MY COLLEGE'S RESOURCES

6 Studying, Understanding, and Remembering

PRE-READING ACTIVITY: Before you start reading, take a few minutes to look through this chapter. Which topic interests you the most? Which topic do you think can be the most helpful to you?

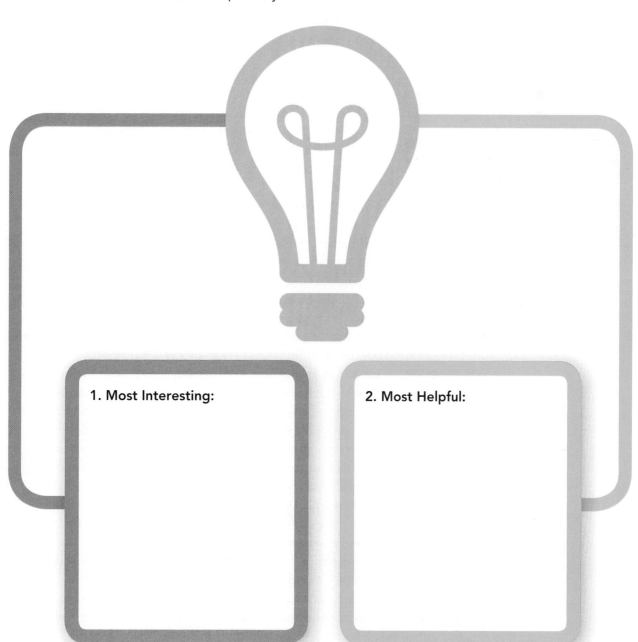

1. Most Interesting:

2. Most Helpful:

6.1 Studying in College

6.2 How Memory Works

6.3 Improving Your Memory

6.4 Studying to Understand and Remember

 PROFILE ✕

Joe Miranda, 19
Engineering Major, *Spokane Falls Community College*

Source: pkchai/Shutterstock

Early in high school, Joe Miranda did well enough in his classes to be able to play basketball and football. He hoped to be a college athlete, but then a knee injury changed that. In his senior year of high school in Spokane, Washington, one of Joe's teachers recommended that he look into engineering as a profession. Joe had always been interested in math and science, but he hadn't done much planning for college. He researched different careers and types of engineering and found that environmental engineering excited him. Then he researched programs close to home.

Joe plans to complete his associate's degree in pre-engineering at Spokane Falls Community College (SFCC) and transfer to Washington State University. SFCC has a six-quarter engineering program intended to prepare students for transfer to a four-year engineering college in their junior year. When he was in high school Joe didn't take the college-prep courses he needed to enter the engineering program at SFCC right away. As a result, he is taking lower-level college courses that will allow him to ramp up to the higher-level courses

> **"I found a great tutor at the learning center on campus who is helping me keep up the good grades I am getting,"**

like calculus and advanced chemistry he'll need for transfer. Joe knows all his time and effort will be worth it. "I found a great tutor at the learning center on campus who is helping me keep up the good grades I am getting," he says.

Joe is good at math and science, but that doesn't mean his transition to college was easy. "In high school," he says, "my studying habits were slim to none. I was the type of high school student who was able to pass a test just from listening and from what I remembered from class."

At SFCC, Joe had to change some of his study habits when he found that he wasn't able to remember everything the instructors required him to learn. "One of the biggest challenges transitioning from high school to college was learning time management and study skills," Joe says. He notes that, compared with high school, his college classes go twice as fast and instructors expect students to do a lot more work on their own. One of the first steps Joe took to adjust his study habits was to stop setting aside huge blocks of unstructured time. "I learned that studying for more than four hours straight is not the best for me. I need to study for an hour, take a half hour break, and then study another hour. I realized that after an hour I had trouble remembering things." By taking breaks to eat, exercise, or watch TV, Joe knows that he's giving his brain time to process information.

His one piece of advice to other first-year students? "The first year is going to be the hardest because it's so different," he says. "Just push through it. You'll find that it all starts making sense."

You might have learned to study effectively while you were in high school, or like Joe, you might find that your high school study habits no longer work. For example, Joe quickly learned that he did have to study, rather than just listening in class, and that for him a four-hour study session was too long. You also need to find ways to structure study times that work best for you, and to set aside regular times each week to review course material, do assigned reading, and keep up with your homework. From time to time, you may also want to do additional reading not assigned by instructors and to research topics that interest you. These strategies will help you learn more.

Studying, understanding, and remembering are essential to getting the most out of your college experience. Although many students think the only reason for studying is to do well on exams, a far more important reason is to learn and understand course information. If you study to increase your understanding, you are more likely to remember and apply what you learn not only to tests but also to future courses and to your career and life beyond college.

This chapter considers two related topics: concentration and memory. It will begin with the role of concentration in studying—if you cannot concentrate, you'll find it next to impossible to remember anything. Next, the chapter offers a number of tools to help you make the best use of your study time. It then concludes with a thorough discussion of what memory is, how it works, and how you can improve your own memory.

YOUR TURN > TRY IT

As you read this chapter, monitor your ability to concentrate. Check your watch when you begin, and check it again when your mind begins to wander. How many minutes did you concentrate on your reading? What strategies could you use to keep your mind from wandering?

_____

_____

STUDYING IN COLLEGE: MAKING CHOICES AND CONCENTRATING

Learning new material takes a lot of effort on your part. You must concentrate on what you hear and read. This might sound simple, but considering all the responsibilities that college students are balancing, the opportunity to concentrate and to really focus on what you're learning and studying can be hard to come by. Understanding how to maximize your ability to concentrate through what you do and where you do it is a good place to start.

Attending college is a huge responsibility, one you shouldn't take lightly. It is a lot of work, but it also offers you a lot of opportunities. For most people, college is a pathway to a better, more fulfilling life. As a college-level learner, you may need to change old habits and make room for new habits that will lead you to success. Tough choices are never easy, but they will have a direct, positive impact on your ability to remember and learn the information you will need in the months and years ahead.

Making a few changes in your behavior and in your environment will allow you to concentrate better and remember longer. With concentration, you'll probably need fewer hours to study because you will be using your time more efficiently. What are you willing to do to make this happen? To find out, work through the exercise in Figure 6.1.

With these realities in mind, what did you learn about yourself from answering the questions in Figure 6.1? Think especially about the questions to which you answered no. What are you unwilling to change in your life? Your job? Your family responsibilities? Making changes in behavior *now* will save you a lot of headaches in the future and will show that you can change old patterns to create successful new habits.

FIGURE 6.1 > Choose to Upgrade Your Learning

Tough Choices	Your Answer: Yes or No?
Are you willing to work together with others to form study groups or partners?	
Are you willing to find a place on campus, at a public library, or elsewhere (not your home) for quiet study?	
Are you willing to turn off your cell phone for a few moments of reading time without interruptions?	
Are you willing to turn off distracting music or TV while you are studying?	
Are you willing to study for tests four or five days before?	
Are you willing to do assigned reading before you come to class?	
Are you willing to sit in the class where you can see and hear better?	
Are you willing to reduce stress through exercise, sleep, or meditation?	
Are you willing to go over your notes after class to clean them up or rewrite them?	
Are you willing to take a few minutes on the weekend to organize the week ahead?	

HOW MEMORY WORKS

Learning experts describe two different processes involved in memory (see Table 6.1). The first is **short-term memory,** defined as how many items you are able to understand and remember at one time. After less than 30 seconds, you will forget the information stored in your short-term memory unless you take action to either keep that information in short-term memory or move it to long-term memory.

Although short-term memory is limited, it has a number of uses. It serves as an immediate holding tank for information, some of which you might not need for long. It helps you maintain your attention span so that you can keep track of topics mentioned in conversation, and it enables you to focus on the goals you have at any moment. But even these simple functions of short-term memory fail on occasion. If you're interrupted in any way, by a ringing phone or someone asking a question, you might find that your attention suffers and that you have to start over in reconstructing the contents of your short-term memory.

The second memory process is important for college success. **Long-term memory,** the capacity to retain and recall information over the long term, from hours to years, can be divided into three categories:

- *Procedural memory* deals with knowing how to do something, such as solving a mathematical problem or driving a car. You are using your procedural memory when you ride a bicycle, even if you haven't ridden in years; when you cook a meal that you know how to prepare without using a recipe; or when you send a text.
- *Semantic memory* involves facts and meanings without regard to where and when you learned those things. Your semantic memory is used when you remember word meanings or important dates, such as your mother's birthday.
- *Episodic memory* deals with particular events, their time, and their place. You are using episodic memory when you remember events in your life—a vacation, your first day of school, the moment your child was born. Some people can recall not only the event, but also the very time and place the event happened. For others, although the event stands out, the time and place are harder to remember.

TABLE 6.1 ❯ Short-Term and Long-Term Memory

Short-Term Memory	Long-Term Memory
Store information for about 30 seconds	Can be described in three ways: Procedural—remembering how to do something
Can handle from five to nine chunks of information at one time	Semantic—remembering facts and meanings
Information either forgotten or moved to long-term memory	Episodic—remembering events, including their time and place

Connecting Memory to Deep Learning

Multitasking has become a fact of life for many of us, but research summarized on the Web site of the American Psychological Association[1] shows that trying to do several tasks at once can make it harder to remember the most important things. It is hard to focus on anything for long if your life is full of daily distractions and competing responsibilities—school, work, commuting, and family responsibilities such as caring for children or parents—or if you're not getting the sleep you need. Have you ever had the experience of walking into a room with a specific task in mind and immediately forgetting what that task was? You were probably interrupted either by your own thoughts or by someone or something else. Or have you ever felt the panic that comes when your mind goes blank during a test, even though you studied hard and knew the material? If you spent all night studying, lack of sleep may have raised your stress level, causing you to forget what you worked hard to learn. Such experiences happen to most people at one time or another.

To do well in college and life, it's important that you improve your ability to remember what you read, hear, and experience. Concentration is a key element of learning and is so deeply connected to memory that you can't really have one without the other.

The benefits of having a good memory are obvious. In college, your memory will help you retain information and earn excellent grades on tests. After college, the ability to remember important details—names, dates, appointments—will save you energy and time and will prevent a lot of embarrassment.

Most memory strategies tend to focus on helping you remember bits and pieces of knowledge: names, dates, numbers, vocabulary words, formulas, and so on. However, if you know the date the Civil War began and the name of the fort where the first shots were fired but you don't know why the Civil War was fought or how it affected history, you're missing the point of a college education. College is a time to develop **deep learning,** understanding the why and how behind the details. So while remembering specific facts is necessary to do well in college and in your career, you will need to understand major themes and ideas. You will also need to improve your ability to think deeply about what you're learning. For more on the sorts of thinking skills you need to develop in college, see the chapters on Information Literacy and Critical Thinking.

Myths about Memory

To understand how to improve your memory, let's first look at what we know about how memory works. Although scientists keep learning new things about how

Avoid Multitasking

This dad is **not** a good role model. If you want to do your best and remember the most important things in your life, multitasking is not the way to go.
Source: © Sasha Gulish/ Corbis

---

[1]https://www.apa.org/research/action/multitask.aspx

our brains function, author Kenneth L. Higbee[2] suggests some myths about memory (some you might have heard, and even believe). Here are five of these memory myths and what experts say about them:

Myth	Reality
Some people have bad memories.	Although the memory ability you are born with is different from that of others, nearly everyone can improve his or her ability to remember and recall. Improving your concentration would certainly benefit your ability to remember!
Some people have photographic memories.	Some individuals have truly exceptional memories, but these abilities result more often from learned strategies, interest, and practice than from the natural ability to remember.
Memory benefits from long hours of practice.	Experts believe that practice often improves memory, but they argue that the way you practice is more important than how long you practice. For all practical purposes, the storage capacity of your memory is unlimited. In fact, the more you learn about a particular topic, the easier it is to learn even more. How you organize the information is more important than the quantity.
People use only 10 percent of their brain power.	No one knows exactly how much of our brain we actually use. However, most researchers believe that we all have far more mental ability than we actually use.

YOUR TURN > ON YOUR OWN

You can use many strategies to improve your memory. For example, many memory games are available that you can play for a few minutes every day; some of them are absolutely free and can be accessed online or on your mobile device as an app. For example, Lumosity is a free app that helps you improve your memory by doing daily exercises.

IMPROVING YOUR MEMORY

Just as you can use strategies for improving your ability to concentrate, you can improve your ability to store information in your brain for future use. Psychologists and learning specialists have developed a number of strategies you can use when studying. Some of these strategies might be new to you, but others will be familiar.

Have you ever had to memorize a speech or lines from a play? How you remember the lines might depend on your learning style. If you're an aural learner, you might decide to record your lines along with those of

---

[2] Kenneth L. Higbee, *Your Memory: How It Works and How to Improve It*, 2nd rev. ed. (New York: Marlowe, 2001).

other characters and listen to them on tape. If you're a visual learner, you might remember best by visualizing where your lines appear on the page in the script. If you learn best by reading, you might simply read the script over and over. If you're a kinesthetic learner, you might need to walk or move as you read the script.

Although knowing specific words will help, remembering concepts and ideas can be much more important. To store such ideas in your mind, ask yourself these questions as you review your notes and books:

1. What is the basic idea here?
2. Why does the idea make sense? What is the logic behind it?
3. How does this idea connect to other ideas in the material or experiences in my life?
4. What are some possible arguments against the idea?

To prepare for an exam that will cover large amounts of material, you need to reduce your notes and text pages into manageable study units. Review your materials with these questions in mind: Is this one of the key ideas in the chapter or unit? Will I see this on the test? Five study tools in particular are effective to help you remember what you have learned: review sheets, mind maps, flash cards, summaries, and mnemonics.

YOUR TURN > WORK TOGETHER

With the help of your instructor, identify other students in your class who share your learning style. (Refer to the chapter on Discovering How You Learn.) With another classmate, discuss strategies for remembering material for exams using your learning style and list the most helpful ideas.

An Elephant (Almost) Never Forgets

While elephants apparently do have pretty good memories, they're like the rest of us in that they sometimes forget. Work to develop your memory by using the specific strategies in this chapter. One of the most important strategies you can use is understanding the big-picture behind bits and pieces of information.

Source: © Shannon Burns

"Is this the memory seminar?"

Review Sheets

Use your notes to develop **review sheets**—lists of key terms and ideas that you need to remember. If you're using the Cornell format to take notes, you'll make these lists in the recall column. Also be sure to use your lecture notes to test yourself or others on information presented in class.

Mind Maps

A **mind map** is essentially a visual review sheet that shows the relationships between ideas; its visual patterns provide you with clues to jog your memory. Because they are visual, mind maps help many students, particularly English language learners, remember the information more easily.

To create a mind map, start with a main idea and place it in the center. Then add major categories that branch out from the center. To these, add pieces of related information to form clusters. You can use different shapes and/or colors to show the relationships among the various pieces of information. You can find many apps for creating mind maps on your computer or mobile device. Figure 6.2 includes the mind map of this chapter created by using an app called Total Recall. Other apps include MindMeister and SimpleMind.

FIGURE 6.2 › Sample Mind Map

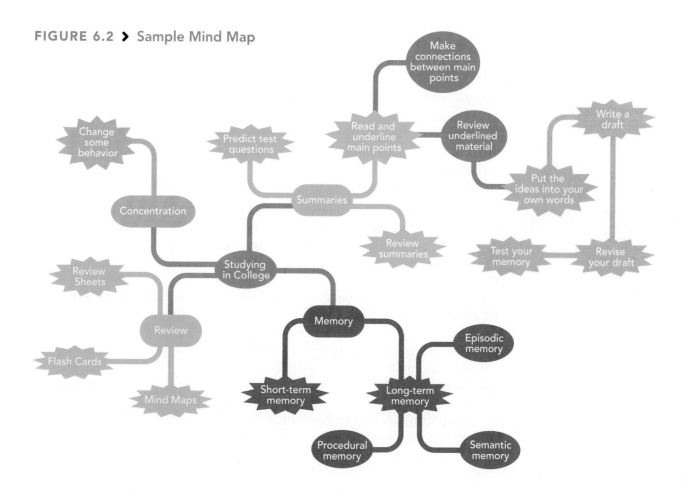

On a separate piece of paper or in a new document, make a mind map for Chapter 5, and see how much more you can remember after studying your map a number of times.

Flash Cards

Just as you can create flash cards during the process of active reading, you can also use them as a tool for improving your memory. Flash cards can serve as memory aids with a question, term, or other piece of information on one side and the answer, definition, or explanation on the other. One of the advantages of flash cards is that you can keep them in a pocket of your backpack or jacket or on your mobile device. Then you can look at them anywhere, even when you don't have enough time to take out your notebook to study.

Flash cards can help you make good use of time that might otherwise be wasted, such as time spent on the bus or waiting for a friend. Flash cards are excellent tools for improving your vocabulary, especially if you are learning English as a second language. See the chapter on Reading to Learn from College Textbooks for more information about creating and using flash cards.

Summaries

An immediate benefit of writing summaries of class topics is that they can help you answer short-answer and essay questions successfully. You can also see the connection between the ideas and can identify the major and minor details. By summarizing the main ideas and putting them into your own words, you will be able to remember information better. Here's how to create a good summary in preparation for taking a test:

1. **Read the assigned material, your class notes, or your instructor's presentation slides.** Underline or mark main ideas as you go, make explanatory notes or comments about the material, or make an outline on a separate sheet of paper. Predict test questions based on your active reading.
2. **Make connections between main points and key supporting details.** Reread to identify each main point and the supporting evidence. Create an outline in the process.
3. **Review underlined material.** Put those ideas into your own words in a logical order.
4. **Write your ideas in a draft.** In the first sentence, state the purpose of your summary. Follow this statement with each main point and its supporting ideas. See how much of the draft you can develop from memory without relying on your notes.

5. **Review your draft.** Read it over, adding missing details or other information.

6. **Test your memory.** Put your draft away, and try to repeat the contents of the summary out loud to yourself or to a study partner who can let you know whether you have forgotten anything.

7. **Schedule time to review your summary and double-check your memory shortly before the test.** You might want to do this with a partner, but some students prefer to review alone. Some instructors might be willing to help you in this process and give you feedback on your summaries.

Mnemonics

Mnemonics (pronounced "ne MON iks") are different methods or tricks to help with remembering information. Mnemonics tend to fall into four basic categories:

1. **Acronyms.** Acronyms are new words created from the first letters of a list or group of words you are trying to remember. For example, a mnemonic acronym for the Great Lakes is *HOMES*, which stands for Huron, Ontario, Michigan, Erie, and Superior.

2. **Acrostics.** An acrostic is a verse in which certain letters of each word or line form a message. Many students are taught the following to remember planets: **M**y **V**ery **E**xcellent **M**other **J**ust **S**erved **U**s **N**achos (**M**ercury, **V**enus, **E**arth, **M**ars, **J**upiter, **S**aturn, **U**ranus, **N**eptune).

3. **Rhymes or songs.** Do you remember learning "Thirty days hath September, / April, June, and November. / All the rest have thirty-one,/ Excepting February alone. / It has twenty-eight days' time, / But in leap years twenty-nine"? If so, you were using a mnemonic rhyming technique to remember the number of days in each month.

4. **Visualization.** You can use visualization to connect a word or concept with a visual image. The more ridiculous the image, the more likely you are to remember the word or concept. For example, if you want to remember the name of George Washington, you may think of a person you know by the name of George. You should then picture that person washing a ton of dishes. Now every time you think of the first president of the United States, you see George washing a ton of dishes.[3]

Mnemonics provide a way of organizing material, a sort of mental filing system. They probably aren't needed if what you are studying is logical and organized, but they can be really useful when material doesn't have a pattern of its own. Although using mnemonics can be helpful in remembering the information, it takes time to think up rhymes, associations, or visual images which have limited use when you need to analyze or explain the material.

---

[3]Example from Jim Somchai, "Memory and Visualization," EzineArticles.com, http://ezinearticles .com/?Memory-and-Visualization&id=569553.

STUDYING TO UNDERSTAND AND REMEMBER

Studying will help you accomplish two goals: understanding and remembering. While memory is a necessary tool for learning, what's most important is that you study to develop a deep understanding of course information. When you really comprehend what you are learning, you will be able to place names, dates, and specific facts in context. You will also be able to exercise your thinking abilities.

Here are some methods that might be useful to you as you're trying to remember detailed information:

- **Pay attention and avoid distractions.** This suggestion is the most basic but the most important. If you're sitting in class thinking about everything except what the professor is saying, or if you're reading and you find that your mind is wandering, you're wasting your time. Force yourself to focus. Review your responses to the questions in Figure 6.1.
- **Be confident that you can improve your memory.** Recall successes from the past when you learned things that you didn't think you could or would remember. Choose memory improvement strategies that best fit your preferred learning styles: aural, visual, reading, kinesthetic. Identify the courses where you can make the best use of each memory strategy.
- **Overlearn the material.** Once you think you understand the material you're studying, go over it again to make sure that you'll remember it for a long time. Test yourself, or ask someone else to test you. Repeat what you're trying to remember out loud and in your own words. Explain it to another person.
- **Make studying a part of your daily routine.** Don't allow days to go by when you don't open a book or keep up with course assignments. Make studying a daily habit!
- **Check the Internet.** If you're having trouble remembering what you have learned, Google a key word and try to find interesting details that will engage you in learning more about the subject. Many first-year courses cover such a large amount of material that you might miss some interesting details unless you look for them yourself. As your interest increases, so will your memory about the topic. Make sure to check multiple online sources.
- ***Go beyond memorizing words, and focus on understanding and then remembering the big concepts and ideas.*** Keep asking yourself questions like "what is the main point here? Is there a big idea?" Whenever you begin a course, review the syllabus, talk with someone who has already taken the course, and take a brief look at all the reading assignments. Having the big picture will help you understand and remember the details of what you're learning. For example, the big picture for a first-year college success class is to give students the knowledge and strategies to be successful in college.
- **Look for connections between your life and what's going on in the content of your courses.** College courses might seem unrelated to you

and your goals, but if you look more carefully, you'll find many connections between course material and your daily life. Seeing those connections will make your courses more interesting and will help you remember what you're learning. For example, if you're taking a sociology class and studying marriage and the family, think about how your own family experiences relate to those described in your readings or in the lectures.

- **Get organized.** If your desk or your computer is organized, you won't waste time trying to remember where you put a particular document or what name you gave to a file. And as you rewrite your notes, putting them in an order that makes sense to you (for example, by topic or by date) will help you learn and remember them.
- **Reduce the stress in your life.** Many two-year college students experience stress because they have to juggle college, work, and family life. To manage the stress that arises, take another look at the strategies in the chapter on Managing Time, Energy, and Money. Stress-reducing habits such as eating well and getting enough exercise and sleep are especially important for college students (see the chapter on Managing Your Health, Emotions, and Relationships in a Diverse World) Remember, too, that your college probably has a counseling or health center where you can seek help in dealing with whatever might be causing stress in your daily life.
- **Collaborate.** In your first year of college, join a group of students who study together. Your instructors or the college learning center can help organize study groups. Study groups can meet throughout the term or can get together only to review for midterm or final exams.
- **Get a tutor.** Tutoring is not just for students who are failing. Often the best students ask for help to make sure that they understand course material. Most tutors are students, and most community college tutoring services are free.

As you learned in this chapter, memory and concentration play very important parts in achieving success in college as they help you understand, remember, and deeply learn the material so that you can apply that learning to your career and life.

Work Together

One way to enhance your memory is to study with others. Each of you can check specific facts and details and share strategies you use for remembering them. You can also motivate and support one another.

Source: Digital Vision/Getty Images

YOUR TURN > WORK TOGETHER

With a small group of your classmates, share your thoughts on the importance of being organized. How would you describe both your living space and your electronic environment?

USE THE CLOUD

Computer labs, laptops, tablets, and smartphones give you the opportunity to work from almost everywhere. What can you do to keep all your important files in one place so that you'll never be without them?

THE PROBLEM *You're at the computer lab, and you don't have the files you need. This time you forgot your flash drive; last time, you had your tablet and not your laptop. And what if your devices get damaged? What then?*

THE FIX *Save your files to a cloud storage site and have access to them from any Internet-connected computer or tablet. The cloud is basically the Internet, which is simply a network of servers. Through an Internet connection, you can access whatever applications, files, or data you have stored in the cloud—anytime, anywhere, from any device.[4]*

HOW TO DO IT

Sign up for a free account from a cloud storage site. These sites allow you to save files to an online location. You'll have your own private storage space that can be accessed only with a password. Some sites are designed for documents (Word files, PDFs, PowerPoint presentations), while others allow easy storage for both print files and audio/video. Cloud storage is great for collaborative projects because you can choose to share some or all of your files with your classmates and friends. The following is a list of sites with free storage (though most require payment to increase your storage size):

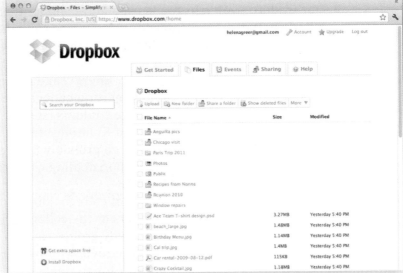

Source: Courtesy of Dropbox

1. **Dropbox (dropbox.com)** is probably the most well-known cloud storage site. Users get 2 gigabytes (GB) of free storage and are able to upgrade to up to 500 GB for a monthly fee. (A *gigabyte* is a unit of measurement approximately equal to 1 billion bytes; a *byte* is a unit of data storage capable of holding a single alphanumeric character.) You can also earn more storage space by referring other customers to the site. Dropbox has a Web interface that you and others can access from any computer and save to your own computer. This makes Dropbox look like any other folder on your computer; however, when you add files it actually adds them to your online folder. Dropbox is available as a stand-alone app on iPhone, iPad, and Android devices and also works with other document-editing apps for mobile devices.

2. **Google Drive (drive.google.com)** allows users to store and share documents up to 5 GB. A great feature of Google Drive is that you can edit documents in real time with your friends and classmates. If you're writing a group paper, all of your coauthors can sign into Google Drive and view the same document. You are able to edit it together, and there is a chat window so you can have a conversation while editing. Google Drive allows for storage of both audio and video. Like Dropbox, Google Drive is also available as a stand-alone app and integrates well with iPhone, iPad, and Android apps.

3. **MediaFire (mediafire.com)** is newer than Dropbox and Google Drive. MediaFire's key feature is 50 GB of free storage space. Users are able to work together in the cloud and access their files using stand-alone apps on iPhone, iPad, and Android devices.

[4]Rama Ramaswami and Dian Schaffhauser, "What Is the Cloud?" *Campus Technology*, October 31, 2011, http://campustechnology.com/articles/2011/10/31/what-is-the-cloud.aspx.

THINK

Doing well on exams is important, but being able to understand and remember what you learn is a more important life skill in general. How do you think these skills may help you in your current or future job? List your ideas.

1. _____

2. _____

3. _____

WRITE

In this chapter, you read about some memory myths and facts. Did anything you learned surprise you? Have you ever believed in any of the myths? If so, which ones? How can the information about memory and the strategies for improving your memory discussed in this chapter help you change your study habits? Jot down a few thoughts here and then expand on them in a journal, in a notebook, or on your favorite device.

APPLY

Now that you have read and discussed this chapter, consider how you can apply what you have learned to your academic and personal life.

1. Give mnemonics a try. Choose a set of class notes that you need to study for an upcoming quiz or exam. As you study, choose a concept and create your own acronym, acrostic, rhyme, song, or visualization to help you remember.

2. Choose a photo, song, or object that reminds you of a person, life event, or time period. Describe what it is about the photo, song, or object that reminds you of something else. Describe your memory in as much detail as possible and explain how it makes you feel.

WHERE TO GO FOR HELP

VISIT . . .	IF YOU NEED HELP . . .
The Academic Learning/Skills Center	developing effective memory strategies. Visit your campus learning center and ask if the staff members offer any specific workshops or one-to-one assistance with memory.
Fellow college students	finding tips for remembering the material in different courses.
Your college library	finding books on the topic of memory. Download or check out a book on memory and see what you can learn. Here are some ideas:

Higbee, Kenneth L. *Your Memory: How It Works and How to Improve It,* 2nd rev. ed. New York: Marlowe, 2001.

Lorayne, Harry. *Memory Mastery.* Hollywood: Frederick Fell Trade, 2010.

O'Brien, Dominic. *You Can Have an Amazing Memory: Learn Life-Changing Techniques and Tips from the Memory Maestro.* London: Watkins, 2011.

Scotts, Jason. *How to Improve Your Memory & Increase Your Brain Power in 30 Days: Simple, Easy & Fun Ways to Improve Memory Now* (Ultimate How To Guides). Kindle Edition, retrieved from Amazon.com, 2013.

ONLINE

GO TO . . .	IF YOU NEED HELP . . .
Memory Techniques from San Antonio College: http://www.alamo.edu/memory	finding memorization techniques.
Memory-Improvement-Tips.com: http://www.memory-improvement-tips.com/	improving your memory.
Brain Metrix: http://www.brainmetrix.com/	learning more about training your brain.
Lumosity: http://www.lumosity.com	improving your memory by playing memory games.

MY COLLEGE'S RESOURCES

7 Taking Tests Successfully

PRE-READING ACTIVITY: Taking tests is an important part of your college experience. For the following statements, mark whether you agree or disagree, and write down the reason for your response.

Tests do not measure students' learning.

Agree ☐   Disagree ☐
Reason:

It is possible to control test anxiety.

Agree ☐   Disagree ☐
Reason:

Smart students are not nervous before taking tests.

Agree ☐   Disagree ☐
Reason:

Text anxiety will go away if students ignore it.

Agree ☐   Disagree ☐
Reason:

If students study before a test, they feel less nervous.

Agree ☐   Disagree ☐
Reason:

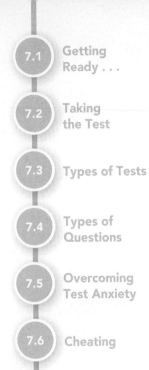
 PROFILE

Carlos Rivera, 26
Health Sciences Major, *Georgia Perimeter College*

Source: Bruce Laurance/
Getty Images

Carlos Rivera was born in Guatemala and has lived in Georgia since he was ten years old. After a few years as a car mechanic, he decided to enroll in Georgia Perimeter College because he realized college was important for his goals and his financial future. "I quickly learned that, unless you are extremely successful, it is hard to plan for any kind of retirement," Jaime says. He chose Georgia Perimeter because of his interest in their medical programs, and so far his favorite course has been biology. After graduating from Georgia Perimeter College, Carlos plans to become a radiologic therapist and help others. Since enrolling, Carlos has taken a straightforward approach to preparing for exams that has served him well. "I review the material periodically throughout the term and the day before exams," he explains. "Typically, I try to get plenty of sleep during the week of exams."

Carlos recounts a challenge he overcame: "I came into one required course with a negative attitude. I didn't know why I needed to take the class, and I didn't pay attention." When he received his first exam grade, Carlos wasn't pleased. "It was definitely not what I was used to," he says. However, he returned to class with an open mind and made an effort to take an interest in the course and to explore how the materials applied to his life and studies. By applying the same strategies he'd used in his other classes to prepare for exams, he was able to improve his grade.

His advice to other first-year students? "Don't slack off, thinking you can make up the work later in the year. Do well from the start—you never know when you may need some room for error later on. If something seems hard, face it and try your best. Most of the time, things are not as difficult as they may seem at first. You can do anything you want with a little perseverance and determination."

> "You can do anything you want with a little perseverance and determination."

Y ou can prepare for tests and exams in many ways. Sometimes you'll have to recall names, dates, and other specific bits of information. Many instructors, especially in courses such as literature and history, will also expect you to have a good overall understanding of the subject matter. Even in math and science courses, your instructors want you not only to remember the correct theory, formula, or equation but also to understand and apply what you have learned. Knowing your preferred learning

style, managing your time and energy, and using study and memory strategies discussed in previous chapters will help you prepare for any kind of test or exam you are facing. This chapter provides you with several strategies to prepare for and take tests and exams successfully. It also describes types of tests and test questions you may encounter and includes tips for managing test anxiety as well as maintaining academic honesty.

GETTING READY . . .

7.1

Believe it or not, you actually begin preparing for tests on the first day of the term. Your lecture notes, assigned readings, and homework are all part of that preparation. As you get closer to the test day, you should know how much additional time you will need for review, what material the test will cover, and what format the test will take. It is very important to double-check the exam dates on the syllabus for each class, as in Figure 7.1, and to incorporate these dates into your overall plans for time management—for example, in your daily and weekly to-do lists.

Prepare for Test Taking

Tests are usually a major portion of your grade in college, so proper preparation for them is essential. Of course you need to understand the material, but there are many ways you can prepare for exams in addition to your regular study routines.

Find Out about the Test. Ask your instructor about the test format, how long it will last, and how it will be graded. Find out the types of questions, the content that will be covered, and how much time you will have to complete the exam. Talk with your instructor to clarify any misunderstandings you might have about your reading or lecture notes. A part-time instructor may not have office hours, but you can usually talk to him or her before or after class. Some instructors might let you view copies of old exams so that you can see the types of questions they use. Never miss the last class before an exam; your instructor might take part or all of that class session to summarize and review valuable information.

Design an Exam Plan. Use information about the test as you design an exam plan. Create a schedule that will give you time to review for the exam without waiting until the night before. Develop a to-do list of the major steps you need to take to be ready, and schedule review dates. Be sure that your schedule is flexible enough to allow for unexpected distractions or emergencies. If you are able to schedule your study sessions over several days, your mind will continue to process the information between study sessions, which will help you during the test. Be sure you have read and learned all the material by one week before the exam. That way, you

FIGURE 7.1 › Exam Schedule from Sample Course Syllabus

History 111, US History to 1865
Fall 2015

Examinations
Note: In this course, most of your exams will be on Fridays, except for the Wednesday before Thanksgiving. This is to give you a full week to study for the exam and permit me to grade them over the weekend and return the exams to you on Monday. I believe in using a variety of types of measurements. In addition to those scheduled below, I reserve the right to give you unannounced quizzes on daily reading assignments. Midterm and final exams will be cumulative (on all material since beginning of the course). Other exams cover all classroom material and all readings covered since the prior exam. The schedule is as follows:

Friday, 9/11: Objective type

Friday, 9/25: Essay type

Friday, 10/2: Midterm: essay and objective

Friday, 11/6: Objective

Wednesday, 11/25: Essay

Friday, 12/18: Final exam: essay and objective

can use the final week to review. In that final week, set aside several one-hour blocks for review and make specific notes on what you plan to do during each hour. Also, let your friends and family know when you have important exams coming up and how that will affect your time with them.

Use Online Quizzing. Many textbooks have Web sites available that offer a number of study tools such as flash cards, videos, or online quizzing. Ask your instructors about these sites and also check the preface of textbooks for information on accessing these sites. You might also use Google to find them.

Strength in Numbers
Study groups can meet anytime, but studying and reviewing with others in your class can be most helpful just before and just after a test or exam.

Join a Study Group. As mentioned in previous chapters, joining a study group is one of the best ways to prepare for exams. Group members can share and review the most important topics, quiz one another on facts and concepts, and gain support from other serious students. Some instructors will provide time in class for the formation of study groups, or you might choose to approach classmates on your own. You can always ask your instructor, academic adviser, or college's tutoring or learning center to help you find other interested students and decide on guidelines for the group. Study groups can meet throughout the term, or they can just review for midterms or final exams. Group members should prepare questions or discussion points before the group meets. If your study group decides to meet just before exams, allow enough time to share notes and ideas.

Talk to Other Students. Other students, especially those who have taken a course you are currently taking from the same instructor, may be able to give you a good idea of what to expect on tests and exams. If your college is small, you shouldn't have any trouble finding students who have taken the same courses you are taking now. If you're at a large college, your instructor may be able to suggest a former student who could serve as a tutor. But keep in mind that your instructor may decide to take a different approach in your class than he or she did in past classes.

Get a Tutor. Most community colleges offer free tutoring services. Ask your academic adviser, counselor, or college learning center about arranging for tutoring. Keep in mind that some of the most successful students seek out tutoring, not just students who are struggling. Most students who receive tutoring do well in their courses. Many academic learning centers employ student tutors (also called peer tutors) who have done well in the same courses you are taking. These students might have some good advice on how to prepare for tests given by particular instructors. If you do well in a particular course, you could eventually become a peer tutor and be paid for your services. Serving as a peer tutor also deepens your own learning and helps you become more successful in your major.

Prepare for Math and Science Exams

Math and science exams often require additional and sometimes different preparation techniques. Here are some suggestions for doing well on these exams:

- Do your homework regularly even if it is not graded, and do all the assigned problems. As you do your homework, write out your work as carefully and clearly as you will be expected to do on your tests. This practice will allow you to use your homework as a review for the test.

- Attend each class, always be on time, and stay for the entire class. Many instructors use the first few minutes of class to review homework, and others may end the class by telling you what will be on the test.

- Build a review guide throughout the term. As you begin your homework each day, write out a problem from each homework section in a notebook that you have set up for reviewing material for that course. As you review later, you can come back to these problems to make sure you have a problem from each section you've studied.

- Throughout the term, keep a list of definitions or important formulas and put these on flash cards. Review several of these as part of every study session. Another technique is to post the formulas and definitions in your living space (for example, on the bathroom wall, around your computer work area, or on the door of the microwave). Seeing this information frequently will help you keep it in your mind.

If none of these strategies seems to help you, ask a tutor to give you a few practice exams and review your responses with you.

Prepare Physically

Keeping your body healthy is another key part of preparing yourself for quizzes, tests, and exams. The following strategies will help you prepare physically:

- **Maintain your regular sleep routine.** To do well on exams, you will need to be alert so that you can think clearly. And you are more likely to be alert when you are well rested. Last-minute, late-night cramming does not allow you to get sufficient sleep, so it isn't an effective study strategy. Most students need 7 to 8 hours of sleep the night before the exam.

- **Follow your regular exercise program.** Exercise is a positive way to relieve stress and to give yourself a needed break from long hours of studying.

- **Eat right.** Eat a light breakfast before a morning exam, and avoid greasy or acidic foods that might upset your stomach. Limit the amount of caffeinated beverages you drink on exam day, because caffeine can make you jittery. Choose fruits, vegetables, and other foods that are high in energy-rich complex carbohydrates.

Avoid eating sweets before an exam; the immediate energy boost they create can be quickly followed by a loss of energy and alertness. Ask the instructor whether you may bring a bottle of water with you to the exam.

Prepare Emotionally

Just as physical preparation is important, so is preparing your attitude and your emotions. You'll benefit by paying attention to the following ideas:

- **Know your material.** If you have given yourself enough time to review, you will enter the classroom confident that you are in control. Study by testing yourself or quizzing others in a study group to be sure you really know the material.
- **Practice relaxing.** Some students experience upset stomachs, sweaty palms, racing hearts, or other unpleasant physical symptoms of test anxiety. The section on test anxiety later in this chapter includes an anxiety quiz; if that quiz reveals that test anxiety is a problem for you, consult your counseling center about relaxation techniques. Some campus learning centers also provide workshops on reducing test anxiety.
- **Use positive self-talk.** Instead of telling yourself, "I never do well on math tests" or "I'll never be able to learn all the information for my history essay exam," make positive statements, such as "I have always attended class, done my homework, and passed the quizzes. Now I'm ready to do well on the test!"

YOUR TURN ❯ WORK TOGETHER

Do you sometimes predict that you'll do poorly on a test or exam, even when you've studied hard? Discuss with a small group of your classmates why some people are hard on themselves and how a positive attitude can help you do your best.

TAKING THE TEST

Throughout your college career you will take tests in many different formats, in many subject areas and with many different types of questions. It may surprise you to find that your first-year tests are likely to be more challenging than those in later years because as a new student, you are still developing your college test-taking skills throughout your first year. The following are test-taking tips that apply to any test situation:

1. **Write your name on the test.** Usually you will have to write your name on a text booklet or answer sheet. Some instructors, however, may require to you fill in your student ID number.

2. **Look over the whole test and stay calm.** Carefully read all the directions before beginning the test so that you understand what to do. Ask the instructor or exam monitor for clarification if you don't understand something. Be confident. Don't panic. Answer one question at a time.

3. **Make the best use of your time.** Quickly review the entire test and decide how much time you will spend on each section. Be aware of the point values of different sections of the test. If some questions are worth more points than others, you need to spend more of your time answering them.

4. **Jot down idea starters before the test.** Check with your instructor ahead of time to be sure that it is okay to write some last-minute notes on the test or on scrap paper. If so, then before you even look at the test questions, turn the test paper over and take a moment to write down the formulas, definitions, or major ideas you have been studying. This will help you go into the test with confidence and knowledge, and your notes will provide quick access to the information you may need throughout the test.

5. **Answer the easy questions first.** Expect that you won't completely understand some questions. Make a note to come back to them later. If different sections have different types of questions (such as multiple-choice, short-answer, and essay questions), first finish the types of questions that are easiest for you to answer. Be sure to leave enough time for essays questions.

6. **If you feel yourself starting to panic or go blank, stop whatever you are doing.** Take a deep breath, and remind yourself that you will be okay and you do know the material and can do well on the test. If necessary, go to another section of the test and come back later to the item that triggered your anxiety.

7. **Try to answer each question, even if only in part.** You may not be able to answer all the questions fully; provide as much information as you can remember. Particularly for math and science test questions, you may get some credit for writing down equations and descriptions of how to solve the problem even if you cannot fully work them out or if you run out of time to finish them.

8. **If you finish early, don't leave immediately.** Stay and check your work for errors. Reread the directions one last time.

7.3

TYPES OF TESTS

While you are in college, you will come across many types of tests. Some may be used in particular subjects such as English or math; others can be used in any class you might take. This section discusses the different test types and presents helpful tips for each one.

Problem-Solving Tests

In science, mathematics, engineering, and statistics courses, some tests will require you to solve problems showing all the steps. Even if you know a shortcut, it is important to document how you got from step A to step B. For these tests, you must also be careful to avoid errors in your scientific notation. A misplaced sign, parenthesis, or bracket can make all the difference.

If you are allowed to use a calculator during the exam, it is important to check that your input is accurate. The calculator does what you tell it to, and if you miss a zero or a negative sign, the calculator will not give you the correct answer to the problem.

Read all directions carefully. Whenever possible, after you complete the problem, work it in reverse to check your solution. Also check to make sure that your solution makes sense. You can't have negative bushels of apples, for example, or a fraction of a person, or a correlation less than negative 1 or greater than 1.

Machine-Scored Tests

For some tests you may have to enter your answers on a Scantron form (See Figure 7.2). The instructor will feed those forms into a machine that scans the answers and prints out your score. When taking any test, especially a machine-scored test, carefully follow the directions. In addition to your name, be sure to provide all other necessary information on the answer sheet. Each time you fill in an answer, make sure that the number on the answer sheet corresponds to the number of the item on the test.

FIGURE 7.2 ❯ Example of a Scantron Answer Sheet

Each time you fill in a Scantron answer sheet, make sure that the number on the answer sheet corresponds to the number of the item on the test. And make sure that all bubbles are filled in completely.

Source: Vixit/Shutterstock

Although scoring machines have become more sophisticated over time, they might still misread additional marks or incomplete bubbles on your answer sheet. When a machine-scored test is returned to you, check your answer sheet against the scoring key, if one is provided, to make sure that you receive credit for all the questions you answered correctly.

Computerized Tests

Computerized tests, such as the one shown in Figure 7.3, can be significantly different from one another depending on the kind of test, the academic subject, and whether the test was written by the instructor, a textbook company, or by another source. Be sure to take advantage of any practice test opportunities to get a better sense of what the tests will be like.

FIGURE 7.3 ❯ Example of a Computerized Question
Computerized test questions can vary significantly depending on the text, academic subject, and test writer. This question is from LearningCurve, a self-assessment online system that may be available with this textbook.

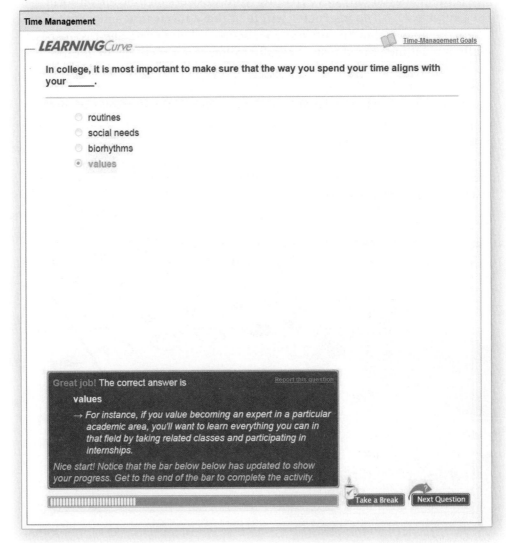

The more experience you have with computerized tests, the more comfortable you will be taking them. (The same is true with the other test types.)

Some multiple-choice computerized tests might allow you to scroll through all the questions; others might allow you to see only one question at a time. After you complete each question, you might have to move on to the next question without being able to return to earlier ones.

For computerized tests in math and other subjects that require you to solve each problem, be sure to check each answer before you submit it. Also, know in advance what materials you are allowed to have on hand, such as a calculator and scratch paper, for working the problems.

Laboratory Tests

In many science courses, you will have laboratory tests that require you to move from one lab station to the next to solve problems, identify parts of models or specimens, or explain chemical reactions. To prepare for lab tests, always attend lab, take good notes, and study your lab notebook carefully before the test.

You might also have lab tests in foreign language courses that can include both oral and written sections. Work with a partner or study group to prepare for oral exams. Have group members ask one another questions that require using key vocabulary words.

Open-Book and Open-Notes Tests

Although you may like the idea of being able to refer to your book or notes during an exam, open-book and open-note tests are usually harder than other tests, not easier. You won't really have time to read whole passages during an open-book exam.

Study as completely as you would for any other test, and do not be fooled into thinking that you don't need to know the material. But as you study, you can develop a list of topics and the page numbers where they are covered in your text or in your lecture notes. Type a three-column grid (or use an Excel spreadsheet) with your list of topics in alphabetical order in the first column and corresponding pages from your textbook and lecture notebook in the second and third columns so that you can refer to them quickly when necessary.

During the test, keep up with your time. Don't waste time looking up information in your text or notes if you are sure of your answers. Instead, wait until you have finished the test, and then, if you have extra time, go back and look up answers and make any necessary changes.

Take-Home Tests

Some instructors may allow you to take tests outside class and refer to your textbook, notes, and other resources. Take-home tests are usually more difficult than in-class tests. Read the directions and questions as soon as you receive the test to estimate how much time you will need to complete it. Remember that your instructor will expect your essay answers to look more like out-of-class papers, proofread and edited, than like the essays you would write during an in-class test.

It is probably no surprise that issues of academic honesty can arise for take-home tests. If you usually work with a study group or in a learning community for the course, check with the instructor in advance to determine if any type of group work is allowed on the test.

YOUR TURN > WORK TOGETHER

Which type of tests described above do you prefer, and why? Why do you think you perform the best on this type of test? Share your test-taking strategies for this test type with another student.

7.4 TYPES OF QUESTIONS

Your instructors choose not only what types of exams they give you but also what types of questions you should answer to demonstrate what you are learning in the course. You may take an exam that has one or multiple types of questions. This section includes strategies to help you answer different types of questions successfully.

Essay Questions

Essay exams include questions that require students to write a few paragraphs in response to each question. Many college instructors have a strong preference for essay questions for a simple reason: They require deeper thinking than other types of questions. Generally, advanced courses are more likely to include essay exams. To be successful on essay exam questions, follow these guidelines:

1. **Budget your exam time.** Quickly go over the entire exam, and note the questions that are the easiest for you to answer. Estimate the approximate amount of time you should spend on each essay question based on its point value. Remember, writing long answers to questions that have low point values can be a mistake because it takes up precious time you might need for answering questions that count more toward the total grade. Be sure you know whether you must answer all the questions or choose among questions. Wear a watch to monitor your time, and don't forget to leave a few minutes for a quick review.
2. **Actively read the whole question.** Many well-prepared students write good answers to questions that were not asked—when that happens, they may lose points or even fail the exam. Many other students write good answers to only part of the question—they also may lose points or even fail the exam.
3. **Develop a brief outline of your answer before you begin to write.** Make sure that your outline responds to all parts of the question. Use your

first paragraph to introduce the main points; use the other paragraphs to describe each point in more depth. If you begin to lose your concentration, you will be glad to have the outline to help you regain your focus. If you find that you are running out of time and cannot complete an essay question, provide an outline of key ideas at the very least. Instructors usually assign points on the basis of your coverage of the main topics from the material. That means you will usually earn more points by responding briefly to all parts of the question than by addressing just one part of the question in detail. You might receive some credit for your outline even if you cannot finish the essay.

4. **Write concise, organized answers.** Some students answer essay questions by quickly writing down everything they know on the topic. Long answers are not necessarily good answers. Answers that are too general, unfocused, or disorganized may not earn high scores.

5. **Know the key task words in essay questions.** Being familiar with key task words that may appear in an essay question will help you frame your answer more specifically. Table 7.1 lists common key task words. If your instructor allows you to do so, consider circling or underlining key words in the question to make sure you know how to organize your answer.

TABLE 7.1 ❯ Key Task Words in Essay Questions

Analyze	Break the whole topic into parts in order to explain it better; show how the parts work together to produce the overall pattern.
Compare	Identify similarities in ideas, events, or objects. Don't just describe the elements; state how they are alike.
Contrast	Identify the differences between ideas, events, or objects. Don't just describe the ideas; state how they are different.
Criticize/Critique	Judge something; give your opinion. Criticism can be positive, negative, or mixed. A critique should generally include your own judgments (supported by evidence) and those of experts who agree with you.
Define	Give the meaning of a word or expression.
Describe	Give more information about the topic.
Discuss	Give broad statements backed up by detailed information. Discussion often includes identifying the important questions related to an issue and trying to answer these questions.
Evaluate	Discuss the strengths and weaknesses of an idea or a position. When you evaluate, you stress the idea of how well something meets a certain standard.
Explain	Clarify a statement. Explanations generally focus on why or how something has come about.
Justify	Argue in support of some decision or conclusion by showing evidence or reasons that support the argument. Try to support your argument with both logical and concrete examples.
Narrate	Relate a series of events in the order they occurred, as you do when you tell a story.
Outline	Present a series of main points in order. Some instructors want a formal outline with numbers and letters.
Summarize	Give information in brief form, without examples and details. A summary is short but covers all the important points.

Multiple-Choice Questions

Multiple-choice questions provide any number of possible answers, often between three and five. The answer choices are usually numbered (1, 2, 3, 4, . . .) or lettered (a, b, c, d, . . .), and the test-taker is supposed to select the correct or the best one. Preparing for multiple-choice tests requires you to actively review all of the material that has been covered for a particular period such as a week or a month. Reviewing flash cards, summary sheets, mind maps, or the recall column in your lecture notes is a good way to cover large amounts of material.

Take advantage of the many cues that multiple-choice questions include. Be careful about words in the question such as *not, except, all,* and *but* to make sure that the answer you choose fits the question. Also read each answer choice carefully; be suspicious of choices that use words such as *always, never,* and *only.* These choices are often (but not always) incorrect. Often the correct answer is the option that is the most comprehensive.

In some multiple-choice questions, the first part of the question is an incomplete sentence (called the stem) and the answer choices complete the sentence. In these questions, any answer choices that do not use correct grammar are usually incorrect. For example, in Figure 7.4, "Margaret Mead was an" is the stem. Which of the four options is grammatically wrong and can be ruled out?

To avoid becoming confused by answer choices that sound alike, predict your own answer to the question before reading the options. Then choose the answer that best matches your prediction.

If you are totally confused by a question, place a check mark in the margin, leave it, and come back later. Sometimes a question later in the exam may provide a clue for the one you are unsure about. If you have absolutely no idea, look for an answer that at least has some pieces of information. If there is no penalty for guessing, fill in an answer for every question, even if it is just a guess. If there is a penalty for guessing, don't just choose an answer at random; leaving the answer blank might be a wiser choice. Finally, always go back, if you have time at the end, and double-check that you chose the right answer for the right question, especially if you are using a Scantron form.

FIGURE 7.4 ❯ Example of a Multiple-Choice Question

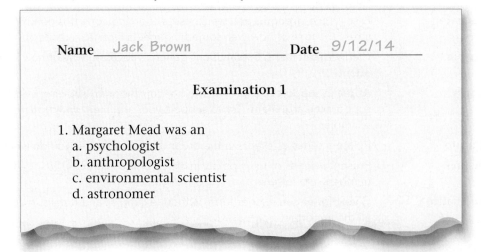

Name _Jack Brown_____ Date _9/12/14_____

Examination 1

1. Margaret Mead was an
   a. psychologist
   b. anthropologist
   c. environmental scientist
   d. astronomer

Fill-in-the Blank Questions

Fill-in-the-blank questions consist of a phrase, sentence, or paragraph with a blank space indicating where the student should provide the missing word or words. In many ways, preparing for fill-in-the-blank questions is similar to getting ready for multiple-choice items, but fill-in-the-blank questions can be harder because you do not have a choice of possible answers right in front of you.

Not all fill-in-the-blank questions are written the same way. Sometimes the answers will consist of a single word; sometimes the instructor is looking for a phrase. There may be a series of blanks to give you a clue about the number of words in the answer, or there may be just one long blank. If you are unsure, ask the instructor whether the answer is supposed to be one word or more.

True/False Questions

True/False questions ask students to determine whether the statement is correct or not. Remember that for a statement to be true, every detail of the sentence must be correct. That is why questions containing words such as always, never, and only tend to be false, whereas less definite terms such as often and frequently suggest the statement might be true. Read through the entire exam to see whether information in one question will help you answer another. Do not begin to second-guess what you know or doubt your answers just because a sequence of questions appears to be all true or all false.

Matching Questions

Matching questions are set up with terms in one column and descriptions in the other, and you must make the proper pairings. Before matching any items, review all of the terms and descriptions. Then match the terms you are sure of. As you do so, cross out both the term and its description, and use the process of elimination to assist you in answering the remaining items. To prepare for matching questions, try using flash cards and lists that you create from the recall column in your notes.

Ace the Test

No matter what type of test you are taking, read each question carefully so that you have the best chance of selecting the right answer. And remember, when you take a machine-scored test, one of the simplest and most important steps you can take is to make sure you match the questions with your answer sheet numbers.

OVERCOMING TEST ANXIETY

Test anxiety takes many different forms. Part of dealing with test anxiety is understanding why it happens and identifying its symptoms. Whatever the reason for test anxiety, you should know that it is common among college students.

Test anxiety has many causes. It can be the result of the pressure that students put on themselves to succeed. Some stress connected with taking exams is natural and can motivate you to perform better. However, when students put too much pressure on themselves or set unrealistic goals, the result can be stress that is no longer motivating.

The expectations of parents, a spouse or partner, friends, and other people who are close to you can also create test anxiety. Sometimes, for example, two-year college students are the first in their families to attend college and thus feel extra pressure that can be overwhelming.

Finally, some test anxiety is caused by lack of preparation. The awareness that you are not prepared, that you have fallen behind on assigned reading, homework, or other academic commitments, is usually the source of anxiety. Procrastination can also be a big problem because if you do poorly on the first test in a course, you will have even more pressure to do well on other tests to pull up your course grade. This situation becomes even more difficult if the units of the course are cumulative—that is, if they build on one another, as in math and foreign languages, or if the final exam includes understanding all the course material.

Some test anxiety comes from a negative prior experience. Forgetting past failures can be a challenge; however, the past is not the present. If you carefully follow the strategies in this chapter, you are likely to do well on future tests. Remember that a little anxiety is okay, but if you find that anxiety is getting in the way of your performance on tests and exams, be sure to ask for help from your college counseling center.

Symptoms of Test Anxiety

Test anxiety can appear in many ways. Some students feel it on the very first day of class. Other students begin showing symptoms of test anxiety when it's time to start studying for a test. Others do not get nervous until the night before the test or the morning of an exam day. And some students experience symptoms only while they are actually taking a test.

Symptoms of test anxiety can include:

- butterflies in the stomach, queasiness, nausea
- mild to severe headaches
- an increased heart rate
- hyperventilation, which is breathing unusually deeply or rapidly because of anxiety
- shaking, sweating, or muscle cramps
- "going blank" during the exam and being unable to remember the information.

Test anxiety can block the success of any college student, no matter how intelligent, motivated, and prepared that student is. Therefore, it is important to seek help from your college's counseling service or another professional if you think that you have severe test anxiety. If you are not sure where to go for help, ask your adviser or counselor, but seek help promptly! If your symptoms are so severe that you become physically ill, you should also consult your physician or campus health center.

Types of Test Anxiety

Students who experience test anxiety don't necessarily feel it in all testing situations. For example, you might do fine on classroom tests but feel anxious during standardized examinations such as a college placement test. One reason such standardized tests can create anxiety is that they can change your future. One way of dealing with this type of test anxiety is to ask yourself: What is the worst that can happen? Remember that no matter what the result, it is not the end of the world. How you do on standardized tests might limit some of your options, but going into these tests with a negative attitude will certainly not improve your chances.

Test anxiety can often be subject-specific. For example, some students have math test anxiety. It is important to understand the differences between anxiety that arises from the subject itself and general test anxiety. Perhaps subject-specific test anxiety relates to old beliefs about yourself, such as "I'm no good at math" or "I can't write well." Now is the time to try some positive self-talk and realize that by preparing well, you can be successful even in your hardest courses. If the problem continues, talk to a counselor to learn about strategies that can help you deal with such fears. Take the following test anxiety quiz to find out more about how you feel before taking tests.

Strategies for Dealing with Test Anxiety

In addition to studying, eating right, and getting plenty of sleep, you can try a number of simple strategies for overcoming the physical and emotional impact of test anxiety:

- **Breathe.** If at any point during a test you begin to feel nervous or you cannot think clearly, take a long, deep breath and slowly exhale to restore your breathing to a normal level.
- **Stretch.** Before you go into the test room, especially before a long exam, stretch your muscles—legs, arms, shoulders, and neck—just as you would when preparing to exercise.
- **Sit well.** Pay attention to the way you are sitting. As you take the test, sit with your shoulders back and relaxed rather than hunched forward. Try not to clutch your pencil or pen tightly in your hand; take a break and stretch your fingers now and then.
- **Create positive mental messages.** Pay attention to the mental messages that you send yourself. If you are overly negative, turn those messages around. Give yourself encouraging, optimistic messages.
- **Keep your confidence high.** Do not allow others (classmates, partners, children, parents, roommates, and friends) to reduce your confidence. If you belong to a study group, discuss strategies for relaxing and staying positive before and during tests.

Do you experience feelings of test anxiety? Read each of the following questions and consider your responses. If your answer to a question is "yes," place a check mark in the box. If your answer is "no," leave the box blank.

Mental

☐ Do you have trouble focusing and find that your mind easily wanders while studying the material or during the test itself?

☐ During the test, does every noise bother you—sounds from outside the classroom or sounds from other people?

☐ Do you often "blank out" when you see the test?

☐ Do you remember answers to questions only after the test is over?

Physical

☐ Do you get the feeling of butterflies, nausea, or pain in your stomach?

☐ Do you develop headaches before or during the test?

☐ Do you feel like your heart is racing, that you have trouble breathing, or that your pulse is irregular?

☐ Do you have difficulty sitting still, are you tense, or are you unable to get comfortable?

Emotional

☐ Are you more sensitive and more likely to lose patience with a roommate or friend before the test?

☐ Do you feel pressure to succeed from either yourself or from your family or friends?

☐ Do you toss and turn the night before the test?

☐ Do you fear the worst–that you will fail the class or flunk out of college because of the test?

Personal Habits

☐ Do you often stay up late studying the night before a test?

☐ Do you have a personal history of failure for taking certain types of tests (essay, math)?

☐ Do you drink more than your usual amount of caffeine or forget to eat breakfast before a test?

☐ Do you avoid studying until right before a test, choosing to do other activities that are less important because you don't want to think about it?

See the following for your Test Anxiety Reflection Score.

TEST ANXIETY REFLECTION SCORE

How many items did you check? Count your total, and then see what level of test anxiety you experience.

13–16 Severe: You may want to see if your college counseling center offers individual sessions to provide strategies for dealing with test anxiety. You have already paid for this service through your student fees, so if you have this level of anxiety, take advantage of help that is available for you.

9–12 Moderate: You may want to see if your counseling center will be offering a seminar on anxiety-prevention strategies. Such seminars are usually offered around midterms or just before final exams. Take the opportunity to do something valuable for yourself!

5–8 Mild: Be aware of what situations—certain types of classes or particular test formats—might cause anxiety and disrupt your academic success. If you discover a weakness, address it now before it is too late.

1–4 Slight: Almost everyone has some form of anxiety before tests, and it actually can be beneficial! In small doses, stress can improve your performance, so consider yourself lucky.

Getting the Test Back

Students react differently when they receive their test grades and papers. Some students dread seeing their tests returned with a grade; other students look forward to it. Either way, unless you look at your answers (the correct and incorrect ones) and the instructor's comments, you will have no way to evaluate your own knowledge and test-taking strengths. You might also find that the instructor made a grading error that might have cost you a point or two. If that happens, you should let the instructor know.

Inhale . . . Exhale . . .

If you are nervous about getting your test back, take a few minutes for some positive self-talk and a few deep breaths. Reviewing your test is a great way to evaluate your learning.

Review your graded tests, because doing so will help you do better next time. You might find that your mistakes were the result of not following directions, being careless with words or numbers, or even thinking too hard about a multiple-choice question. Mistakes can help you learn, so refer to your textbook and notes to better understand the source and reason for each mistake. If you are a member of a study group, plan a test review with other group members; this allows you to learn from your mistakes as well as those of the others in the group.

If you have any questions about your grade, that is an excellent reason to visit your instructor during his or her office hours or before or after class; your concern will show the instructor that you want to succeed. When discussing the exam with your instructor, you might be able to negotiate a few points in your favor. Avoid making demands, though, and always be respectful.

YOUR TURN > WORK TOGETHER

What do you do when an instructor returns an exam to you? Do you just look at the grade, or do you review the items you answered correctly and incorrectly? With another classmate, make a list of some reasons why it's important to review an exam.

CHEATING

Imagine what our world would be like if researchers reported fake results that were then used to develop new machines or medical treatments or to build bridges, airplanes, or subway systems. Fortunately, few researchers actually do falsify their findings; most follow the rules of academic honesty. This honesty is a foundation of higher education, and activities that jeopardize it can damage everyone: your country, your community, your college, your classmates, and yourself.

What Is Cheating?

Different colleges define *cheating* in different ways. Some include the following activities in their definition of cheating: looking over a classmate's shoulder for an answer, using a calculator when it is not permitted, obtaining or discussing an exam (or individual questions from an exam) without permission, copying someone else's lab notes, purchasing term papers over the Internet, watching the video instead of reading the book, and copying computer files. Whatever your college's rules about cheating, it's essential that you follow them.

Many colleges do not allow certain activities in addition to lying or cheating. Here are some examples of prohibited behaviors:

- Intentionally inventing information or results.
- Submitting the same piece of academic work, such as a research paper, for credit in more than one course.
- Giving your exam answers to another student to copy during the actual exam or before that exam is given to another class.
- Bribing anyone in exchange for any kind of academic advantage.
- Helping or trying to help another student commit a dishonest act.

Why Students Cheat and the Consequences of Cheating

Students cheat mainly when they believe they cannot do well on their own. Some college students developed a habit of cheating in high school or even elementary or middle school and do not trust their own ability to succeed in classes. Other students simply don't know the rules. For example, some students incorrectly think that buying a term paper isn't cheating. Some think that using a test file (a collection of actual tests from previous terms) is fair behavior.

Cultural and college differences may cause some students to cheat. In other countries and at some U.S. colleges, students are encouraged to review past exams as practice exercises. Some student government associations or student social organizations maintain test files for use by students. Some colleges permit sharing answers and information for homework and other assignments with friends. Make sure you know the policy at your college.

Stop! Thief!

When students are seated close to each other while taking a test, they may be tempted to let their eyes wander to someone else's answers. Don't let this happen to you. Cheating is the same as stealing. Also, don't offer to share your work or make it easy for other students to copy your work. Reduce temptation by covering your answer sheet.

Pressures from others—family, peers, and instructors—might cause some students to consider cheating. And there is no doubt that we live in a competitive society. But in truth, grades are nothing if you cheat to earn them. Even if your grades help you get a job, it is what you have actually learned that will help you keep that job and be promoted. If you haven't learned what you need to know, you won't be ready to work in your chosen field.

Sometimes lack of preparation will cause students to cheat. Perhaps they tell themselves that they aren't really dishonest and that cheating just "one time" won't matter. But if you cheat one time, you're more likely to do it again.

Although you might see some students who seem to be getting away with cheating, such behaviors can have severe and life-changing results. In some cases, students who have cheated on examinations have been suspended or expelled; graduates have had their college degrees revoked.

Here are some steps you can take to reduce the likelihood of problems with academic honesty:

- **Know the rules.** Learn the academic code for your college by going to its Web site or checking in the student handbook.
- **Set clear boundaries.** Refuse when others ask you to help them cheat. This might be hard to do, but you must say no. Leave your cell phone in your book bag; instructors are often suspicious when they see students looking at their cell phones during an exam.
- **Improve time management.** Be well prepared for all quizzes, exams, projects, and papers.
- **Seek help.** Find out where you can get help with study skills, time management, and test taking. If your skills are in good shape but the content of the course is too hard, consult your instructor, join a study group, or visit your campus learning center or tutorial service.
- **Withdraw from the course.** Your college has a policy about dropping courses and a deadline to drop without penalty. You might decide to drop only the course that's giving you trouble. Some students choose to withdraw from all classes and take time off before returning to school if they find themselves in over their heads or if a long illness, a family crisis, or something else has caused them to fall behind. But before withdrawing, you should ask about college policies in terms of financial aid and other scholarship programs. See your adviser or counselor before you decide to withdraw.
- **Reexamine goals.** Stick to your own realistic goals instead of giving in to pressure from family members or friends to achieve impossibly high standards. You might also feel pressure to enter a particular career or profession that doesn't interest you. If that happens, sit down with counseling or career services professionals or your academic adviser and explore your options.

YOUR TURN > DISCUSS IT

Some students think it is acceptable to get answers from another student who took the exam earlier in the term or in a prior term. What do you think?

FEAR NOT THE ONLINE TEST

THE PROBLEM *You don't know how to take an online test.*

THE FIX *Learn to avoid errors.*

HOW TO DO IT

Source: © Fotosearch

Here are our top ten strategies:

1. **Don't wait until the last minute to study.** Whether this online test is part of a self-paced online course or a face-to-face course, start a study group (either in person or online) as soon as possible.

2. **Get organized.** An open-book quiz can take longer than a normal test if you're not sure where to locate the information you need. Note: Having a good understanding of the material going in is key; your notes and books should be for occasional reference only.

3. **Resist the temptation to surf the Web for answers.** The answer you pick might not be what your instructor is looking for. It's much better to check your notes to see what you were taught in class.

4. **Collaborate when it is permitted.** If your instructor allows you to work with someone else on tests, open up an instant message window with a fellow student. Take the test together.

5. **Don't get distracted.** When you're taking an online exam, it's easy to get distracted by Facebook, iTunes, YouTube, or Twitter. Whatever you do, take the test seriously. Go somewhere quiet where you can concentrate—not Starbucks. A quiet, remote spot in the library is ideal. Noise-canceling headphones might help even more.

6. **While taking the test, budget your time.** Keep an eye on the clock so that you'll be sure to finish the whole test.

7. **Tackle easy questions first.** Once you get those out of the way, you can revisit the harder ones.

8. **Find out in advance if there's any penalty for wrong answers.** If not, bluffing is allowed, so you want to be sure to answer every question.

9. **Beware: There's always the risk of losing your Internet connection midtest.** To be on the safe side, type all of your answers and essays into a Word document. Then leave time at the end to cut and paste them into the test itself.

10. **Finish early?** Take a few minutes to check your answers and spelling. (That's good advice for traditional tests, too.)

THINK

As you were reading the tips for improving your performance on exams and tests, were you surprised to see different tips for various subjects, such as math and science, and for different kinds of questions, such as multiple-choice and essay? What did you find to be the most useful information in this chapter? What material was unclear to you?

WRITE

Do you consider yourself to be a good test taker or a poor one? Why? Do you experience test anxiety? If you do, what might be the reasons? What did you learn in this chapter that either explains your inability to relax while taking tests or can help you relax and improve your test grades? Jot down a few thoughts here and expand on them in a journal, in a notebook, or on your favorite device.

APPLY

1. Identify your next upcoming test or exam. What time of day is it scheduled, and what type of test will it be? What strategies have you read in this chapter that will help you prepare for and take this test?

2. What course do you find most difficult? If you are anxious about taking tests in this class, what positive self-messages can you use to help yourself stay focused?

AT YOUR COLLEGE

VISIT . . .	IF YOU NEED HELP . . .
Academic Learning/Skills Center	preparing for tests. Almost every college has a learning assistance support center whose specialty is to help you study for tests. The best students, good students who want to be even better, and students with academic difficulties use learning centers and tutoring services. These services are offered by both full-time professionals and highly skilled peer tutors and are usually free.
Counseling Center	finding workshops and individual or group counseling for test anxiety. Sometimes these services are also offered by the campus health center. Ask your instructor where you can find counseling services at your college.
Fellow students	finding a tutor or joining a study group. Students who work with tutors and in study groups are much more likely to be successful. Often the best help we can get is the closest to us. Keep an eye out in your classes and extracurricular activities for the best students—those who appear to be the most serious, purposeful, and directed.

ONLINE

GO TO . . .	IF YOU NEED HELP . . .
Florida Atlantic University's Center for Learning and Student Success (CLASS): fau.edu/class/Success/test%20tips.jpg	finding a list of tips to help you prepare for exams.
Study Guides and Strategies: studygs.net/tstprp8.htm	getting tips for reducing text anxiety.

MY COLLEGE'S RESOURCES

8 Information Literacy

PRE-READING ACTIVITY: Imagine that you are in your college library to research a topic for one of your courses. Your instructor has asked you to use at least six different sources (books, journals, online resources, etc.). Describe three ways you could go about finding information on the assigned topic.

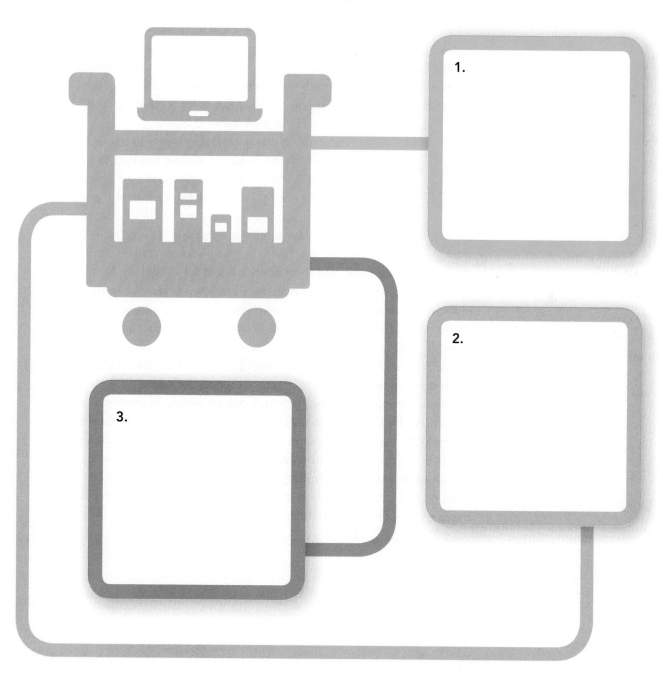

1.

2.

3.

📁 **PROFILE** ✕

Analee Bracero, 26
Criminal Justice Major, *Ocean County College*

When Analee was looking into colleges, she found that Ocean County College in New Jersey had everything she wanted: an affordable community college that also offers online courses, off-campus sites, transfer opportunities, and a variety of student clubs. The college also has a good library system that allows her to conduct research and write papers while on campus.

Analee grew up in a small town in Puerto Rico where she attended high school, completed a certificate program in medical office billing and coding, and then worked for a few years. When she decided that she wanted to change careers, she realized a degree in criminal justice was just what she needed. "I intend to join a law enforcement agency," she says. "My goal is to join the FBI as a behavior analyst."

Now, while working about twenty-five hours a week at an after-school program, Analee has had to develop a number of strategies to help her write well-researched papers that are very different from those she wrote in high school. "In high school, they didn't emphasize how important it was to include your opinions," she says. "In college, they want you to research your work, cite as many sources as you can, and think about your topic and form opinions. It is very different for me." She tells us that her best strategy is to start early and prepare to write, rewrite, and edit the same material a few times before handing it in for a grade. "Start researching the topic you will be writing about as soon as possible," she advises. "Every day, look for more data and take additional notes. That way you can prevent procrastination and reduce your stress when it's time to put the research together on the paper."

Analee does most of her research online, where information is at her fingertips. She is careful about checking the validity of material she finds on the Web, especially on sites like Wikipedia. "I use Wikipedia and other online encyclopedias to start learning about a topic," she explains, "but I rely on other sources for writing my paper and carefully check any information I pull from the Web to ensure accuracy." She can access the databases she needs from her laptop or at the library.

> **"Start researching the topic you will be writing about as soon as possible."**

As Analee's story illustrates, developing the skills to locate and use information will increase your ability to keep up with what is going on in the world; participate in activities that interest you; and succeed in college, career, and community. The research skills you learn and use as a student will serve you well as a successful professional. That is true for whatever career you choose. Whether you're a student of nursing, criminal justice, or business, one of your main tasks in college is to manage information. In a few years, as a nurse, probation officer, or accountant, one of your main tasks will be the same: to manage and present information for your employers and clients. All colleges and many companies provide libraries for this purpose.

But finding information and using it involve more than operating a computer or browsing the stacks. To make sense of the enormous amount of information at your fingertips in a reasonable amount of time, you'll need to develop a few key research and information literacy skills.

INFORMATION LITERACY

Information literacy is the ability to find, interpret, and use information to meet your needs; it includes computer literacy, media literacy, and cultural literacy:

- **Computer literacy.** The ability to use electronic tools for conducting searches and for communicating and presenting to others what you have found and analyzed. This ability involves using different computer programs, digital video and audio tools, and social media.
- **Media literacy.** The ability to think deeply about what you see and read through both the content and context of television, film, advertising, radio, magazines, books, and the Internet.
- **Cultural literacy.** Knowing what has gone on and is going on around you. You have to understand the difference between the American Civil War and the Revolutionary War, U2 and YouTube, Eminem and M&Ms so that you can keep up with everyday conversations and with your college reading material.

Information matters. It helps people make good choices. The choices people make often determine their success in careers, their happiness as friends and family members, and their well-being as citizens on our planet.

YOUR TURN > DISCUSS IT

In a small group, discuss how information literacy can contribute to people's success in today's world?

Learning to Be Information Literate

People are amazed at the amount of information available to them everywhere, especially online. Many think that because they checked out some links they found on a search engine, they are informed or can easily become informed. Most of us, though, are unprepared for the number of available sources and the amount of information that we can find at the press of a button. What can we do about information overload? To become an informed and successful user of information, keep three basic goals in mind:

1. **Know how to find the information you need.** Once you have figured out where to look for information, you'll need to ask good questions and learn how to search information systems, such as the Internet, libraries, and databases. You'll also want to get to know your college librarians who can help you ask questions, decide what sources you need to investigate, and find the information you need.

2. **Learn how to interpret the information you find.** It is important to find information, but it is even more important to make sense of that information. What does the information mean? Have you selected a source you can understand? Is the information correct? Can the source be trusted?

3. **Have a purpose for collecting information and then do something with it once you have it.** Even the best information won't do much good if you don't know what to do with it. True, sometimes you'll hunt down a fact simply to satisfy your own curiosity. But more often, you'll communicate what you've learned to someone else. First you should decide how to put your findings into an appropriate format such as a research paper for a class or a presentation at a meeting. Then you need to decide what is it that you want to accomplish. Will you use the information to make a decision, solve a problem, share an idea, prove a point, or something else?

In this chapter we'll explore ways to work toward each of these goals.

Information Literacy

In today's world, information literacy is one of the most important skills. This means developing computer, media, and cultural literacy, along with learning how to find, interpret, and use information you need.

What's Research and What's Not?

In the past, you might have completed assignments that asked you to find a book, journal article, or Web page related to a particular topic. While finding information is an essential part of research, it's just one step, not the end of the road. Research is not just copying a paragraph from a book or putting together bits and pieces of information without adding any of your own comments. In fact, such behavior could easily be considered plagiarism, a form of cheating that could result in a failing grade or worse. (Plagiarism is discussed in the chapter on Writing and Speaking.) At the very least, repeating information or ideas without thinking about or interpreting them puts you at risk of careless use of old, incorrect, or biased resources.

Research is a process including steps used to collect and analyze information to increase understanding of a topic or issue. Those steps include asking questions, collecting and analyzing data related to those questions, and presenting one or more answers. Good research is information literacy in action. If your instructor asks you to select and report on a topic, you might search for information about it, find a dozen sources, evaluate them, interpret them, select a few and remove a few, organize the ones you wish to keep, select related portions, write a paper or presentation that cites your sources, write an introduction that explains what you have done, draw some conclusions of your own, and submit the results. That's research. The conclusion that you make based on your research is new information!

CHOOSING, NARROWING, AND RESEARCHING A TOPIC

8.2

Assignments that require the use of library materials can take many forms and will be a part of most of your classes. We'll learn several ways to search for information later in the chapter. Before you start searching, however, you need to have an idea of exactly what you're looking for.

Choosing a topic is often the hardest part of a research project. Even if an instructor assigns a general topic, you'll need to narrow it down to a particular area that interests you enough to research it. Imagine, for example, that you have been assigned to write a research paper on the topic of global warming. What steps should you take? Your first job is to get an overview of your topic. You can begin by conducing a Google search. Once you've found some basic information to guide you toward an understanding of your topic, you have a decision to make: What aspects of the subject will you research? Soon after you start researching your topic, you may realize that it is really large (for example, simply typing "global warming" into Google will return millions of hits) and that it includes many related subtopics. You can use this new information to create keywords. A **keyword** is a word or phrase that tells an online search tool what you're looking for. You can create a list of keywords by brainstorming different terms and subtopics within your general topic that will help you find resources for your topic. For example, for the topic "global warming," keywords may include "climate change," "greenhouse effect," "ozone layer," "smog," or "carbon emissions." Even those terms will generate a large number of hits, and you will probably need to narrow your search several times.

What you want are twelve or so focused and highly relevant hits on an aspect of the topic that you can use to write a well-organized essay. Begin by figuring out what you already know and what you would like to learn more about. Perhaps you know a little about global warming causes and effects and you're curious about its impacts on animals and plants; in that case you might decide on a two-part topic: impacts on animals, impacts on plants. By consulting a few general sources, you'll find that you can narrow a broad topic to something that interests you and is a manageable size. You may end up focusing on the impact of global warming on one particular animal or plant in one specific geographic area.

If you are having trouble coming up with keywords, one place to begin your research is an encyclopedia. Encyclopedias provide general overviews of topics. They can help you understand the basics of a concept or event, but you will need to use other resources for most college-level research projects. An encyclopedia is a great place to start your research but not a good place to end it.

You have probably used an encyclopedia recently—you may use one all the time without thinking about it: Wikipedia. A *wiki* is a type of Web site that allows many different people to edit its content. This means that information on wikis can be constantly changing. Wikipedia is controversial in college work. Many instructors feel that the information on Wikipedia cannot be guaranteed to be reliable because anyone can change it; they instead want students to use sources that have gone through a formal editing and reviewing process. Your instructors might even forbid Wikipedia; if so, avoid it altogether. Even if an instructor permits the use of Wikipedia, it's best to use it only as a *starting point* for your research. Do not plan on citing Wikipedia in your final paper. Rather, check the references at the bottom of Wikipedia pages, or otherwise verify claims made at Wikipedia on another trustworthy site.

Even with an understanding of various types of sources, it can be difficult to determine what exactly you need for your assignment. Figure 8.1 provides an overview of when to use different common research sources and gives examples of what you'll find in each source.

FIGURE 8.1 ❯ Using Common Research Sources

Through one particular example, this chart differentiates the most common research sources. You will access these types of sources for classwork and also your personal life.

| Topic: Environmental Issue: Effects of BP/Deepwater Horizon oil spill on the brown pelican, the state bird of Louisiana |||
Source	Timing of information	What it offers
Newspapers (print and online)	Provide reports hourly/daily after an event	Primary-source, first-hand discussions of current events, what happened at the time of the event; short articles; months or years after an event, it can be fascinating to compare early newspaper reports with later analysis offered in scholarly articles and books.
Magazines	Weekly/monthly after event	Analysis of an event a few weeks after it occurs by a journalist or reporter; informally credits sources; longer articles than in newspapers; might include more interviews or research and historical context.
Scholarly articles	Months after event	In-depth analyses of issues; research-based scientific studies with formally credited sources, written and reviewed by experts; contains graphs, tables, and charts
Books	Months/years after event	Comprehensive overview of a topic with broad and in-depth analyses

YOUR TURN ❯ WORK TOGETHER

With a classmate decide where would you go to find information about an environmental issue affecting your neighborhood. Use the chart above to determine what kind of information each source provides.

USING THE LIBRARY

Whenever you have research to do for a class, for your job, or for your personal life, visit a library. We can't stress this enough. Although the Internet is loaded with billions of pages of information, don't be fooled into thinking it will serve all of your needs. For one thing, you'll have to sort through a lot of junk to find your way to good-quality online sources. More important, if you limit yourself to the Web, you'll miss out on some of the best materials. Although we often think that everything is electronic and can be found through a computer, a great deal of valuable information is still stored in traditional print formats and your college library database.

Every library has books and journals as well as a great number of items in electronic databases that aren't available on public Web sites. Librarians at your college work with your instructors to determine the kinds of materials that support their teaching. Most libraries also have other types of information, such as government documents, microfilm, photographs, historical documents, maps, music, and films. A key component of being information literate is determining the kinds of sources you need to satisfy your research questions.

YOUR TURN > WORK TOGETHER

Have a discussion with a group of your classmates to answer this question: Is the library a necessary resource for learning in college? Do the members of the group agree or disagree? Share your group's ideas with others in the class.

A college library is far more than a document warehouse, however. For starters, most campus libraries have Web sites and apps that offer lots of help for students. Some provide guidelines on writing research papers, conducting online searches, or navigating the **stacks**—the area of a library in which most of the books are shelved.

Of course, no one library can possibly own everything you might need or enough copies of each item, so groups of libraries share their materials with each other. If your college library does not have a journal or book that looks promising for your project, or the item you need is checked out, you can use **interlibrary** loan, a service that allows you to request an item at no charge from another library at a different college or university. The request process is simple, and the librarians can help you get started.

If it is difficult for you to go to your college library because of your commuting, family, work challenges, time constraints, or because you

Library of the Future?
No, the Present!

College libraries are changing as information goes digital and space for group work becomes a priority. This facility contains quiet spaces for individuals or groups and a digital classroom. Have you explored your college library? Are you making the most of this important academic resource?

Source: Learning Commons, 2012, Atlanta University Center Robert W. Woodruff Library Photographs, Atlanta University Center. Robert W. Woodruff Library

are an online student who lives far from the actual campus and its library, you will still have off-campus, online access to library materials through a school-provided ID and password. You can also have online chats with librarians who can help you in real time. To learn more, check out your library's Web site, or e-mail or phone the reference desk. Be sure to use the handouts and guides that are available at the reference desk or online. You will also find tutorials and virtual tours that will help you become familiar with the collections, services, and spaces available at your library.

The 20-Minute Rule

If you have been working hard trying to locate information for a research project for 20 minutes and haven't found what you need, stop and ask a librarian for help. Let the librarian know what searches you've tried, and he or she will be able to help you figure out new strategies to get to the books, articles, and other sources you need. In addition, the librarian can help you develop strategies to improve your research and writing skills. Doing research without a librarian is like driving cross-country without a map or GPS—technically, you can do it, but you will get lost along the way and may not get to your destination on time. Get to know at least one librarian as your go-to expert. College librarians are dedicated to helping students.

Scholarly Articles and Journals

Many college-level research projects will require you to use articles from **scholarly journals,** collections of original, peer-reviewed research articles written by experts or researchers in a particular academic discipline. Examples are the *Journal of Educational Research* and the *Social*

Psychology Quarterly. The term **peer-reviewed** means that other experts in the field read and evaluate the articles in the journal before it is published. You might find that some of your instructors use the terms *peer-reviewed* or *academic* to refer to scholarly articles or journals. Be sure to clarify what your instructor expects of your sources before you begin your work.

Scholarly articles focus on a specific idea or question and do not usually provide a general overview of a topic. For example, for the topic of climate change you might find scholarly articles that compare temperature data over a certain period, analyze the effect of pollution, or explore public and political conversations on the topic. Scholarly articles always include a reference list that includes other sources related to the topic; you may find those sources useful in finding other relevant articles as well.

The most popular way to find scholarly articles is to use a online **database,** an searchable set of information often organized by certain subject areas. Some databases are specific to one subject, like chemistry, while others include articles from many different disciplines. Many libraries have dozens, if not hundreds, of databases. It can be difficult to figure out which ones you should use, but your librarian can help you determine which databases are best for your research.

When you use a database, you can easily add filters to ensure that your results include scholarly articles only, and you can clearly see who the authors are. Your database search should result in article and journal titles, descriptions, and sometimes full articles.

While some databases are available to anyone, whether that person is a student or instructor at a college, most of the databases you'll use for research are through subscription and available only to students at a college that pays for the service. Remember, even though databases might look just like Web sites, they're actually carefully chosen subscriptions paid for by the library. For this reason, you will most likely need to log in with your college ID and password.

The second most popular way to find scholarly articles is to use your library's catalog, an online resource accessible on or off campus. Sometimes off-campus access requires you to log in with your college ID and password. When searching the library catalog, you are more likely to find only the names of journals and *not* the titles of the articles within the journal. You might find a link to the electronic version of the journal. You may also be able to find some of the scholarly articles by using Google Scholar as your search engine. This is a specific part of Google that searches only within scholarly journal articles.

Periodicals

You may have heard the word *periodical* before. Many sources that we use in both academic research and our personal lives are periodicals. A **periodical** is a resource such as a journal, a magazine, or a newspaper that is published multiple times a year. Periodicals are designated either by date of publication or by annual volume numbers and issue numbers (based on the number of issues published in a given year).

Peer-reviewed scholarly journals are of course periodicals, but most periodicals are classified as popular rather than scholarly. The articles in *Rolling Stone* (a periodical with a focus on politics and popular culture published twice each month) do not go through the peer-review process like the articles in scholarly journals. Lack of peer review does *not* disqualify magazines as possible legitimate sources for your research, unless your assignment specifically requires all sources to be scholarly articles or books. Look back at Figure 8.1 for a breakdown of different types of sources.

Books

Books are especially useful for research projects. Often students in introductory classes must write research papers on broad topics like the Civil War. While many scholarly articles have been written about the Civil War, they will not provide the kind of general overview of the topic that is available in books.

Searching the library catalog for a book is a lot like searching databases. When you find a source that looks promising, check to see whether it is currently available or checked out to another student. If it's available, write down the title, author, and the call number. The call number is like an address that tells you where the book is located in the library. After you have this information, head into the stacks to locate your book or journal. If it's checked out to another student or if your library doesn't own the item you're looking for, remember to ask about interlibrary loan. One of the biggest benefits of searching for books is the ability to browse. When you find your book on the shelf, look at the other books around it. They will be on the same topic.

Many books are also available electronically; some of these e-books can be easily accessed online. Your college library may have books available in this format as well. You can browse the entire e-book chapters and even print a few pages.

EVALUATING SOURCES

8.4

Both the power and the pitfalls of doing research on the Internet relate to the importance of knowing how to evaluate sources properly. The Internet makes research easier in some ways and more difficult in others. Through Internet search engines such as Google and Bing, you have immediate access to a great deal of free information. Keep in mind that many of the entries on any topic are not valid sources for serious research, and the order of the search results is determined not by their importance but by search formulas that depend both on popularity and on who pays for Web pages to be on the top of the list. Anybody can put up a Web site, which means you can't always be sure of the Web site owner's credibility and reliability. A Web source may be written by anyone — a fifth grader, a famous professor, a professional society, or a person with little knowledge about the topic.

Some students might at first be excited about receiving 243,000,000 hits from a Google search on global warming, but they may be shocked when they realize the information they find is not sorted or organized. Think carefully about the usefulness of the information based on three important factors: relevance, authority, and bias.

YOUR TURN > DISCUSS IT

What kinds of searches do you do on the Internet? How valuable do you think the Web is for serious research?

Relevance

The first thing to consider in looking at a possible source is whether it is relevant: Does it relate to your subject in an appropriate way? How well does it fit your needs? The answers to these questions depend on your research project and the kind of information you are seeking.

- **Is it introductory?** Introductory information is basic and elementary. It does not require prior knowledge about the topic. Introductory sources can be useful when you're first learning about a subject. They are less useful when you're drawing conclusions about a particular aspect of the subject.
- **Is it definitional?** Definitional information provides some descriptive details about a subject. It might help you introduce a topic to others or clarify the focus of your investigation.
- **Is it analytical?** Analytical information supplies and interprets data about origins, behaviors, differences, and uses. In most cases it's the kind of information you want.
- **Is it comprehensive?** The more detail, the better. Avoid unconfirmed opinions, and look instead for sources that consider the topic in depth and offer plenty of evidence to support their conclusions.
- **Is it current?** You should usually give preference to recent sources although older ones can sometimes be useful (for instance, primary sources for a historical topic or if the source is still cited by others in a field).
- **Can you conclude anything from it?** Use the "So what?" test: So what does this information mean? Why does it matter to my project?

Authority

Once you have determined that a source is relevant to your project, check that it was created by somebody who is qualified to write or speak on the subject and whose conclusions are based on solid evidence. This, too, will depend on your subject and the nature of your research. For example, a fifth grader would generally not be considered an authority, but if you are writing about a topic such as bullying in elementary schools, a fifth grader's opinion might be exactly what you're looking for.

Make sure you can identify the author and be ready to explain why that author is qualified to write on the subject. Good qualifications might include academic degrees, other research and writing on the subject, or related personal experience.

Determine whether your project calls for scholarly publications, periodicals such as magazines and newspapers, or both. As mentioned in the previous section, you don't necessarily have to dismiss popular periodicals. Many journalists and columnists are extremely well qualified, and their work might be appropriate for your needs. But as a general rule, scholarly sources will have been thoroughly reviewed, giving the work credibility in a college research project. Use Figure 8.1 for a review of different sources and what each offers.

YOUR TURN › WORK TOGETHER

While you are reading this chapter, conduct an Internet search for the phrase "finding resources for research papers" with a couple of your classmates. What ideas did you find through your Internet search?

Bias

When you are searching for sources, you should realize that all materials have an author who has personal beliefs that affect the way he or she views the world and approaches a topic. This is a normal part of the research process; however, serious authors have adopted ways to ensure that their own opinions don't get in the way of accuracy. You will want to find such objective sources whenever possible; however, many sources will be heavily biased toward a specific viewpoint or ideology.

Research consists of considering multiple perspectives on a topic, analyzing the sources, and creating something new from your analysis. Signs of bias, such as overly positive or overly harsh language, hints of a personal agenda, or a stubborn refusal to consider other points of view, indicate that you should question the credibility and accuracy of a source. Although nothing is wrong with someone having a particular point of view, as a researcher you will want to be aware that the bias exists. You may need to exclude strongly biased sources from your research. For example, if you are writing about climate change, you will want to examine sources for evidence of political or personal agendas. The following questions can help you evaluate your sources:

- Who is the author?
- Why is the author interested in this topic? What is the author's goal in writing about this topic?
- Does the author present facts or personal opinions about the topic?
- Does the author provide evidence that is based on research or information from other sources? Does the author cite these sources?
- Are the conclusions the author made based on sound evidence or are they just based on the author's personal interests and opinions?
- What do you think is missing from the article?

YOUR TURN > DISCUSS IT

Do you know Web sites, blogs, newspapers, magazines, or TV networks that you believe are biased? Why do you consider them biased?

8.5 SYNTHESIZING INFORMATION AND IDEAS

The main point of conducting research is that the process contributes to the development of new knowledge. As a researcher, you tried to find the answer to a question. Now is the time to formulate that answer and share it.

Many students are satisfied with a straightforward report that only summarizes what they found. Sometimes, that's enough. More often, however, you'll want to apply the information to ideas of your own. To do that:

- First consider all of the information you found and how your sources relate to one another. What do they have in common, and where do they disagree?
- Ask yourself these questions: What conclusions can you draw from those similarities and differences? What new ideas did they spark?
- Consider how you can use the information you have on hand to support your conclusions.

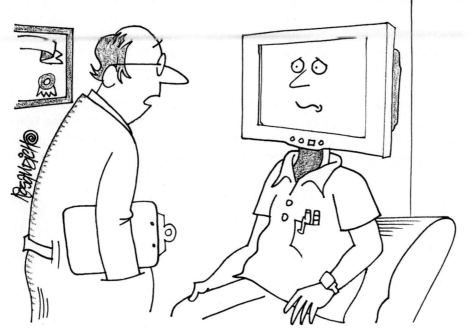

"It's a new syndrome we're seeing more of... "Google-itis"."

Google-itis

Search engines such as Google have made finding immediate answers to any question easier than ever before. Be careful, though: Some Google hits may be authentic and valuable, but others may take you to advertisements or incorrect reports that don't give you exactly the answer that you were looking for. Read more about search engines in this chapter's Tech Tip.

Source: www.cartoonstock .com

Essentially, what you're doing at this stage of your research project is processing information, an activity known as **synthesis:** accepting some ideas, rejecting others, combining related concepts, assessing the information, and pulling it all together to create new ideas that other people can use. Once your research has reached the point of synthesis, you are ready to begin putting your ideas into writing. The next chapter provides you with guidelines and strategies for using your research in writing papers and giving presentations.

CHECK YOUR ENGINE

THE PROBLEM *You understand the basics of online research but don't know how to apply it to an academic setting.*

THE FIX *Learn what research is considered scholarly: peer-reviewed academic journals (e.g., the Harvard Business Review), government Web sites (the Web addresses for U.S. government–sponsored Web sites usually end in .gov), or newspaper Web sites (like the New York Times or the Washington Post).*

HOW TO DO IT

Ask a Librarian

Unlike the examples above, much of the information you find online isn't objective or factual; it's a digital free-for-all out there. When looking for academic research, you need to filter out all the garbage.

Your college library offers free access to a lot of academic databases, LexisNexis, e-journals, and so on. As an example, visit the University Libraries Web site for Bowling Green State University (**http://libguides.bgsu.edu/library_basics**) to find helpful guides to getting started in online research and to improve your online research skills. Here are some tips:

- **Consult the Help or FAQs links.** The first time you use any catalog, database, or search engine, use the Help or Frequently Asked Questions (FAQs) links to learn specific searching techniques. You will get the best results if you use the tips and strategies suggested by the database provider.

- **Use search operators.** A particular database or search engine may use a set of search operators, which are symbols (such as quotation marks, asterisks, or colons) or words (such as *and*, *not*, or *or*) added to keywords in order to narrow the results of a search. Check the database or site for basic and advanced search tips.

- **Search more than one database or engine.** Different ones might pull up very different sources.

- **Check your library's electronic resources page.** Here you will see what else is available online. Most libraries have links to other commonly used electronic reference tools. These include online encyclopedias, dictionaries, almanacs, style guides, biographical and statistical resources, and news sources.

GOOD TO KNOW

Whether you use Bing, Google, or Google Scholar, you can learn tricks to refine your search.

KEY TIPS

1. **Don't procrastinate.** If you leave a big paper until the last minute, you'll be more tempted to cut and paste and less careful about citing your sources.

2. **Avoid *unintentional* cheating.** Whenever you copy online research into your notes, be sure to add the Web address in brackets at the end. While you're at it, place quotation marks around all cited materials, or highlight them in a bright color. It's surprisingly easy to forget which words are your own and which words came from another author.

3. **When in doubt, footnote.** Using anything off the Internet without giving credit to the author is cheating, just as it is for using anything from any other source. Most colleges have a zero-tolerance policy on the subject.

THINK

The importance of using information literacy skills in college is a no-brainer, but think beyond your college experience. How will improving your information literacy skills help you once you are out of college? Think of a career that you are interested in, and describe how you might use those skills in that career.

WRITE

Did the material in this chapter make you think about libraries and research in a new light? What did you find to be the most useful information in this chapter? What would you like to learn more about? Jot down your ideas here and expand on them in a journal, notebook, or on your favorite device.

APPLY

1. It is important to get comfortable with all of the resources in your campus library. Think about a book you love that was turned into a movie (e.g., *The Hobbit, The Hunger Games*, or a book from the Harry Potter series). Search your library catalog to find a print copy of the book, an audiobook version, a translation of the book in a language other than English, a DVD or a soundtrack from the movie. Use a newspaper database to find movie reviews or interviews with the author.

2. Choose a national current event. Carefully read about it in two places:
   a. On your favorite news Web site (e.g., www.cnn.com).
   b. In a traditional national newspaper (e.g., the *New York Times*, the *Wall Street Journal*, the *Christian Science Monitor*, or *USA Today*). A library will have these newspapers, or you can find them on the Web.
   In a Word document, compare and contrast the differences in the way the event was described by the online news site and traditional national newspaper you chose.

   - Are the authors' names or other sources provided?
   - Do you find clues that indicate the authors are taking a biased stand in reporting? If so, describe these clues.
   - For whom do you think the authors were writing (who is the intended audience)? For example, were they writing for any reader or for people of a certain age or educational level?
   - Were the facts presented the same way by both the online source and the print source? Explain your answer.
   - Did one source include more details than the other? If so, explain your answer.
   - Did the authors include their sources? If so, what were they?

AT YOUR COLLEGE

VISIT . . .	IF YOU NEED HELP . . .
Your instructor	understanding their expectations for any writing assignment. Talk to your instructor after class, drop by during office hours, or make a one-on-one appointment.
Your college library	working on an assignment. Check out the library Web site or ask about a calendar of upcoming events. Many libraries have drop-in classes or workshops to help you learn specific skills. Head over to the reference desk and talk with a librarian about the assignment you are working on.
The Writing Center	finding effective writing and research tools.
Specialized Collections	finding information specific to your major. Check the main library's Web site for what specialized libraries or collections—such as a biology or nursing collection—are on campus. Make it a point to visit all of them.
The Technology Support Center	dealing with a computer crisis. *Everyone* deals with their computer crashing at some point. It seems that disaster may strike right before a major paper is due. Prepare yourself! Check out your school's technology support services *before* you need them. Attend an orientation, chat with help-desk staff, and review their Web site so you know where to go when you're in crisis mode.

ONLINE

GO TO . . .	IF YOU NEED HELP . . .
Purdue University: http://owl.english.purdue.edu/owl/resource/584/02	researching and documenting sources both print and electronic.
PlainLanguage.gov: http://plainlanguage.gov/howto/guidelines/Federal PLGuidelines/index.cfm	with government jargon. This is a guide to writing user-friendly documents for federal employees.
Re:Writing 2: http://bedfordstmartins.com/rewriting	finding inspiration, building a bibliography, learning citation styles and more. This free resource offers videos of real writers to inspire you, writing tutorials, checklists for better writing, grammar exercises, and research tips.

MY COLLEGE'S RESOURCES

9 Writing and Speaking

PRE-READING ACTIVITY: Describe your experiences with writing before you started in community college. How have you used writing in school or at work? Do you enjoy writing, or does the thought of writing a research paper cause you to panic? How do you feel about speaking in front of a group of people? Do you prefer that to writing papers? Why or why not? Write your responses to these questions in the space provided:

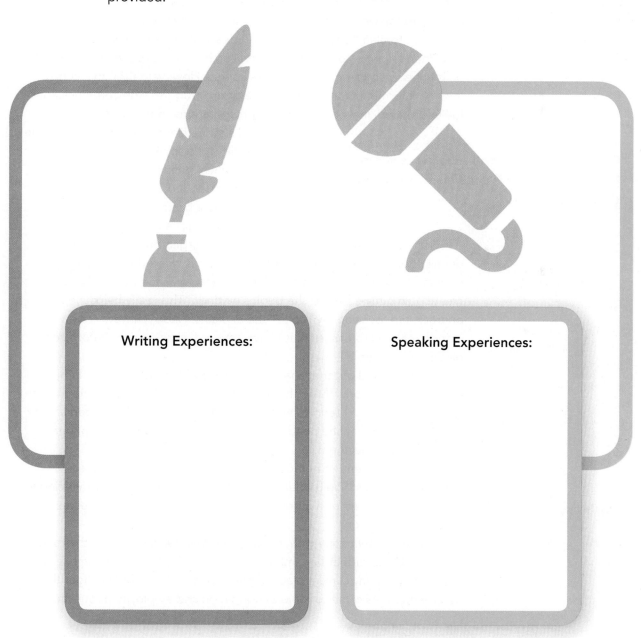

Writing Experiences:

Speaking Experiences:

📁 PROFILE

Victoria Walter, 43
Business Administration Major, *Santa Fe College*

Victoria Walter found that life was changing around her. After twenty-five years of marriage, she saw her two sons off to college and wondered what was next for her. So Victoria decided to enroll in a business administration program at Santa Fe College, a community college in Gainesville, Florida, while also working forty hours a week as a department manager at a major retail store. After graduation, she would like to transfer to the University of Florida to continue her education. "If all goes according to plan," she says, "I will graduate alongside my sons!"

When it comes to doing library research, Victoria has learned a lot of skills in her first-year college success course. However, after collecting enough information on her topic, she often struggles with communicating the information in writing or in oral presentations to the class. She found that she could summarize the information, but she found it a bit difficult to make it clear which ideas were hers and which ideas came from other sources. "After I attended a workshop in the library, I developed a better understanding of how to cite my sources," she noted.

> **"After I attended a workshop in the library, I developed a better understanding of how to cite my sources."**

Victoria's biggest challenge, however, is organizing the facts and details she needs to support her point. She has worked to overcome this challenge, and one of the most effective strategies for Victoria has been creating an outline before she begins writing. "This really helps me stay on track and focus on my topic," she explains. "Also, I always review my written material to ensure that I have covered all key points before completing the paper."

Victoria found out that sharing her ideas with a classmate or family member as she works through them is helpful. "I noticed that when I write papers," she says, "I tend to write as if I am speaking with someone." She also discovered that she needs someone to proofread her final papers before she submits them.

As far as presenting her ideas in front of a group, Victoria feels extremely nervous. She has learned that preparing notes and practicing in front of her husband or a mirror helps her with controlling her nerves during the presentation.

Already pretty happy with the path her life is taking, Victoria thinks that college will help further her ambitions. "I would like to become an executive manager at my current place of employment. I'll be the manager that other employees come to for job information and employment questions."

As Victoria's story illustrates, when you write papers and prepare oral presentations, the ability to make sense of all the information you find is important. Writing and speaking are basic requirements for all college courses. Instructors want to see how you form your thoughts about your topic instead of providing just a summary of the information. They are interested in seeing which ideas you are accepting, which you are rejecting, and how you relate the concepts and come to a new understanding of the topic. In short, they want to see you think deeply about the information you find. These skills are particularly important in today's world in which processing information is part of our daily lives and careers. Whatever career you choose, you will be expected to manage, communicate, and use information effectively whether in writing or in the form of oral presentations.

USING YOUR RESEARCH IN WRITING

You have probably heard the saying "Knowledge is power." But knowledge gives you power only if you put it to use in the form of what might be called a product. You have to decide what form that product will take—a piece of writing or a presentation—and what kind of power you want it to hold. Who is your audience and how will you present the information? What do you hope to accomplish by sharing your conclusions? Remember that a major goal of information literacy is to use information effectively to accomplish a specific purpose. Make it a point to do something with the results of your research. Otherwise, why bother? You researched information to find the answer to a question. Now is the time to formulate that answer and share it with others.

Many students satisfy themselves with a straightforward report that summarizes what they found. Sometimes that's enough. Sometimes you'll want to analyze the information and use that analysis to form your own ideas. To do that, first consider how the facts, opinions, and details you found from your different sources relate to one another. What do they have in common, and how do they differ? What conclusions can you draw from those similarities and differences? What new ideas did they spark? How can you use the information you have on hand to support your conclusions? Essentially, what you're doing at this stage of any research project is **synthesis,** a process in which you put together parts of ideas to come up with a

Synthesis

Once you've done your research, it's time to process the information you found and decide how to use it. What ideas did your research spark?
Source: © Blue Jean Images/Corbis

whole result. By accepting some ideas, rejecting others, combining related concepts, and pulling it all together, you'll create new information and ideas that other people can use.

Your final paper will include analysis and synthesis of the information you found through your research along with your original ideas. You must make sure that you clearly state which thoughts and ideas came from the sources you found and which are yours.

9.2 THE WRITING PROCESS

Your writing tells others how well you think and understand the ideas you are learning in your courses. In college, you are required to write often. Students have to write lab reports in science courses, reflection papers in response to readings in liberal arts courses, and journal entries and one-minute papers in writing courses. Like research, writing takes practice, and it is always a good idea to ask for help. This section will get you started by walking you through the writing process with step-by-step guidelines for effective and efficient writing.

Steps to Good Writing

The writing process typically includes the following steps:

1. Prewriting
2. Drafting
3. Revising

Now, let's look more in-depth at each one of these steps.

Step 1: Using Prewriting to Discover What You Want to Say Engaging in prewriting activities is the first step in the writing process. Prewriting simply means writing things down as they come to mind based on the information from the sources you found through your research along with your own ideas, without consciously trying to organize your thoughts, find exactly the right words, or think about structure. It can involve filling a page, whiteboard, or screen with words, phrases, or sentences.

The most commonly used prewriting activity is called **freewriting**. Freewriting simply means writing without worrying about punctuation, grammar, spelling, and background. In this step, you are writing without trying to organize your thoughts, to find exactly the right words, or to think about structure. Freewriting also helps you avoid the temptation to try to write and edit at the same time. It's impossible to write well and at the same time try to organize, check grammar and spelling, and offer intelligent thoughts to your readers. If you are freewriting on your computer or tablet, turn off the grammar and spelling checkers.

When you freewrite, you might notice that you have more ideas than can fit into one paper, and this is very common. Fortunately, freewriting helps you choose, narrow, and investigate a topic. It helps you figure out what you really want to say as you make connections between different ideas. When you freewrite, you'll see important issues more clearly—issues that you can use as keywords in developing your theme. Remember, keywords are synonyms, related terms, or subtopics that we use to find materials for research papers.

YOUR TURN > WORK TOGETHER

Think for a minute about your writing process—the steps you go through when you write a major paper—and then share them with another student. Do the two of you use the same process? If not, what can you learn from each other?

Step 2: Drafting When you have completed your research with the help of your librarian, gathered a lot of information sources and ideas, and done some freewriting, it's time to move to the drafting stage. Before you start writing your draft, you need to organize all the ideas you generated in the freewriting step and form a **thesis statement,** a short statement that clearly defines the purpose of the paper (see Figure 9.2).

Most students find that creating an outline helps them organize their thoughts, resulting in a clear structure from the thesis to the conclusion (see Figure 9.3 for an example). Once you've set the structure for your paper, you'll add analysis and synthesis of your research findings and you're well on your way to a final draft. Now, with your workable outline and thesis, you can begin paying attention to the flow of ideas from one

FIGURE 9.2 > Example of a Thesis Statement

Thesis: Napoleon's dual personality can be explained by examining incidents throughout his life.
1. Explain why I am using the term "dual personality" to describe Napoleon.
2. Briefly comment on his early life and his relationship with his mother.
3. Describe Napoleon's rise to fame from soldier to emperor. Stress the contradictions in his personality and attitudes.
4. Describe the contradictions in his relationship with Josephine.
5. Summarize my thoughts about Napoleon's personality.
6. Possibly conclude by referring to opening question: "Did Napoleon actually have a dual personality?"

FIGURE 9.3 ❯ **Example of an Outline**

An outline is a working document; you do not need a complete outline to begin writing. Note how this author has a placeholder for another example; she has not yet decided which example from her research to use.

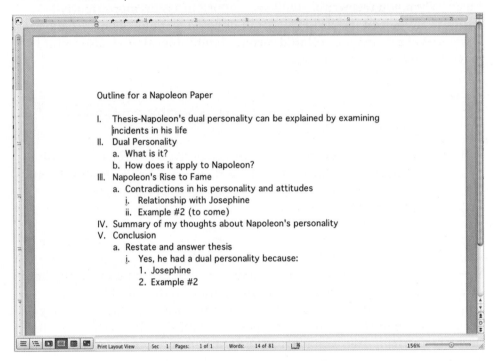

Outline for a Napoleon Paper

I. Thesis-Napoleon's dual personality can be explained by examining incidents in his life
II. Dual Personality
　　a. What is it?
　　b. How does it apply to Napoleon?
III. Napoleon's Rise to Fame
　　a. Contradictions in his personality and attitudes
　　　　i. Relationship with Josephine
　　　　ii. Example #2 (to come)
IV. Summary of my thoughts about Napoleon's personality
V. Conclusion
　　a. Restate and answer thesis
　　　　i. Yes, he had a dual personality because:
　　　　　　1. Josephine
　　　　　　2. Example #2

sentence to the next and from one paragraph to the next, including headings and subheadings where needed. If you have chosen the thesis carefully, it will help you check to see that each sentence relates to your main idea. When you have completed this stage, you will have the first draft of your paper in hand.

Step 3: Revising The key to good writing is rewriting or revising, which is the stage at which you take a good piece of writing and do your best to make it great. After you draft your paper, read it once. You may need to reorganize your ideas, add smoother transitions, cut unnecessary words from sentences and paragraphs, rewrite some sentences or paragraphs, or use stronger words.

After you revise your paper, put it aside for at least a day and then reread it. Distancing yourself from your writing for a while allows you to see it differently later. You will probably find and correct more grammatical and spelling errors, reorganize your written ideas, and make your writing stronger as a result.

It also might help to share your paper with one or more of your classmates or a family member to get their feedback. You should also check to see if your college provides any writing or editing assistance. Many community colleges have a writing center or learning center where students can get help during any stage of the writing process: finding a topic, narrowing a topic, creating a thesis, outlining, drafting, rewriting, and revising. Once you have talked with your reviewers about their suggested changes, it will be your decision to either accept or reject them.

At this point, you are ready to finalize your writing and turn in your paper. Reread the paper one more time, and double-check spelling and grammar.

Know Your Audience

Before you came to college, you probably spent much more time writing informally than writing formally. Think about all the time you've spent writing emails, Facebook posts, texts, and tweets. Now think about the time you've spent writing papers for school or work. The informal style that you use in writing an email, text, or post can become a problem when you try to write a formal research paper. Be sure that you know when you can use abbreviations and when you have to write out an entire word or phrase. When you write research papers in college, you should assume that your audience is composed of instructors and other serious students who will make judgments about your knowledge and abilities based on your writing. You should not be sloppy or casual when writing a formal paper.

The Importance of Time in the Writing Process

Many students turn in poorly written papers because they skip the first step (freewriting) and last step (rewriting/revising) and make do with the middle one (drafting). The best writing is usually done over an extended period of time, not as a last-minute task.

When planning the amount of time you'll need to write your paper, make sure to add enough time for the following:

- Asking your instructor for clarification on the assignment
- Seeking help from a librarian or from the writing center
- Narrowing or expanding your topic, which might require finding some new sources
- Balancing other assignments and commitments
- Dealing with technology problems

Writing for class projects might be a challenge at first. It is important to leave time to get help from writing center staff or trained peers in the academic support/learning centers. Also, ask your instructor for examples of papers that have received good grades. You might show your instructor a draft of your paper and explain how the writing center has helped you.

Write. Revise. Repeat.

Good writers spend more time revising and editing their written work than they spend writing the original version. Never turn in your first draft; spend the necessary time to reread and improve your work.
Source: © Radius Images/ Corbis

Citing Your Sources

At some point, you'll present your findings whether you are writing an essay, a formal research paper, a script for a presentation, a page for a Web site, or something else. Remember that you must include a complete **citation,** a reference that enables a reader to locate a source based on information such as the author's name, the title of the work, and the publication date.

Citing your sources serves many purposes. For one thing, acknowledging the information and ideas you've borrowed from other writers distinguishes between other writers' ideas and your own and shows respect for their work. Source citations show to your audience that you have based your conclusions on good, reliable evidence. They also provide a starting place for anyone who would like more information about the topic or is curious about how you reached your conclusions. Most important, citing your sources is the simplest way to avoid **plagiarism**—taking another person's ideas or work and presenting them as your own—which we will explore in more detail later in this chapter.

Source citation includes many details and can get complicated, but it all comes down to two basic rules you should remember as you write:

- If you use somebody else's exact words, you must give that person credit.
- If you use somebody else's ideas, *even if you use your own words to express those ideas*, you must give that person credit.

Your instructors will tell you about their preferred method for citation: footnotes, references in parentheses included in the text of your paper, or endnotes. If you're not given specific guidelines or if you simply want to be sure that you do it right, use a handbook or writing style manual. One standard manual is the *MLA Handbook for Writers of Research Papers,* published by the Modern Language Association (**www.mlahandbook.org**). Another is the *Publication Manual of the American Psychological Association* (**www.apastyle.org**). You can also download MLA and APA apps on your mobile devices from Google Play or iTunes.

About Plagiarism

Plagiarism is taking another person's ideas or work and presenting them as your own. Plagiarism is unacceptable in a college setting. Just as taking someone else's property is considered physical theft, taking credit for someone else's ideas is considered intellectual theft. In written reports and papers, you must give credit anytime you use (a) another person's actual words; (b) another person's ideas or theories, even if you don't quote them directly; or (c) any other information that is not considered common knowledge.

Occasionally, writers and journalists who have plagiarized have jeopardized their careers. In 2012, columnist Fareed Zakaria was suspended for a week from *Time* and CNN for plagiarizing material from *The New*

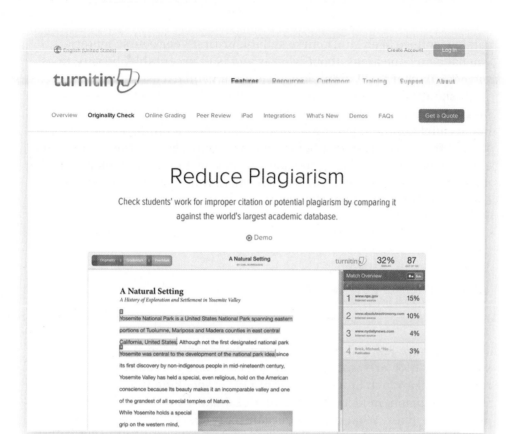

A Speed Trap for Plagiarizers

If knowing that plagiarism is wrong isn't enough of a reason to prevent you from doing it, how about knowing that you will probably get caught? Turnitin's Originality Check checks submitted papers against billions of Web papers, millions of student papers, and leading library databases and publications. Just as known speed traps usually get you to slow down when you are driving, knowing about systems like Turnitin can help you resist the urge to plagiarize.

Source: Courtesy Turnitin

Yorker, an oversight for which he took full responsibility. In spring 2013, Fox News analyst Juan Williams was criticized for plagiarizing material from a Center for American Progress report in a column he wrote for a political insider publication, but he blamed his research assistant. Also in 2013, Republican senator Rand Paul of Kentucky found himself in trouble over accusations that he plagiarized portions of his book and several speeches. Even a few college presidents have been found guilty of borrowing the words of others and using them as their own in speeches and written documents. Such discoveries may result not only in embarrassment and shame but also in lawsuits and criminal actions.

Plagiarism can be a problem on all college campuses, so instructors are now using electronic systems such as Turnitin (**turnitin.com**) to identify passages in student papers that have been plagiarized. Many instructors routinely check their students' papers to make sure that the writing is original. Some students consider cheating or plagiarizing because they think that doing so will help them get a better grade, but you can avoid the temptation if you keep in mind the high likelihood of getting caught.

Because there is no universal rule about plagiarism, ask your instructors about the guidelines they set in their classes. Once you know the rules, plagiarism is easy to avoid. Keep careful notes as you do your research, so that later on you don't mistake someone else's words or ideas for your own. Finally, be sure to check out your college's official definition of plagiarism, which you will find in the student handbook, college catalog, college Web site, course syllabi, or first-year course materials. If you have any questions about what is and isn't acceptable, be sure to ask someone in charge. "I didn't know" is not a valid excuse.

It should go without saying (but we'll say it anyway) that intentional plagiarism is a bad idea on many levels. Aside from the possibility of being caught and the potential for punishment—a failing grade, suspension, or even expulsion—submitting a paper purchased from an Internet source, copying and pasting passages from someone else's paper, or lifting material from a published source will cause you to miss out on the discovery and skill development that research assignments are meant to teach.

9.3

USING YOUR RESEARCH IN PRESENTATIONS

What you have learned in this chapter about writing also applies to public speaking—both are processes that you can learn and master, and each results in a product. Since the fear of public speaking is a common one (it is more common, in fact, than the fear of death), you might be thinking along these lines: What if I plan, organize, prepare, and practice my speech, but my mind goes completely blank, I drop my note cards, or I say something totally embarrassing? Remember that people in your audience have been in your position and will understand your anxiety. Your audience wants you to succeed. Just be positive, rely on your wit, and keep speaking. Your recovery is what they are most likely to recognize; your success is what they are most likely to remember.

YOUR TURN > DISCUSS IT

Do you enjoy public speaking? Are you an anxious or a confident speaker? What strategies do you suggest to anyone who wants to become more comfortable when speaking in front of a group?

Guidelines for Successful Speaking

Just as there is a process for writing a paper, there is a process for developing a good speech. The following guidelines can help you improve your speaking skills greatly and lose your fear of speaking publicly.

Step 1: Clarify Your Objective Begin by identifying the goals of your presentation. Do you want to persuade your listeners that your campus needs additional student parking or inform your listeners about the student government? What do you want your listeners to know, believe, or do when you are finished?

They Make It Look So Easy

When television icon Ellen DeGeneres hosted the eighty-sixth Academy Awards, she surprised everybody by having pizza delivered during the show to the hungry celebrity audience. While this comedian's use of humor and creativity to engage with the audience seems effortless, she wasn't always so comfortable onstage. "I got so nervous I would choke," she has said when talking about her early days doing stand-up comedy. When you feel nervous about speaking in front of others, consider taking a cue from Ellen: How can you work some audience interaction into your presentation?

Source: Kevin Winter/Getty Images

Step 2: Understand Your Audience In order to understand the people you'll be talking to, ask yourself the following questions:

- Who are my listeners?
- What do they already know about my topic?
- What do they want or need to know?
- What are their attitudes toward me, my ideas, and my topic?

Step 3: Organize Your Presentation Now comes the most important part of the process: building your presentation by selecting and arranging blocks of information to help your listeners connect the ideas they already have to the new knowledge, attitudes, and beliefs you are presenting. You can actually write an outline for your speech.

Step 4: Choose Appropriate Visual Aids You might use software programs, such as Prezi or PowerPoint, to prepare your presentations. When creating PowerPoint slides or Prezi templates, you can insert images and videos to support your ideas while making your presentations animated, engaging, and interactive. You might also choose to prepare a chart, write on the board, or distribute handouts. As you select and use your visual aids, consider these guidelines:

- Make visuals easy to follow. Make sure that words are large enough to be read, and don't overload your audience by including a lot of information on one slide.
- Use font colors to make your slides visually attractive. Use light colors for text on a dark background or dark colors on a light background.
- Explain each visual clearly.

Reach for the Stars
A planetarium probably won't be available to you when you're giving a speech about astronomy, but you can still use dynamic visual aids that grab your audience's attention and support your major points.

- Give your listeners enough time to process visuals.
- Proofread carefully. Misspelled words do not make you seem like a knowledgeable speaker.
- Maintain eye contact with your listeners while you discuss the visuals. Don't turn around and address the screen.

A fancy slideshow can't make up for lack of careful research or sound ideas, but using clear, attractive visual aids can help you organize your material and help your listeners understand what they're hearing. The quality of your visual aids and your skill in using them can help make your presentation effective.

Step 5: Prepare Your Notes If you are like most speakers, having an entire written copy of your speech in front of you may tempt you to read much of your presentation. But a speech, read word for word, will often sound artificial. A better strategy is to memorize the introduction and conclusion, and then use a carefully prepared outline to guide you in between. You should practice in advance. Because you are speaking mainly from an outline, your choice of words will be slightly different each time you give your presentation, with the result that you will sound prepared but natural. Since you're not reading, you will be able to maintain eye contact with your listeners. Try using note cards; number them in case you accidentally drop the stack on your way to the front of the room. After you become more experienced, your visuals can serve as notes. A handout or a slide listing key points can provide you with a basic outline.

Step 6: Practice Your Delivery Practice your delivery before an audience: a friend, your dog, even the mirror. Use eye contact and smile. As you rehearse, form a mental image of success rather than failure. Practice your presentation aloud several times to control your anxiety. Begin a few days before your speech date, and make sure you rehearse out loud, as thinking through your speech and talking through your speech have very different results. Consider making an audio or video recording of yourself on your cell phone or mobile device to hear or see your mistakes. If you ask a practice audience (friends or family) to give you feedback, you'll have some idea of what changes you might want to make.

Step 7: Pay Attention to Word Choice and Pronunciation As you reread your presentation, make sure that you have used the correct words to express your ideas. Get help ahead of time with words you aren't sure how to pronounce. Try your best to avoid *like, um, uh, you know,* and other fillers.

Step 8: Dress Appropriately Now you're almost ready to give your presentation. But don't forget one last step: Dress appropriately. Leave the baseball cap, the T-shirt, and the tennis shoes at home. Don't overdress, but do look professional. Experts suggest that your clothes should be a little nicer than what your audience is wearing. Some speakers find that when they dress professionally, they deliver a better presentation!

Step 9: Request Feedback from Someone in Your Audience After you have completed your speech, ask a friend or your instructor to give you some honest feedback. If you receive written evaluations from your audience, read them and pay attention to suggestions for ways you can improve.

YOUR TURN > DISCUSS IT

Think about public speakers you have heard either in person or on TV. Which ones were the most effective? Why? What are some of the specific ways that the best public speakers use to communicate with an audience?

SAY YES TO TWITTER

There is more to Twitter than sharing what you had for lunch. It is a great way to share your interests and stay connected to what you care about.

THE PROBLEM *You hear Twitter mentioned often, but you don't know why or even how you would use it.*

THE FIX *Dive in!*

HOW TO DO IT

Twitter is a microblogging site used by millions of people globally. Microblogging is sending live messages, called tweets, from Web-enabled devices. It's called "micro" because you are allowed only 140 characters per message.

1. **Entertainment.** Many actors, bands, sports teams, and authors often have Twitter accounts to notify their fans of upcoming events and news or share pictures and great jokes.

2. **Education.** Following leaders in your chosen field helps you stay up-to-date on current issues and gives you the chance to interact with experts. Some instructors are even using Twitter in class as a way for you to engage with course material online.

3. **Job Hunting.** Following the official Twitter feed of organizations you want to work for can lead to instant notification of new job opportunities.

4. **Community involvement.** Twitter allows for global conversations on important issues. For example, Twitter was a key component in the Arab Spring of 2011–2012, a period that saw dozens of political demonstrations and revolutionary movements across a wide range of the Arab world. Live tweeting is very common and allows for international exchange of information in real time.

Diagram of a Tweet

Here is a diagram showing Twitter in action. The key below walks you through each element of the sample tweet.

❶ **Fiona Curry** @fiona_curry ❷ ❸
The Fault in Our Stars by @realjohngreen is my favorite book! #favoritebook ❹

Source: © Jo Kirchherr/Westend61/ Corbis

↰Reply 🔁Retweet ★Favorite ❺

Kevin King @kevinbooklover
RT @fiona_curry The Fault in Our Stars by @realjohngreen is my favorite book! #favoritebook ❻

Source: © Gerhilde Skoberne/Corbis

Tessa Pool @tessapool
➤. @fiona_curry Mine too! Check out this article via @nytimes on the book and #yalit: http://nyti.ms/1jRNITC ❽ ❼

Source: © Matelly/ Corbis

❶ Tweet author profile image.
❷ Tweet author name and username.
❸ When mentioning somebody in a tweet or addressing your comments to a specific user, use "@username." The name will become a hyperlink to that person's profile and your message will be visible to them and their followers.
❹ Use hashtags (#) in front of keywords related to the topic of your tweet. They become links that will take you to all tweets using that hashtag.
❺ See something you like? You have options to reply to, "retweet," or "favorite" a tweet.
❻ "Retweeting" means posting someone else's exact tweet to your list of followers. Do this by either prefacing your tweet with "RT @username" or pushing the retweet button at the bottom of their original tweet. Be sure to always give somebody credit for what they share!
❼ When replying to a user, your tweet will begin with @username. Be sure to use a period before @username so that the tweet goes to all of that user's followers.
❽ When sharing a link, use URL shorteners like *bitly.com* or *tinyurl.com* to save space.

THINK

This chapter has information that you can use to improve your writing and speaking skills. Which is easier for you, writing or public speaking? Which strategies could you or should you put into practice to improve your writing or speaking?

WRITE

Identify a public figure who, in your opinion, is a good speaker. List the specific qualities (for example, humor, eye contact) that make that person's presentations effective. Explain why it is important for that person to speak well. Jot down your thoughts here, and then expand on them in a journal, notebook, or new document on your favorite device.

APPLY

Develop a five-slide presentation, using Prezi or PowerPoint, to introduce yourself to your classmates in a new way. You might include slides that contain points about your high school years, your hobbies, your jobs, your family, your baby pictures, and so forth. Use the effective speaking strategies in this chapter to help you outline your presentation. In addition to text, use visuals such as photos, video clips, and art to engage your audience.

WHERE TO GO FOR HELP

AT YOUR COLLEGE

VISIT . . .	IF YOU NEED HELP . . .
Writing Center/Academic Learning Center	writing or revising your paper.
Library	researching your topic for a paper.
Departments of Speech and Communications	finding resources and specific courses to help you develop your speaking skills.
Student Activities	learning and practicing speaking skills. When you become active in student organizations, especially those like the student government association and the debate club, you will have many opportunities for speaking in front of a group.

ONLINE

GO TO . . .	IF YOU NEED HELP . . .
The University of Iowa's History Department, which offers tips on common writing mistakes: http://clas.uiowa.edu/history /teaching-and-writing-center/guides	finding writing tips.
American Psychological Association: http://www.apastyle.org/learn/faqs/index.aspx	with answers to the frequently asked questions about APA style.
Toastmasters International: http://www.toastmasters.org/tips.asp	finding speaking tips.
Purdue University's online writing lab MLA: http://owl.english.purdue.edu/owl/resource/747/01/	using MLA citation style.
Purdue University's online writing lab APA: http://owl.english.purdue.edu/owl/resource/560/01/	Using APA citation style.

MY COLLEGE'S RESOURCES

THINKING CRITICALLY

STUDENT OBJECTIVES

MANAGING YOUR HEALTH, EMOTIONS, AND RELATIONSHIPS IN A DIVERSE WORLD

STUDENT OBJECTIVES

12 MAKING THE RIGHT CAREER CHOICE

STUDENT OBJECTIVES

10 Thinking Critically

PRE-READING ACTIVITY: You are determined to lose some weight. You talk to a few friends and family members about different weight-loss options. Most options seem to take a long time and require a lot of effort. A friend shows you a magazine ad for a product that promises a weight loss of 30 pounds in 60 days with no diet or exercise. The price seems to be right, and the ad claims that several famous people have lost weight by using this product.

Are you willing to try this weight loss product?

Why or why not?

How would you determine if this product is the right option for you?

📁 **PROFILE**

Donna Williford, 41
Health Care Business Informatics Major, *Pitt Community College*

 As a student in a health care field at Pitt Community College in North Carolina, Donna Williford understands the importance of critical thinking skills both inside and outside the classroom. When Donna arrived on campus last fall, she had held many jobs that all had one thing in common: the need to think deeply and to make good decisions.

Last year, Donna decided to fulfill a lifelong dream and enroll in college; she doesn't regret waiting until later in life to do so. "I'm more focused now, at forty-one, than I would have been fresh out of high school," she says. Donna uses that focus to her advantage in school, writing essays and preparing for tests. Donna' ability to think deeply has come in handy more than once, especially when evaluating the quality of sources as she does research. Similarly at work, she has been able to use her thinking skills in her interactions with medical staff and patients who have different backgrounds and needs.

After graduation, Donna hopes to get a job working with computers in the growing field of electronic medical records management, where she plans to continue learning and thinking outside the box. As new technologies are introduced, the medical staff need to change the ways they work. "Excellent thinking skills will play a vital role in my everyday decisions in the health care field," she says.

Donna's one piece of advice for other first-year students is this: "Be open to changes and new ideas because that's what a good life is all about."

> **"Be open to changes and new ideas because that's what a good life is all about."**

As Donna's story suggests, the most important skill you'll acquire in college is the ability to think for yourself. Courses in every discipline will encourage you to ask questions, to sort through different information and ideas, to form opinions of your own, and to defend them.

If you have just completed high school, you might be experiencing a lot of changes as you adjust to college. If you're an older returning student, discovering that your instructors trust you to find valid answers could be both surprising and stressful. If a high school teacher asked, "What are the three branches of the U.S. government?" there was only one acceptable answer: "legislative, executive, and judicial." A college instructor, on the other hand, might ask, "Under what circumstances might conflicts arise among the three branches of government, and what does this tell you about the democratic process?" There is no single or

simple answer, and that's the point of higher education. Questions that suggest complex answers engage you in the process of deep thinking.

Important questions usually do not have simple answers. To come up with good answers to such questions, you will have to discover many ways of thinking. You will need to become comfortable with uncertainty. You also must be willing to challenge assumptions and conclusions, even when they are presented by experts. People without such thinking skills are easily convinced to buy a product, accept an idea, vote for a political candidate, or do something against their will by those who provide misleading information. People who can think critically tend to develop the additional skills they need for success, whether it's earning an A, getting a promotion, or making connections in the community. And, it shouldn't surprise you that such thinking skills are among the most valued by employers and college admissions counselors who will play significant roles in your future.

For many people, it's natural to these critical thinking difficult and to feel frustrated by answers that are not entirely wrong or entirely right. Yet the complicated questions are usually the ones that are most interesting, and working out the answers can be both exciting and satisfying. In this chapter, we explain how developing and applying your critical thinking skills can make the search for truth, an adventure that is worth your time and mental energy.

DEFINING CRITICAL THINKING

10.1

Helping students become critical thinkers is the main purpose of college education, and most colleges will measure whether students actually improve their critical thinking abilities by the end of the first or second year. If you transfer to a four-year college or university after completing your associate's degree, your professors will assume that you have learned and practiced some critical thinking skills. Similarly, employers look for applicants who have such thinking skills; they consider these abilities to be the most important skills employees can have. Yet figuring out exactly what the term *critical thinking* means is often a challenge for students and instructors alike.

Let's start with what critical thinking is *not*. By *critical*, we do not mean "negative" or "harsh." Rather, the word *critical* refers to thoughtful attention to the information, ideas, and arguments that you hear or read. In essence, **critical thinking** is a search for truth that requires asking questions, considering multiple points of view, and drawing conclusions supported by evidence. Experts in critical thinking believe that much of our thinking, by itself, is biased, one-sided, incomplete, uninformed, or prejudiced.

Yet both the quality of our life and the quality of what we produce, make, or build depends exactly on the quality of our thoughts. You probably know people who simply follow authority without asking questions.

They typically do not think for themselves and depend on others to think for them. More troubling, they might assume that what they believe is true simply because they wish it, hope it, or feel it to be true. You might also know people who like things simply because they are popular, and still others whose beliefs may also be based on what they heard growing up without ever examining the ideas. As you might have noticed, such people tend not to have much control over their lives or any real power in business or society. Are you reminded of anyone you know whose thinking is either fuzzy or closed off? Have you ever followed a trend only because it was popular?

Critical thinkers are different. They examine problems, ask questions, suggest new answers that challenge the existing situation, discover new information, question authorities and traditional beliefs, make independent judgments, and develop creative solutions. When employers say they want workers who can find reliable information, analyze it, organize it, draw conclusions from it, and present it convincingly to others, they are seeking employees who are good critical thinkers.

Whatever else you do in college, make it a point to develop and sharpen your critical thinking skills. You won't become a great critical thinker overnight. With practice, however, you can learn how to tell if the information is truthful and accurate. Take any chance you get to practice in class, while reading, spending time online, working at your job, commuting to school, or talking with friends and loved ones. This practice will pay off. It will help you make better decisions, come up with fresh solutions to difficult problems, and communicate your ideas well.

YOUR TURN > DISCUSS IT

In your opinion, why do some people rely on others to think for them rather than think for themselves?

10.2

BECOMING A CRITICAL THINKER

The critical thinking process helps you consider alternatives, make informed decisions, and solve problems. In college and in life, you'll face a lot of information and ideas. Some of what you hear and read will be contradictory; different people may claim that opposite ideas are true. If you have ever talked back to a television commercial or doubted a politician's campaign promises, you know this already. How do you decide what to believe?

Critical thinking experts remind us that there might be more than one right answer to any given question. The task is to decide which of those answers are the most reasonable. If you are trying to think through a difficult problem, you will have to consider options and consequences before you can reach the best decision. You'll need to ask questions, consider several different points of view, and draw your own conclusions

YOUR TURN > WORK TOGETHER

With another classmate, discuss a problem you had to solve in the past and how you were able to do it. Pay special attention to the things that each of you did to solve the problem.

Ask Questions

The first step of thinking critically is to be curious. Instead of accepting statements and claims at face value, question them. Here are a few suggestions:

- When you come across an idea or a statement that you consider interesting, confusing, or suspicious, first ask yourself what it means.
- Do you fully understand what is being said, or do you need to pause and think to make sense of the idea?
- Do you agree with the statement? Why or why not?
- Can the statement or idea be interpreted in more than one way?

Don't stop there.

- Ask whether you can trust the person or group making a particular claim, and ask whether there is enough evidence to back up that claim (more on this later).
- Ask who might agree or disagree and why.
- Ask how a new concept relates to what you already know.
- Think about where you might find more information about the subject, and what you could do with what you learn.
- Finally, ask yourself about the effects of accepting a new idea as truth.
  - Will you have to change or give up what you have believed in for a long time?
  - Will it require you to do something differently?
  - Will it be necessary to examine the issue further?
  - Should you try to bring other people around to a new way of thinking?

YOUR TURN > DISCUSS IT

Imagine that your state has just approved a license plate design including a cross and the slogan "I Believe." Almost immediately, a number of organizations begin protesting that this is a violation of the First Amendment of the U.S. Constitution. What questions should you ask to get at the truth? Be prepared to share these questions with the class.

Comparison Shopping

Use your critical thinking abilities to practice healthy skepticism in your life—shopping is a great opportunity to practice. What questions do you need to ask to find out if a deal is really a deal? What examples from your own life can you think of?

Source: © Randy Glasbergen

Consider Multiple Points of View

Once you start asking questions, you'll usually discover a number of different possible answers. Don't select one answer too quickly. To be a critical thinker, you need to be fair and open-minded, even if you don't agree with certain ideas at first. Give them all a fair hearing; your goal is to find the truth or the best action, not to confirm what you already believe.

Often, you will recognize contradictory points of view held by people you know personally. You might also discover them in what you read, watch, or listen to for pleasure. Reading assignments might introduce conflicting arguments and theories about a subject on purpose, or you might come across differences of opinion as you do research for a project.

In class discussions, your instructors might present more than one valid point of view. For instance, not everyone agrees about bilingual education. Your instructor might want you to think about which types of students would or would not benefit from bilingual teaching and provide very specific reasons for your point of view. Instructors themselves can disagree with the experts and sometimes identify problems or mistakes in commonly accepted theories. Instructors also sometimes support your personal views and ask you to explain how your own life experiences help you relate to what you are reading or learning in class.

The more ideas you consider, the better your own thinking will become. Eventually, you will discover that you can change your mind, and that a willingness to do so shows that you are a reasonable, educated person.

YOUR TURN > DISCUSS IT

Have you read a book or watched a movie introducing ideas that go against what you have been taught? Did it change your thinking? Have you discussed it with family members or friends who wouldn't approve of these ideas? Has that been stressful or rewarding for you?

Draw Conclusions

Once you have considered different points of view, it's up to you to reach your own conclusions, to come up with a new idea based on what you've learned, or to make a decision about what you'll do with the information you have.

Drawing conclusions isn't necessarily about figuring out the best idea. Depending on the goals of the activity, your conclusion might be simply the one you think is the most practical or it might be a new idea of your own creation. In a chemistry lab, it might be a matter of interpreting the results of an experiment. In buying a computer, it might require evaluating your needs and your budget, asking others about their experiences, and reading buyers' reviews. Drawing conclusions involves looking at the results of your questions in a challenging, critical way. If you are trying to solve a problem, which possible solutions seem most promising after you have conducted a comprehensive search for information? Do some answers conflict with others? Which ones can be achieved? If you have found new evidence, what does that new evidence show? Do your original beliefs hold up? Do they need to be modified? Which ones should be excluded? Most important, consider what you would need to do or say to persuade someone else that your ideas are valid. Thoughtful conclusions aren't useful if you can't share them with others.

YOUR TURN > DISCUSS IT

Our experiences shape the way in which we think and perceive the world around us. Sometimes it is easy to interpret things without stopping to think about why we feel the way we do. Name three people (such as family, friends, celebrities, national leaders) who have most influenced the way you think. Describe how these individuals' values, actions, expectations, and words have shaped the way you think about yourself and the world.

FIGURE 10.1 › Rate Your Critical Thinking Skills
Now that you have read about critical thinking, it would be beneficial to rate yourself as a critical thinker.

Circle the number that best fits you in each of the situations described below.

Situations	Never		Sometimes		Always
In class, I ask lots of questions when I don't understand.	1 2 3 4 5 6 7 8 9 10				
If I don't agree with what the group decides is the correct answer, I challenge the group opinion.	1 2 3 4 5 6 7 8 9 10				
I believe there are many solutions to a problem.	1 2 3 4 5 6 7 8 9 10				
I admire those people in history who challenged what was believed at the time, such as "the earth is flat."	1 2 3 4 5 6 7 8 9 10				
I make an effort to listen to both sides of an argument before deciding which way I will go.	1 2 3 4 5 6 7 8 9 10				
I ask lots of people's opinions about a political candidate before making up my mind.	1 2 3 4 5 6 7 8 9 10				
I am not afraid to change my belief system if I learn something new.	1 2 3 4 5 6 7 8 9 10				
Authority figures do not intimidate me.	1 2 3 4 5 6 7 8 9 10				

The more 7–10 scores you have circled, the more likely it is that you use your critical-thinking skills often. The lower scores indicate that you may not be using critical-thinking skills very often or use them only during certain activities, such as a class.

FAULTY REASONING AND LOGICAL FALLACIES

A critical thinker has a healthy attitude of wanting to avoid nonsense, to find the truth, and to discover the best course of action. Logical reasoning is essential to solving any problem, whether simple or complex. A critical thinker needs to go one step further to check that an argument hasn't been based on any **logical fallacies,** which are mistakes in reasoning that contain invalid arguments or irrelevant points that weaken the logic of an argument. When confronted with logical fallacies, critical thinkers aim to be logical instead of defensive or emotional.

Here are some of the most common logical fallacies:

- **Attacking the person.** It's perfectly acceptable to argue against other people's positions or to attack their arguments. It is not acceptable, however, to go after their personalities. Any argument that resorts to personal attack ("Why should we believe a cheater?") shouldn't be considered.

- **Appealing to emotion.** "Please, officer, don't give me a ticket because if you do, I'll lose my license, and I have five little children to feed and won't be able to feed them if I can't drive my truck." None of the driver's statements offer any evidence, in any legal sense, as to why she shouldn't be given a ticket. Appealing to emotion *might* work if the officer is feeling generous, but an appeal to facts and reason would be more effective: "I fed the meter, but it didn't register the coins. Because the machine is broken, I'm sure you'll agree that I don't deserve a ticket."

- **Arguing along a slippery slope.** "If we allow college tuition to increase by 2 percent, the next thing we know it will have gone up

PENGUINS ARE BLACK AND WHITE.
SOME OLD TV SHOWS ARE BLACK AND WHITE.
THEREFORE, SOME PENGUINS ARE OLD TV SHOWS.

—GLASBERGEN

Copyright 1997 by Randy Glasbergen.

www.glasbergen.com

Logic: another thing that penguins aren't very good at.

Logic That Just Doesn't Fly

This cartoon is an obvious example of faulty reasoning. Some conversations or arguments tend to include reasoning like this. Can you think of an illogical leap like this one that someone used in an argument with you? How did you use critical thinking to counter it? Or did your emotions get the best of you?

Source: © Randy Glasbergen

200 percent a term." Such an argument is an example of slippery slope thinking: claiming that one small event will definitely lead to a larger, more significant event without allowing for the possibility of other alternatives.

- **Appealing to false authority.** Citing authorities, such as experts in a field or qualified researchers, can offer valuable support for an argument, but a claim based on the authority of someone who isn't an expert only gives the appearance of authority rather than real evidence. Many ads that use celebrity spokespeople reply on such appeals.

- **Jumping on a bandwagon.** Sometimes we are more likely to believe something that many others also believe. Even the most widely accepted truths, however, can turn out to be wrong. At one time, nearly everyone believed that the sun revolved around the earth—until astronomers proved that the sun is at the center of the solar system and the earth revolves around it.

- **Assuming that something is true because it hasn't been proved false.** Go to a bookstore or online, and you'll find dozens of books claiming to report close encounters with flying saucers and extraterrestrial beings or ghosts. Because critics could not disprove the claims of the witnesses, the events are said to have really occurred. Even if you can't completely prove that something is false, you can question the evidence.

- **Falling victim to false cause.** Frequently, people assume that just because one event followed another, the first event must have caused the second. This reasoning is the basis for many superstitions. The ancient Chinese once believed that they could make the sun reappear after an eclipse by striking a large gong, because they knew that one time the sun reappeared after a large gong had been struck. Most effects, however, are usually the result of a complex web of causes. Don't be satisfied with easy before-and-after claims; they are rarely correct.

- **Making hasty generalizations.** If you selected one green marble from a barrel containing a hundred marbles, would you guess that the next marble would be green? There are ninety-nine marbles still in the barrel; they could be any color. If, however, you had drawn fifty green marbles from the barrel, you might conclude that the next marble you draw would be green, too. (Of course, you would still have to be careful; the next marble might be a different color after all.) Reaching a conclusion based on one instance or one source is like figuring that all the marbles in the barrel are green after pulling out only one.

Fallacies like these can slip into even the most careful reasoning when someone is trying to make a point. One false claim can change an entire argument, so be on the lookout for weak logic in what you read, write, hear, or say. Check the facts presented in an argument. Do not just accept them because several other people do. Remember that accurate reasoning is a key factor for success in college and in life.

YOUR TURN > DISCUSS IT

Have you ever used or heard someone use any of these logical fallacies to justify a decision? Why was it wrong to do so?

10.4

ARGUMENTS AND EVIDENCE

What does the word *argument* mean to you? If you're like most people, the first image it brings up might be an ugly fight you had with a friend, a yelling match you witnessed on the street, or a heated disagreement between family members. True, such unpleasant confrontations are arguments. In logic, though, the word **argument** refers to a calm, reasoned effort to persuade someone of the value of an idea.

When you think of it this way, you'll quickly recognize that arguments are central to academic study, work, and life in general. Scholarly articles, business memos, and requests for spending money all have something in common: The effective ones make a general claim, provide reasons to support it, and back up those reasons with evidence. That's what an argument is.

As we have already seen, it's important to consider multiple points of view, or arguments, in dealing with new ideas and complex questions. Not all arguments are equally valid. Good critical thinking involves creative examination of the assumptions that might have been left out and of the quality of the evidence used to support a claim. Whether analyzing an argument or communicating one, a good critical thinker is careful to make sure that ideas are presented in understandable, logical ways.

Critical thinkers are careful to check that the **evidence**, which consists of facts supporting an argument, is of the highest possible quality. To do that, simply ask a few questions about the arguments as you consider them:

- What general idea am I being asked to accept?
- Are good and sufficient reasons given to support the overall claim?
- Are those reasons backed up with evidence in the form of facts, statistics, and quotations?
- Does the evidence support the conclusions?
- Is the argument based on logical reasoning or logical fallacy?
- Do I recognize any questionable assumptions?
- Can I think of any counterarguments? What facts can I find as proof?
- What do I know about the person or organization making the argument?

If, after you have evaluated the evidence used in support of a claim, you're still not certain of its quality, it's best to keep looking. Drawing on questionable evidence for an argument has a tendency to backfire. In most cases, a little persistence will help you find something better.

COLLABORATION AND CRITICAL THINKING

Researchers who study critical thinking in elementary school, high school, and college find that critical thinking and **collaboration**, or working with others, go hand in hand. Students at all levels are more likely to exercise their critical thinking abilities when they are exposed to the experiences and opinions of others.

YOUR TURN ❯ WORK TOGETHER

Make a list of the ways you think you could benefit from joining a study group. Make another list of the reasons you might decide not to join one. Compare what you wrote with several classmates, and see which of your reasons are the same or different.

Reasons for Joining a Study Group	Reasons for NOT Joining a Study Group
Example: Could share child care responsibilities	Example: Might interfere with one of my part-time jobs

---

Having more than one student involved in the learning process results in a greater number of ideas. People think more clearly when they talk as well as listen (a good reason to participate actively in your classes). Creative brainstorming and group discussion encourage original thought. These habits also teach participants to consider alternative points of view carefully and to express and defend their own ideas clearly. As a group negotiates ideas and learns to agree on the most reliable thoughts, it moves closer to a better solution.

Collaboration occurs not only face-to-face but also over the Internet through online discussion groups, blogs, Skype, FaceTime, Google Hangouts, and wikis (which allow users to add, update, and otherwise improve material that others have posted).

Whether in person or through electronic communication, teamwork improves your ability to think critically. As you leave college and either transfer or decide to return to work, you will find that collaboration is essential in almost any career you pursue, not only with people in your work setting but also with others around the globe.

Get a Second Opinion and a Third

One way to become a better critical thinker is to practice with other people. By getting feedback from others, you can see the possible flaws in your own position or approach. Whether debating an issue in a political science class or making a gown in a fashion design course, appreciate how people bring their own life experiences, personal taste, knowledge, and expertise to the table. Most questions do not have clear-cut answers, and there are often several ways to do something. Getting input can help make your finished product a masterpiece.

Source: © Zero Creatives/Corbis

10.6

CRITICAL THINKING IN COLLEGE AND LIFE

Being a college graduate and an educated citizen will lead to many future opportunities to think critically about matters that affect the quality of life for you and your friends and family. Answers are often not clear-cut but rather loaded with ambiguity and disagreement. Taking a position on an issue will require careful, critical thinking.

Exploring an Issue: What's Your Position?

Life often presents opportunities to get involved with community, political, and social issues and to take particular positions. For instance, what should we do about the problem of childhood and adult obesity? Should we deal with this problem as a society, or is it a matter that should be left to individuals? What steps might a community take to address this public health crisis?

Let's assume that you and some neighbors decide to petition the school board to place on its next agenda a decision to ban soft-drink vending machines in the public schools. In response to your request, you are

granted permission to speak at the next school board meeting. Your team collaborates to identify the questions that you need to explore:

1. What is the current obesity rate of adults in this community?
2. What is the current obesity rate of school-age children in this community, and how does it compare to the rate twenty years ago?
3. What health interventions are currently in place in schools to offset the potential for obesity?
4. When were soft-drink vending machines placed in the schools?
5. How much profit does each school generate by the sale of such beverages?
6. How do the schools use these profits?
7. Have there been any studies on the student population in the community connecting the obesity levels with other health problems such as diabetes?

You collect data using resources at your nearest library, and in your search for evidence to support your position, you discover that, according to the local health department, obesity rates for adults and children in your community are above the national average and have gone up significantly in the past twenty years. Rates of diabetes among high school students are also increasing every year. You also learn that soft-drink machines first appeared in schools within your community fifteen years ago. Other than regular physical education classes, the schools don't have programs in place to encourage weight loss. Schools receive money from the soft-drink companies, but you cannot get a clear answer about how much money they receive or how it is being used.

The data about the health of the community and its schoolchildren are powerful. You carefully cite all of your sources, and your team believes it is ready to make its case. You assume that the school board will make an immediate decision to remove soft drink vending machines from school grounds based on what you have discovered. You cannot imagine another side to this issue, and you wonder how anyone could possibly object to removing from schools something that, in your view, clearly harms children.

Little did you know that your position would meet firm opposition during the board meeting. You were shocked to hear arguments such as these:

1. Students don't have to buy these drinks. Nobody makes them.
2. Students will be unhappy if their soft drinks are taken away, which will negatively affect their academic performance.
3. America is all about freedom of choice. It is morally wrong for any government agency to interfere with people's freedom of choice, no matter what their age.
4. If we allow the school board to tell children what they can and cannot drink, pretty soon they will be telling children what to think or not think.
5. This proposed policy will lead to significant revenue loss for our school, and this will result in higher taxes to make up the shortfall.
6. There is no evidence that it is the consumption of soft drinks that actually causes obesity. Other factors might be the problem.
7. If students don't have these drinks to purchase in school, they will sneak them in from home.

Understanding Assumptions

To some extent, it's unavoidable to have beliefs based on gut feelings or on blind acceptance of something we've heard or read. Sometimes, these assumptions should be examined more thoughtfully, especially if they will influence an important decision or serve as the foundation for an argument:

- What are the assumptions behind the opposition's arguments?
- What assumptions are behind the arguments that you made?
- How could you and your neighbors use critical thinking to strengthen your own arguments and to respond to those of the opposition?
- What facts support the assumptions and arguments on both sides?
- Are there exaggerations on both sides?
- Do you detect the use of any logical fallacies on either side?
- How can you evaluate the facts?
- If your goal is to ban soft drinks from schools in your community and to address childhood obesity, what additional evidence do you need to gather, and what are the next steps you need to take?

As this scenario suggests, well-meaning people may often disagree. It's important to listen to both sides of an argument before making up your mind. If you hang on to the guidelines in this chapter, we can't promise your classes will be easier or that you'll solve community problems, but you will be better equipped to handle them. You have the skills to use critical thinking to figure things out instead of depending only on how you feel or what you've heard. As you listen to a lecture, a political debate, or an argument about what is in the public's best interest, try to predict where it is heading and why. Ask yourself whether you have enough information to justify what you have heard.

BLOOM'S TAXONOMY

Benjamin Bloom, an important educational psychologist at the University of Chicago in the late 1940s and 1950s, led a team of colleagues in designing what is known as **Bloom's taxonomy**, a system of classifying goals for the learning process, now used at all levels of education to define and describe the process that students use to understand and think critically about what they are learning.

Bloom identified six levels of learning, as represented in the triangle shown in Figure 10.2. The higher the level, the more critical thinking it requires.

Bloom's Taxonomy and Your First Year of Community College

In your first year of attending community college, you will recognize material you've learned before, and you will practice your skills of defining and remembering. But you'll soon find that Bloom's first level isn't going to get you very far. To remember new information, you'll need to move to level 2: understanding the information clearly enough so that you can describe the concepts to someone else. Many of your classes will require you to apply what you learn to new situations (level 3), and you'll also need to use levels 4 and 5 to analyze (break apart) and synthesize (bring together) new concepts. Finally, you'll reach level 6 as you begin trusting your own judgments in evaluating what you are learning. As you progress through your first year, be aware of how you use each of these levels to build your critical thinking skills.

FIGURE 10.2 ❯ The Six Levels of Learning of Bloom's Taxonomy

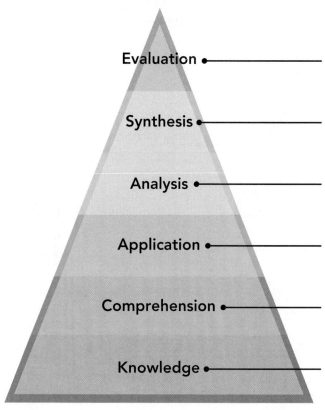

Evaluation, Bloom's highest level, is defined as using your ability to judge the value of ideas and information you are learning according to internal or external standards. Evaluation includes appraising, arguing, defending, and supporting.

Synthesis is defined as bringing ideas together to form a new plan, proposal, or concept. Synthesis includes collecting, organizing, creating, and composing.

Analysis is defined as breaking down material into its parts so that you can understand its structure. Analysis includes categorizing, comparing, contrasting, and questioning.

Application is defined as using what you have learned, such as rules and methods, in new situations. Application includes choosing, illustrating, practicing, and interpreting.

Comprehension is defined as understanding the meaning of material. Comprehension includes classifying, describing, explaining, and translating.

Knowledge, the bottom level, is defined as remembering previously learned material. Knowledge includes arranging, defining, memorizing, and recognizing.

RESEARCH WISELY

Don't assume that information you find on the Internet is accurate or unbiased. Thanks to the First Amendment, people can publish whatever they want online. It's up to you to filter out what's valuable, objective, and up-to-date.

THE PROBLEM *You're not sure how to evaluate the types of information you find on the Web.*

THE FIX *Get some context.*

HOW TO DO IT

1. **Portals.** These one-stop shops serve up a full range of cyberservices. Expect to find search engines, weather and news updates, stock quotes, reference tools, and even movie reviews. (Bonus: Most services are free.) Examples: **Google.com** and **Yahoo.com**.

2. **News.** Sites that offer news, politics, business trends, sports, entertainment, analysis of current events, and so on are often sponsored by magazines, newspapers, and radio stations. News sites include extras — for example, charts, slideshows, original documents — beyond what you might find in the print versions. Examples: **NYTimes .com**, Harvard Business Review (www.**hbr.org**), and **CNN.com**.

3. **Corporate and marketing.** Some company Web sites let you order their products or services online; others even list job openings. Examples: **Ford.com** and **BenJerry.com**.

4. **Informational.** Fact-based sites, often created by government agencies, contain information on everything from city bus schedules to information on health and safety. Examples: **NYCsubway.org**, **Travel.State.gov**, and the U.S. Centers for Disease Control site (**www.cdc.gov**).

5. **Blogs.** Web logs (blogs) are informal Web sites through which people can air their views and opinions on an occasional or regular basis. Some businesses create blogs to connect with their customers; other blogs are strictly personal, designed to share with family and friends. Examples: **Gawker.com**, **Tumblr.com**, and The Lawsons Spill Their Guts (**http:// thelawsonspilltheirguts.blogspot.com/**).

Source: Courtesy Centers for Disease Control

6. **Wikis.** These are informational Web sites that allow for open editing by registered users or, in some cases, by the general public. Examples: **Wikipedia.com** and **TechCrunch.com**.

Keep in mind that there's a big difference between the *Journal of the American Medical Association* and a journal written by "Fred" from Pomona. And, no, you can't use an ad for Shake Weight as a source for a fitness article: It's an ad. Be careful, and use your critical thinking skills. To make sure that the research you use is unbiased and current, look for tip-offs. Most reputable Web sites are easy to navigate, contain little advertising, and list authors' names and credentials.

THINK

In your opinion, is it harder to think critically than to base your arguments on how you feel about a topic? Why or why not? What are the advantages of finding answers based on your feelings? What about those that are based on critical thinking? How might you use both approaches in seeking answers?

WRITE

One major shift from being a high school student to being a college student involves the level of critical thinking your college instructors expect of you. How would you describe critical thinking to a high school student? Jot down some thoughts here and expand on them in a journal, in a notebook, or on your favorite device.

APPLY

1. After reading this chapter, think of professions (for example, doctors, engineers, marketing professionals) for whom problem solving and critical thinking are necessary. Choose one career, and describe why you think critical thinking is a necessary and valuable skill in that area.

2. Describe an experience you have had since coming to college that has challenged you to think about an issue in a new and different way.

AT YOUR COLLEGE

VISIT . . .	IF YOU NEED HELP . . .
College Catalog	taking argument courses and critical thinking courses. Such courses will help you develop the ability to form logical arguments and avoid logical fallacies.
Student Activities	joining a debate club or team.
Library	**finding resources for improving your critical thinking skills. For example, *12 Angry Men* by Reginald Rose (New York: Penguin Classics, 2006) is a reprint of the** original teleplay, which was written in 1954 and made into a film in 1958. It is also available on DVD. The stirring courtroom drama pits twelve jurors against one another as they argue the outcome of a murder trial in which the defendant is a teenage boy. While critical thinking is needed to arrive at the truth, all the jurors except one use noncritical arguments to arrive at a guilty verdict. However, the analysis of that one holdout produces a remarkable change in their attitudes.

ONLINE

GO TO . . .	IF YOU NEED HELP . . .
Florida International University on Bloom's Taxonomy: http://online.fiu.edu/faculty/resources/blooms taxonomy	understanding and using Bloom's taxonomy to build an awareness of how you progress through the levels in building your critical thinking skills.
ICYouSee Guide to Critical Thinking: http://.icyousee.org/think/think.html	finding a guide to critical thinking about what you see on the Web.

MY COLLEGE'S RESOURCES

11 Managing Your Health, Emotions, and Relationships in a Diverse World

PRE-READING ACTIVITY: By now you know that college is demanding. Successful students are the ones who remain healthy, manage their emotions, and build relationships in a diverse environment. This chapter covers all these topics with the goal of helping you understand how they are connected. List some challenges you have already encountered in each of these areas, and how you overcame each challenge.

Health Challenge:

How I overcame this challenge:

Diversity Challenge:

How I overcame this challenge:

Emotional Challenge:

How I overcame this challenge:

Relationship Challenge:

How I overcame this challenge:

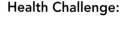

📁 **PROFILE**

Rahm Patel, 19
Accounting Technology Major, *Palm Beach State College*

Source: R. Gino Santa Maria/Shutterstock

When Rahm Patel started attending Palm Beach State College, he was expecting to have a lot of fun. After the first week of classes when he received the syllabus for each course, he could tell he was going to have to work hard. "To make more study time, I cut back on going to the gym each week," he explained. "I started skipping lunch to save time and ate snacks from vending machines between classes instead." He also found himself sleeping less and eating more junk food during the exam weeks.

Rahm was particularly stressed out and nervous about a class presentation he had been working on. He emailed his instructor and asked for an extension, which his instructor granted. After delivering the speech, Rahm was upset about the critiques from the instructor because they seemed much harsher than the ones he got from his classmates. He could feel his face burning. "After class, I wrote an angry email to the instructor about how I expected a good grade on my speech because I had worked so hard," he explained. To his surprise, his professor wrote him back, highlighting problems with his behavior:

> "I realized that eating, exercising, and sleeping well made me less irritable and better able to control my emotions."

Dear Rahm,

I am sorry to see that you are not happy about what happened in class today. Please keep in mind that the goal of the class is to help students become better at public speaking. If we do not discuss strategies and suggestions for improving each speaker's presentation, the class is not going to be helpful. Let's imagine for a second that you were asked to prepare and deliver this presentation at work. First, you ask your boss to change the presentation date that was scheduled with difficulty to ensure that all team members could present. Then your boss reviews your presentation and gives you some suggestions for improving it in front of the team, but you noticeably get upset in the meeting and send an angry email to your boss as soon as you return to your office. What do you think the outcome would be?

Professor Cruz

"I was really embarrassed. I realized that I hadn't handled the situation well," Rahm admitted. He then shared how he went to the college's counseling center to ask for help. The counselor advised Rahm to visit the instructor during office hours and apologize for his unprofessional behavior. Although Rahm was nervous about the meeting, the visit pleasantly surprised him. The instructor accepted his apology and promised to help him overcome his anxiety about public speaking.

After this incident, Rahm realized that he needed to get a handle on his life. "I realized that eating, exercising, and sleeping well made me less irritable and better able to control my emotions," he said. And he realized that he needed to take responsibility for his actions and choices. Rahm didn't want a repeat of what had happened, and he hoped to build good relationships with his instructors and other students.

Like Rahm, many college students need help in managing their lives when they enter college. This chapter focuses on helping you manage three significant components of your life: your health, your emotions, and your relationships with the many people you encounter throughout your college experience and beyond. When life is busy or when all your energy is focused on one thing in particular, you might find yourself off balance, not paying enough attention to important areas of your life. Taking a helicopter view of your life can let you see where you need to make adjustments. The main goal of this chapter is to help you achieve balance.

MANAGING YOUR HEALTH

11.1

College provides you with multiple opportunities to exercise your mind and expand your horizons. You may have noticed that many students can handle the transition to college easily by using a variety of healthy coping strategies. However, some students drink too much, smoke, overeat, or develop an eating disorder. Recent research shows that over four years, at least 70 percent of college students gain weight, with an average gain of about twelve pounds and with men gaining more weight than women.[1] This study clearly has implications for two-year college students, as unhealthy behaviors often begin at the start of college. In addition, relationships with family and friends often suffer when the pressures of being in college get added to other life's stressors. Managing your health means making the right choices and achieving balance.

---

[1]Sareen S. Gropper, Karla P. Simmons, Lenda Jo Connell, and Pamela V. Ulrich, "Changes in Body Weight, Composition, and Shape: A 4-Year Study of College Students," Applied Physiology, Nutrition, and Metabolism, September 17, 2012, http://www.nrcresearchpress.com/doi/full/10.1139/h2012-139.

Nothing but Blue Skies
When you are feeling stressed, take a moment to breathe. Focusing on inhaling and exhaling slowly and picturing a serene scene like a blue sky or a sunny beach can help slow your heart rate and calm you down. You might also picture yourself succeeding at the task that is currently stressing you out. Breathing and visualization techniques can be powerful tools.
Source: Filipe Matos Frazao/Shutterstock

Managing Stress

One of the biggest challenges facing college students is stress. Many students report that stress negatively affects either an exam grade or a course grade.[2] When you are stressed, your body undergoes physiological changes. Your breathing becomes rapid and shallow; your heart rate increases; the muscles in your shoulders, forehead, neck, and perhaps chest tighten; your hands become cold or sweaty; your hands and knees may shake; your stomach becomes upset; your mouth goes dry; and your voice may sound strained.

A number of psychological changes also occur when you are under stress. You might experience a sense of confusion, trouble with concentration, an inability to remember things, and poor problem solving. As a result of stress, you may also make decisions that you regret later. Emotions such as anger, anxiety, depression, fear, frustration, and irritability are common, and you might either be unable to go to sleep at night or wake up frequently.

Stress has many sources, but the following three seem to be the most important:

1. Life events such as a death in the family, the loss of a job, or an illness. Repeated stress from life events, especially if many happen over a short time period, can cause physical and mental health problems.
2. Too many responsibilities at home, work, or college. When there is not enough time to attend to family, meet deadlines, and prepare for tests and projects, the level of stress increases.
3. Daily hassles. Minor things that we experience every day, such as losing the car keys, getting stuck in traffic, having three tests on the same day, arguing with a roommate or spouse, or worrying about money, can result in major stress.

---

[2]American College Health Association, *National College Health Assessment, Undergraduate Reference Group Executive Summary, Spring 2012* (Hanover, MD: American College Health Association, 2012).

The best starting point for handling stress is to be in good physical and mental shape. This means you need to pay attention to your diet, exercise, sleep, and mental health.

YOUR TURN > TRY IT

Are you stressed before an exam? The next time you are in a stressful situation, keep a written record of how you feel, both physically and mentally, and the events that triggered the increased symptoms of stress. What specific changes do you notice in your behavior and feelings? Think about the ways that stress affects your ability to concentrate, your breathing patterns, your patience, and so on. Jot down some of your observations here.

Diet

There is a clear connection between what you eat and drink, your overall health and well-being, and stress. Eating a lot of junk food will add pounds to your body and reduce your energy level. And when you can't keep up with your work because you're slow or tired, you will experience more stress. Caffeine is probably the best example of something commonly ingested that is linked to high stress levels.

Caffeine increases alertness and reduces feelings of fatigue if used moderately—50 to 200 milligrams per day, equivalent to one to two cups of regular coffee—but even at this low dosage it can make you more energetic during part of the day and more tired later. Too much caffeine can cause nervousness, headaches, bad temper, upset stomach, and sleeplessness—all symptoms of stress. Instead of drinking caffeinated drinks, consider drinking water, decaf coffee, caffeine-free sugar free soft drinks, or herbal tea.

If you are gaining weight and losing energy, what can you do about your eating habits? It might not be easy at first, but if you start making small positive changes, you can build toward a new way of eating. You will not only feel better but also be healthier and probably happier. Here are some commonsense suggestions:

- Limit snacks to healthy options, such as fruit, vegetables, yogurt, and small portions of nuts, such as pistachios, almonds, cashews, or walnuts.
- Eat plenty of vegetables and fruits daily. Opt for these over fruit juices, which tend to be high in sugar.
- Drink plenty of water and sugar free noncaffeinated drinks. Aim for about 64 ounces each day.

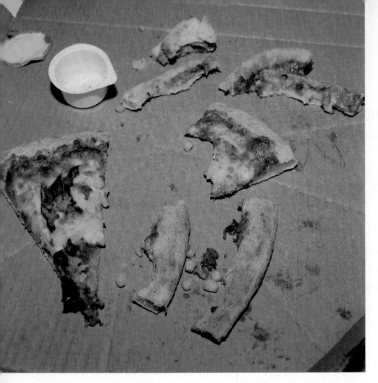

A Serving Is a Slice, Not the Whole Pizza
Have you ever found yourself staring at the remains of a pizza like this one and realizing that you're a bit out of control? Start to rein yourself back in. Stop at the grocery store on the way home to pick up some healthy snacks. Throw out half-eaten bags of chips. Take a long walk or give yourself an extra half hour in the morning to take another walk or jog. It's never the wrong time or too late to take better care of yourself, and no step in the right direction is too small.
Source: © Image Source/Corbis

- Restrict your intake of red meat, butter, white rice, white bread, and sweets. Instead, eat a sensible amount of nuts and beans that can add to your fiber intake.
- Avoid fried foods. Choose grilled or broiled lean meat and fish instead.
- Watch your portion sizes. Avoid large, jumbo, or king-size fast-food items and all-you-can-eat buffets.
- Eat breakfast! Your brain will function better if you eat a power-packed meal first thing in the morning.
- Always read the nutrition label on packaged foods. Look for the number of grams of fat and carbohydrates. Check the sodium content: Sodium (table salt) will make you gain weight and can possibly increase your blood pressure.

Think about what, when, and how much you eat day to day. You might think that eating a fast-food diet will save time in your busy schedule, but it will add pounds to your body and reduce your overall health and sense of well-being. If possible, take time to cook your own food; it's almost always healthier than eating out or buying food on the fly.

By paying attention to nutrition guidelines, you can maintain your optimal weight both now and in the future. If you're responsible for feeding your family, then all of you will benefit from establishing healthy habits. The MyPlate icon in Figure 11.1 proposes one set of guidelines for healthy eating.

Eating Disorders

Although we advise you to think about what you are eating from day to day, we also advise you not to overthink it. Remember that the key to good health is achieving balance, and an obsession with food intake may be a sign that things are out of balance. Over the last few decades, an increasing number of college students (both men and women) have been

FIGURE 11.1 › MyPlate Eating Guidelines

Figure 11.1 shows the new MyPlate icon introduced by the federal government in 2011 to replace the Food Guide Pyramid. **ChooseMyPlate.gov** provides tips and recommendations for healthy eating and understanding the plate's design.

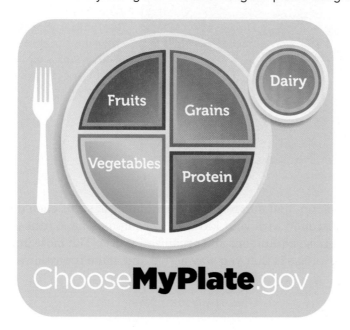

developing eating disorders such as anorexia nervosa (an extreme fear of gaining weight), bulimia (overeating followed by self-induced vomiting or laxative use), or binge eating disorder (compulsive overeating long past the feeling of being full).

Anyone who is struggling with an eating disorder should seek medical attention. Eating disorders can be life-threatening if they are not treated by a health care professional. Contact your student health center for more information, or contact the National Eating Disorder Association (**http://www.nationaleatingdisorders.org** or 1-800-931-2237) to find a professional in your area who specializes in the treatment of eating disorders.

Exercise

Exercise is an excellent stress-management technique, the best way to stay fit, and an important element in effective weight-loss programs. Any kind of exercise—walking, jogging, running, swimming, biking, or using a stair climber—benefits your body and spirit and is a great choice for stress and weight management. Choose activities that you enjoy so that you look forward to your exercise time and make it a regular part of your routine. People who exercise report more energy, less stress, better sleep, healthier weight, and an improved self-image compared with people who do not exercise.

Think about ways to combine activities and use your time efficiently. Maybe you can leave your car at home and walk or ride a bike to class. If you must drive, then park at the far end of the parking lot to get in extra steps. Try going to the gym with a friend and asking each other study questions while on the treadmill. Take the stairs whenever possible.

Wear a pedometer, and aim for a certain number of steps each day. If you're a parent, run around with your kids. Many campuses have fitness centers that offer exercise equipment and organized sports. The most important thing about exercise is that you stay active and make it part of your day-to-day life.

Sleep

Getting adequate sleep is another way to protect yourself from stress. According to the National Sleep Foundation, 63 percent of American adults do not get the recommended eight hours of sleep per night. Lack of sleep can lead to anxiety, depression, and academic problems. Researchers at Trent University in Ontario found that students who studied all week but then stayed up late partying on the weekends forgot as much as

30 percent of the material they had learned during the prior week. Try the following suggestions to establish better sleep habits:

- Avoid long daytime naps that last longer than 30 minutes.
- Try reading or listening to a relaxation tape before going to bed.
- Exercise during the day.
- Get your clothes, school materials, and food for the next day together before you go to bed.
- Sleep in the same room and bed every night.
- Set a regular schedule for going to bed and getting up.

Taking Control

Modifying your lifestyle is the best overall approach to stress management. You have the power to change your life so that it is less stressful. Lifestyle modification involves identifying the parts of your life that do not serve you well, making plans for change, and then carrying out the plans. For example, if you are stressed because you are always late for classes, get up 10 minutes earlier. If you get nervous before a test when you talk to a certain negative classmate, avoid that person before a test. Learn test-taking skills so that you can manage test anxiety better.

Check your college website, counseling center, health center, student newspaper, or fitness center for classes that teach relaxation. Learning new techniques for managing stress takes knowledge and practice. You'll find apps, websites, books, and other resources that can guide you through relaxation techniques.

YOUR TURN > WORK TOGETHER

With a group of students in your class, review the list of ways to lower your stress level. Discuss the ideas that make the most sense for you. On the basis of your experience, which ideas would your group suggest to other college students?

Depression and Suicide

According to the American Psychological Association, depression is one of the most common psychiatric disorders in the United States, affecting more than 15 million adults. College students are at especially high risk for both depression and suicide because of the major life changes and high stress levels some of them are experiencing.

Depression is not a weakness; it is an illness that needs medical attention. Many college students suffer from some form of depression. The feelings are often temporary and may be situational. A romantic breakup, a disappointing grade, or an ongoing problem with another person can create feelings of despair. Although most depression goes away on its own, if

you or any of your friends have any of the following symptoms for more than two weeks, it is important to talk to a health care provider:

- Feelings of helplessness and hopelessness
- Feeling useless, inadequate, bad, or guilty
- Self-hatred, constant questioning of one's thoughts and actions
- Loss of energy and motivation
- Loss of appetite
- Rapid weight loss or gain
- Difficulty going to sleep or excessive need for sleep
- Loss of interest in sex
- Difficulty concentrating for a significant length of time

The U.S. Centers for Disease Control and Prevention (CDC) reports that students ages fifteen to twenty-four are more likely than any other age group to attempt suicide. Most people who commit suicide give a warning of their intentions. The following are common indicators of someone's intent to commit suicide:

- Recent loss and not being able to let go of grief
- Change in personality—sadness, withdrawal, indifference
- Expressions of self-hatred
- Change in sleep patterns
- Change in eating habits
- A direct statement about committing suicide (e.g., "I might as well end it all".)
- A preoccupation with death

If you or someone you know threatens suicide or displays any of these signs, it's time to consult a mental health professional. Most campuses have counseling centers that offer one-on-one sessions as well as support groups for their students, most commonly for no fees.

Finally, remember that there is no shame attached to high levels of stress, depression, anxiety, or suicidal tendencies. Unavoidable life events or physiological imbalances can cause such feelings and behaviors. Proper counseling, medical attention, and in some cases prescription medication can help students cope with depression and suicidal thoughts.

Substance Abuse

In this section, our purpose is not to make judgments, but to warn you about the ways in which irresponsible use of substances can have a major negative impact on your college experience and your life. We hope that this information will help you think twice and avoid the trouble that can come from all forms of substance abuse.

In today's world, it is easy to obtain substances, both legal and illegal, that can cause serious harm to your health and well-being. For college students, the substances most commonly used and abused are tobacco, alcohol, and marijuana. While smoking tobacco is not illegal, smoking marijuana is against federal law and state laws in most states.

Alcohol Throughout the history of higher education, the drug most used by students has been alcohol. Whether you drink or not, this is important information to read. Many college students have reported helping a drunken friend or classmate. Most college students think that the average student drinks twice as much as they actually do. A number of surveys have confirmed that your peers aren't drinking as much as you think they are.

People experience the pleasurable effects of alcoholic beverages as the alcohol begins to affect several areas in the brain. How fast you drink makes a difference to how strong the effects become. Your body gets rid of alcohol at a rate of about one drink an hour. Drinking more than one drink an hour might cause a rise in blood alcohol content (BAC)—a measure of how much alcohol is in the bloodstream—because the body is absorbing alcohol faster than it can eliminate it.

At BAC levels of .025 to .05, a drinker tends to feel animated and energized. At a BAC level of around .05, a drinker can get loud. This is where most people report feeling a buzz from alcohol. At a BAC level between .05 and .08, alcohol starts to act as a depressant. So as soon as you feel that buzz, remember that you are on the brink of losing coordination, clear thinking, and judgment. Driving is measurably impaired at BAC levels lower than the legal limit of .08. Most people become severely uncoordinated with BAC levels higher than .08 and might begin falling asleep, falling down, or slurring their speech. People try home remedies (such as coffee, water, or cold showers) for helping to sober someone up, but time is the only remedy because your liver can metabolize only one ounce of alcohol per hour.

Tobacco Tobacco is a legal drug that contains nicotine, a highly addictive substance—and is the cause of many serious medical conditions, including heart and lung diseases and some forms of cancer. One concern that particularly relates to college students is *social smoking*. This term describes smoking by students who do so only when hanging out with friends, drinking, or partying. Most college students feel they will be able to give up their social smoking habit once they graduate, but some find that they have become addicted to cigarettes.

You may have noticed advertisements for electronic cigarettes (e-cigarettes or e-cigs) or seen them in stores. According to the U.S. Food and Drug Administration, e-cigarettes are battery-operated products designed to deliver nicotine, flavors, and other chemicals in the form of vapor. E-cigarettes, have not been fully studied, so consumers currently don't know the potential risks.

Although only a small percentage of college students use smokeless tobacco, the habit is no less addicting than smoking is. One dip delivers the same amount of nicotine as three to four cigarettes. Smokeless tobacco contains 28 known cancer-causing substances and is associated with the same level of health risk as cigarette smoking.

A final reason for smokers to quit, or for others never to start, is the cost (see Table 11.1). Contact your campus health or counseling centers for more information about quitting.

TABLE 11.1 ❯ The Approximate Cost of Smoking Across the United States

Half-Pack-a-Day Smoker
$6.25/pack × 3.5 packs/week = $21.88/week
$21.88/week × 52 weeks/year = $1,137.76/year
$1,137.76/year × 2 years of community college = $2,275.52
In 25 years, you will have spent $28,444
Pack-a-Day Smoker
$6.25/pack × 7 packs/week = $43.75/week
$43.75/week × 52 weeks/year = $2,275.00
$2,275.00/year × 2 years of college = $4,550.00
In 25 years, you will have spent $56,875

11.2 MANAGING YOUR EMOTIONAL HEALTH

We have discussed several aspects of managing your health so far in this chapter: reducing stress, eating well, and keeping fit, for instance. An important component of your overall health is your emotional health. Particularly in the first year of college, many students have difficulty establishing positive relationships with others, dealing with pressure, or making wise decisions. Other students are optimistic and happy and seem to adapt to their new environment without any trouble. Being optimistic doesn't mean that you ignore your problems or pretend that they will go away, but optimistic people believe in their own abilities to address problems successfully as they arise. Your ability to deal with life's challenges is based on your **emotional intelligence**—how well you recognize, understand, and manage moods, feelings, and attitudes. Emotional intelligence is part of your personality; if you take a psychology course in college, you are likely to learn more about it.

Keeping It Together on the Big Stage
Imagine the stress of performing live in front of celebrity judges and fellow competitors, a live audience, and millions of television viewers. Oh, and the quality of each performance determines your fate. In a matter of weeks, the young contestants of reality talent shows like *American Idol* or *The Voice* have to learn on the fly to handle the emotions that come from this kind of experience. How do you think the emotional intelligence of each contestant factors into how far each goes in the competition?
Source: Photo by FOX via Getty Images

YOUR TURN > WORK TOGETHER

With a classmate make a list (first names only) of people you know who don't have good people skills. What kinds of challenges do these people face? Be prepared to share your thoughts.

Emotions are a big part of who you are; you should not ignore them. The better the emotional read you have on a situation, the more appropriately you can respond to it. Being aware of your own and others' feelings helps you gather correct information about the world around you and allows you to respond in appropriate ways. If you are an older student who is back in college, you probably have a great deal of life experience in dealing with tough times.

As you read this section, think about the behaviors that help people, including yourself, to do well and the behaviors that interfere with success. Get to know yourself better, and take the time to examine your feelings and the impact they have on the way you act. You can't always control the challenges of life, but with practice you *can* control how you respond to them. Remember that emotions are real, can be changed for the better, and significantly affect whether a person is successful.

Perceiving and Managing Emotions

Developing an awareness of emotions allows you to use your feelings to improve your thinking. If you are feeling sad, for instance, you might view the world in a negative way, while if you feel happy, you are likely to view the same events differently. Once you start paying attention to emotions, you can learn not only how to cope with life's pressures and demands but also how to use your knowledge of the way you feel for more effective problem solving, reasoning, decision making, and creativity. This is all part of developing your emotional intelligence.

Perceiving emotions involves the ability to monitor and identify feelings correctly (nervous, happy, angry, relieved, and so forth) and to determine why you feel the way you do. It also involves predicting how others might feel in a given situation. Emotions contain information, and the ability to understand and think about that information plays an important role in behavior.

Managing emotions is based on the belief that feelings can be modified, even improved. At times, you need to stay open to your feelings, learn from them, and use them to take appropriate action. Other times, it is better to disengage from an emotion and return to it later. Anger, for example, can blind you and lead you to act in negative or antisocial ways; used positively, however, anger can help you take a stand against bias or injustice. Learning how to put yourself in the right mood to handle different situations is important.

Based on the work of Professor Reuven Bar-On, Table 11.2 lists skills that influence a person's ability to cope with life's pressures and demands. Which skills do you think you already have? Which ones do you need to improve?

TABLE 11.2 ❯ Emotional Skills and Competencies

Skills	Competencies
Intrapersonal	- **Emotional self-awareness.** Knowing how and why you feel the way you do. - **Assertiveness.** Standing up for yourself when you need to without being too aggressive. - **Independence.** Making important decisions on your own without having to get everyone's opinion. - **Self-regard.** Liking yourself in spite of your flaws (and we all have them). - **Self-actualization.** Being satisfied and comfortable with what you have achieved in school, work, and your personal life.
Interpersonal	- **Empathy.** Making an effort to understand another person's situation or point of view. - **Social responsibility.** Establishing a personal link with a group or community and cooperating with other members in working toward shared goals. - **Interpersonal relationships.** Seeking out healthy and mutually beneficial relationships—such as friendships, professional networks, family connections, mentoring, and romantic partnerships—and making a persistent effort to maintain them.
Adaptability	- **Reality testing.** Ensuring that your feelings are appropriate by checking them against external, objective criteria. - **Flexibility.** Adapting and adjusting your emotions, viewpoints, and actions as situations change. - **Problem solving.** Approaching challenges step by step and not giving up in the face of obstacles.
Stress Management	- **Stress tolerance.** Recognizing the causes of stress and responding in appropriate ways; staying strong under pressure. - **Impulse control.** Thinking carefully about potential consequences before you act and delaying gratification for the sake of achieving long-term goals.
General Mood and Effective	- **Optimism.** Looking for the bright side of any problem or difficulty and being confident that things will work out for the best.
Performance	- **Happiness.** Being satisfied with yourself, with others, and with your situation in general.

Source: "What Is Emotional Intelligence?" from Bar-On EQ-i Technical Manual @ 1997, 1999, 2000 Multi Health Systems Inc. Toronto, Canada. Reproduced with permission from Multi-Health Systems Inc.

Write a description of yourself as a successful person ten years after you graduate from college. What kinds of skills will you have? Don't just focus on your degree or a job description; include the competencies that help explain why you have become successful.

How Emotions Affect College Success

Emotions are strongly tied to physical and psychological well-being. A number of studies link emotional skills to college success in particular. Here are a few highlights (using terms from Table 11.2):

- Students with intrapersonal skills (emotional self-awareness, assertiveness, independence, self-regard, and self-actualization), stress tolerance, and adaptability skills (reality testing, flexibility, and problem solving), and stress management skills (stress tolerance and impulse control) do better academically than those who lack these skills.
- **Students who can't manage their emotions struggle academically.** Some students experience panic attacks before tests, and far too many students turn to risky behaviors (such as drug and alcohol abuse) in an effort to cope.
- Even students who manage to succeed academically in spite of emotional difficulties can be at risk if unhealthy behavior patterns follow them after college.

If you think you need help developing some of these skills, especially if you feel that you are not happy or optimistic, do something about it. Although you can look online and get some tips about being an optimistic person, for example, there is nothing like getting some help from a professional. Consider visiting your academic adviser or a wellness or counseling center on campus. Look for any related workshops that are offered on campus or nearby.

MANAGING YOUR RELATIONSHIPS

How well you are able to manage your emotions is directly related to the quality of the relationships in your life. The relationships you maintain and develop in college can have positive effects on your success. While you are making new friends, you continue to have relationships with your parents, spouse, children, or other family members. Sometimes the expectations of family members change, and negotiating such changes is not always easy. If you are fresh out of high school, you might feel that your parents still want to control your life. If you have a spouse or partner, going to college will give you a new identity that might seem strange or threatening to your partner. If you have children, they might not understand what's going on as you try to balance your need for study time with their need for your undivided attention.

If your friends or others close to you also go to college, you will have a great deal to share and compare. But if your friends are not college students, they, too, might feel threatened as you take on a new identity. Romantic relationships can support you or can create major conflict and heartbreak, depending on whether your partner shares your feelings and whether the relationship is healthy or dysfunctional.

Building Relationships with College Instructors

An important set of relationships that you develop in college is with your instructors. You might choose to get to know your instructors or to ignore them outside of class, but the quality and frequency of the interaction you have with them can affect how well you do academically.

Knowing and Meeting Expectations While instructors' expectations might be different from course to course, most instructors expect their students to exhibit attitudes and behaviors that are required for student success. By now, you know that you must get to class on time. If you repeatedly arrive late or leave early, you are breaking the basic rules of etiquette and politeness, and you are intentionally or unintentionally showing a lack of respect for your instructors and your classmates. Instructors also expect honesty and openness. Many instructors invite you to express your feelings about the course through anonymous one-minute papers or other forms of class assessment.

In addition, college instructors expect you to be motivated to do your best. Your high school teachers might have spent a great deal of time thinking about how to motivate you, but college instructors usually consider this to be your personal responsibility.

YOUR TURN › WORK TOGETHER

Make a list of things you had heard or thought about college instructors before coming to college. In a small group, share these ideas and talk about whether they are proving to be accurate or inaccurate now that you have been in college for a number of weeks.

Making the Most of the Learning Relationship Most college instructors appreciate your willingness to ask for appointments. This may seem a little scary to some students, but most instructors welcome the opportunity to establish an appropriate relationship with their students and get to

Exchanging Ideas

Most college instructors love to exchange ideas. Many successful college graduates can name a particular instructor who made a positive difference in their lives and influenced their academic and career paths. Develop meaningful relationships with your instructors. It could change your life for the better.
Source: © John Stanmeyer/VII/Corbis

know them. As discussed in the first chapter of this book, it's up to you to take the initiative to visit your instructors during their office hours. Most instructors are required to keep office hours, so don't feel like you are asking them for a special favor. Even adjunct instructors, who are not required to have office hours, can be available to help you with your coursework or answer your questions. You can visit your instructors, anytime during the term, either in real time or online, to ask questions, seek help with a difficult topic or assignment, or discuss a problem. If you have a problem with the instructor, the course, or your grade, set up a meeting with your instructor to work things out. If the problem is a grade, keep in mind that your instructors have the right to assign you grades based on your performance, and no one can force them to change those grades.

The relationships you develop with instructors can be valuable to you both now and in the future. Instructors who know you well can also write that all-important letter of reference when you are applying to a university or to your first job after college.

Friendships in and beyond College

One of the best things about going to college is meeting new people from different backgrounds and interests. You learn as much or more from other students you meet as you learn from instructors. Although not everyone you hang out with will become a close friend, you will likely find a few special relationships that might even last a lifetime.

Social Media Social networking sites and apps such as Facebook, Twitter, Instagram, Vine, and Snapchat are popular with college students; it's likely that you use sites and apps such as these throughout the day to keep up with your friends. While social media outlets have both positives and negatives, one thing is certain: As students enter college, most do not carefully examine what they share through social media. Online statements, posts, and messages can have a strong impact, so you should fully examine the benefits and pitfalls of everything you put into public view. Students often ignore the fact that what goes online or is shared through a mobile app lives on forever, although some sites claim differently.

The Tech Tip at the end of this chapter offers some additional advice for using social media, professional networking sites, and mobile apps wisely. It also offers ideas for using technology to stay connected on campus, make the most of resources offered by your college, and gain access to your instructors.

Serious Relationships

College presents an opportunity not only to make lots of new friends but also to start a romantic relationship. You might already be in a long-term committed relationship, or you might have your first serious romance with someone you meet on campus. Given that college allows you to meet people from different backgrounds who share common interests, you might find it easier to meet romantic partners in college than you ever have before. Whether you choose to commit to one serious relationship or keep yourself open for meeting others, you'll grow and learn a great deal about yourself and those with whom you become involved.

Relationships to Avoid

It is never wise to become romantically involved with an instructor or someone who works above or for you. Imagine how you might feel if the relationship breaks up and your ex still has control over your grades or your job! If you date someone who works for you and the relationship ends, you might find yourself being fired, sued, or accused of **sexual harassment,** which refers to any kind of unwanted sexual advances or remarks. Even dating coworkers is risky: If it goes well, the relationship may take your attention away from your job; if it does not go well, things may be awkward if you must continue to work together.

Protecting against Sexual Assault

Sexual assault that happens on college campuses is a problem that has existed for many years. Although colleges have addressed this issue with some success, the problem still remains. Today, 20 to 25 percent of female college students report experiencing a rape or attempted rape. Anyone is at risk for being raped, but the majority of victims are women. Between the time they start college and when they graduate, an estimated one-out-of-four college women will be the victim of attempted rape, and one-out-of-six will be raped.

Most women will be raped by someone they know—a date or an acquaintance—and most will not report the crime. Alcohol is a factor in nearly three-fourths of the incidents. Whether raped by a date or by a stranger, a victim can suffer long-term traumatic effects. Following is some advice from Tricia Phaup, Director, Medical Case Management at University of South Carolina School of Medicine, on avoiding sexual assault:

- Go to social gatherings with friends, and leave with them.
- Avoid being alone with people you don't know very well.
- Trust your intuition.
- Be alert to subtle and unconscious messages you may be sending and receiving.
- Be aware of how much alcohol you drink, if any.
- Avoid putting yourself in a vulnerable position because you have consumed too much alcohol.

If you are ever tempted to force another person to have sex:

- Realize that it is never OK to force sex on someone.
- Never assume that you know what your date wants.
- If you're getting mixed messages, ask for clarification.
- Don't have sex with someone who is too drunk to know what they are doing.
- Remember that rape is morally and legally wrong.

If you have been raped, regardless of whether you choose to report the rape to the police or get a medical exam, it is very helpful to seek counseling by contacting resources such as a campus sexual assault coordinator, a local rape crisis center, the campus police department, student health services, women's student services, a local hospital emergency room, or a campus chaplain.

In 2014, the federal government established the "Campus Sexual Violence Elimination" (SaVE) Act to ensure that all colleges and universities have policies for reporting and responding to issues of sexual violence.

SaVE requires that incidents of domestic violence, dating violence, sexual assault, and stalking be disclosed in annual campus crime statistics reports required of each college and university. Also students or employees who report being victims will get assistance from campus authorities, a change in living or working situations as needed, the ability to obtain a "no contact" or restraining order, knowledge about their college's disciplinary process, and information about counseling, health, and legal services.

SaVE ensures that there will be a prompt and fair investigation by officials who are trained on sexual violence. SaVE also requires colleges and universities to provide programming for students and employees addressing these issues that specifically targets new students and new employees. Don't keep silent if you are a victim.

Marriage and Parenting during College

Can marriage and parenting coexist positively with being a college student? The answer, of course, is yes, although meeting everyone's needs—your own, your spouse's, your children's—is not easy. If you are married, with or without children, you need to become an expert at time management. If you do have children, make sure you find out what resources your college offers to help you with day care or after-school care.

Sometimes going to college can create conflict with a spouse or partner as you take on a new identity and set of responsibilities. Financial problems are likely to put extra pressure on your relationship, so both you and your partner have to work hard at paying attention to each other's needs. Be sure to involve your spouse and children in your decisions. Bring them to campus at every opportunity, and let your spouse read your papers and other assignments. Finally, set aside time for your partner and your children just as carefully as you schedule your work and your classes.

Relationships with Parents and Other Family Members

Your relationship with your parents will never be quite the same as it was before you began college. On the one hand, you might find it uncomfortable when your parents try to make decisions on your behalf, such as choosing your major, determining where and how much you work, and setting rules for what you do on weekends. On the other hand, you might find that it hard to make decisions on your own without talking to your parents first. While communication with your parents is important, don't let them make all your decisions. Your college can help you draw the line between what decisions should be yours alone and what decisions your parents should help you make.

If you come from a cultural background that values family relationships and responsibilities above everything else, you will have to find a way to balance your home life and college. In some cultures, if your grandmother or aunt needs help, that might be considered just as important—or more important—than going to class or taking an exam. Some instructors might help you if you have occasional problems with meeting a deadline because of family obligations, but you cannot expect that they will. It's important that you explain your situation; your instructors cannot guess what you need. As the demands on your time increase, it is important that you talk with family members to help them understand your role and responsibilities as a student and ask for their help and support.

Not every family is ideal. If your family is not supportive, find other people who can help you create the family you need. Seek help from your campus's counseling center if you find yourself in the middle of a difficult family situation.

YOUR TURN > WORK TOGETHER

In a small group, talk about how your family has been adjusting to your college experience. Share helpful strategies you have been using during this adjustment period.

Getting Involved

Colleges can seem to be huge places, especially if you went to a small high school or grew up in a small town. To feel comfortable in the college environment, it is important for you to find your comfort zone. It's not hard to find the place where you belong, but it will take some initiative on your part. Consider your interests and the high school activities you enjoyed most, and choose some activities to explore. You might be interested in joining a sports team, performing community service, or running for a student government office. Or you might prefer joining a more structured campuswide club or organization.

Almost every college has organizations you can join; usually, you can check them out through activity or club fairs, printed guides, open houses, Web pages, and so on. Find out what the organization is like, what the expectations of time and money are, and whether you feel comfortable with the members. Students who become involved with at least one organization are more likely to complete their first year and remain in college.

You can also get involved in the surrounding community. Consider volunteering for a community service project such as caring for animals at a shelter, serving the homeless at a soup kitchen, or helping build or renovate homes for needy families. Your college might offer service opportunities as part of first-year courses.

Be careful not to overextend yourself when it comes to campus activities. While it is important to get involved, joining too many clubs or organizations will make it difficult to focus on any given activity and will interfere with your studies. Future employers will consider a balance in academics and campus involvement an important quality in applicants.

YOUR TURN > WORK TOGETHER

In a small group, discuss opportunities to get involved on campus. Share experiences you have had participating in clubs or organizations. How can you get involved in your college's clubs and organizations?

Working

One of the best ways to develop relationships on your campus is to get an on-campus job. Generally, your on-campus supervisors may be much more flexible than off-campus employers in helping you balance your study demands and your work schedule. You might not make as much money working on campus as you would in an off-campus job, but the relationships you'll develop with important people who care about your success in college and who will write those all-important reference letters make on-campus employment well worth it. Consider finding a job related to your major. For example, if you are a computer science major, you might be able to work in a computer lab. That work could help you gain knowledge and experience and make connections with experts in your field.

If an on-campus job is not available or you don't find one that appeals to you, an off-campus job can allow you to meet new people in the community. If you already had a job before starting college, talk to your employer about the new demands on your time. Also keep in mind that some employers offer tuition assistance; ask to see if any such opportunities are available to you.

Wherever you decide to find a job, it's important that you limit work to a reasonable number of hours per week. Although you might have to work to pay your tuition or living expenses, many college students work too many hours just to support a certain lifestyle. Be careful to maintain a reasonable balance between work and study. Don't fall into the trap of thinking, "I can do it all." Too many college students have found that trying to do it all means not doing anything well.

11.4

THRIVING IN DIVERSE ENVIRONMENTS

So far in this chapter, you have learned strategies for managing your emotional and physical health and have a better understanding of how doing so contributes to your ability to maintain healthy relationships in your life. A logical next step is to increase your awareness of differences and similarities among people, which is an important component of building healthy relationships. Two-year colleges attract students with different backgrounds. Race, ethnicity, culture, economic status, and religion may vary widely. These differences provide opportunities for students to experience diversity.

Diversity is the set of differences in social and cultural identities among people in a given community. Each person brings to campus a unique combination of life story, experience, value system, view of the world, and set of judgments. And yet most have similar goals and aspirations. Interacting with others in a diverse environment can enrich your entire life.

A college serves as a microcosm of the real world—a world that requires us all to work, live, and socialize with people from various ethnic and cultural groups. Two-year colleges are one of the few settings where diverse members interact in such close proximity. Familiarizing yourself with differences can greatly expand your experiences in the classes you take, the organizations you join, and the relationships you have. For many students, college is the first time they have been exposed to so many people whose life experiences differ greatly from their own.

Through self-assessment, discovery, and open-mindedness, you can begin to understand your perspectives on diversity. This work, although difficult at times, will add to your educational experiences, personal growth, and development. Thinking critically about your personal values and belief systems will allow you to have a greater sense of belonging and to make a positive contribution to our multicultural society.

What kinds of diversity can be seen? What other kinds of diversity might exist but can't be seen? Discuss why some college students have an interest in diversity, both seen and unseen, and why other students avoid the topic. Share your ideas with the whole class.

Why We Believe What We Believe

Many of our beliefs are the result of our personal experience. Others are a result of a **stereotype,** a generalization, usually exaggerated or oversimplified and often offensive, that is used to describe or distinguish a group.

A negative experience with individual members of a particular group may result in **stereotyping** people in that group. We may acquire stereotypes about people we have never met before or have bought into a stereotype without even thinking about it. Children who grow up in an environment in which dislike and distrust of certain types of people are openly expressed might adopt those very judgments even if they have had no direct interaction with those being judged.

In college, it is likely that you will meet and interact with people who look different from you, think differently, and hold different values. Spending time with people who view the world in a way you may never have considered contributes to your college experience and helps you avoid stereotyping.

YOUR TURN › ON YOUR OWN

Think back to the earliest messages you received from family members or friends about how you should react to people who are different from you. Which messages still positively or negatively affect your behavior? Which messages have you revised? Jot down some thoughts here.

Expand Your Worldview

How has going to college changed your experience with diversity? Are you getting to know people of different races or ethnic groups? Do your classes have both traditional-aged and adult students? Make it a point to seek out people who are different from you and share your personal stories and worldviews.

Source: © Ocean/Corbis

Ethnicity, Culture, Race, and Religion

Often the terms *ethnicity* and *culture* are used interchangeably, although their definitions are different. **Ethnicity** refers to the identity that is assigned to a specific group of people who are historically connected by a common national origin or language. For example, one of the largest ethnic groups in the United States, Latinos, consists of people from more than thirty countries within North, Central, and South America.

Culture is defined as those aspects of a group of people that are passed on or learned. Traditions, food, language, clothing styles, artistic expression, and beliefs are all part of culture.

Race commonly refers to biological characteristics that are shared by groups of people, including skin tone, hair texture and color, and facial features. Making generalizations about someone's racial group affiliation is risky. Even people who share some biological features—such as similar eye shape or skin color—might be ethnically distinct.

All of us come into the world with our own unique characteristics; aspects of our physical appearance, our personalities, and our experiences make us who we are. As unique as each one of us is, people around the world have one thing in common: We want to be respected even if we are different from others in some ways. Whatever the color of your skin or hair, whatever your life experiences or cultural background, you will want others to treat you fairly and acknowledge and value your contribution to your communities and the world. And, of course, others will want the same from you.

Religion is a specific fundamental set of beliefs and practices generally agreed on by a number of persons or sects. Freedom to practice one's religion has been central to the American experience. In fact, many settlers of the original thirteen colonies came to North America to escape religious-based discrimination.

Can You Find Yourself?

Are you a student who has recently come to the United States from another country? Perhaps you have immigrated with family members or on your own. Whatever you particular situation, learning the unique language, culture, and expectations of a U.S. college can be a challenge. Do instructors' expectations and student behaviors seem different from what experienced in your home country? Seek out English as a second language (ESL) courses or programs if you need help with your English skills. Also, visit the international student advisors to find out how you can continue to increase your understanding of life in the United States, both on and off campus.

Source: © Elaine Thompson/AP/Corbis

While in college, your openness to diversity will add to your understanding of the many ways in which people are different from one another. Learn not to make assumptions, rely on stereotypes, or rush to judgment. Give yourself time to get to know someone before forming an opinion about him or her.

Age

Although some students enter college around age eighteen, others choose to enter or return at an older age. Age diversity in the classroom gives everyone the opportunity to learn from others who have different life experiences. Many factors determine when students enter higher education for the first time, stop, and then reenter.

Economic Status

The United States is a country of vast differences in wealth. This considerable economic diversity can be either a positive or a negative aspect of college life. On the positive side, you will be exposed to, and can learn from, students from a wide range of economic differences. Meeting others who have grown up with either more or fewer opportunities than you did is part of learning how to live in a democracy.

Try to avoid developing exaggerated feelings of superiority or inferiority. What matters now is not what you had or didn't have before you came to college; what matters is what you do in college. You have more in common with other students than you think. Now your individual efforts, dreams, courage, determination, and ability to stay focused can be your success factors.

Learning and Physical Abilities

Although the majority of college students have reasonably average learning and physical abilities, the numbers of students with physical or learning disabilities are rising on most college campuses, as are the services that are available to them. Physical disabilities can include deafness,

Role Model

He spent only three months on Capitol Hill, but Zach Ennis, a deaf college intern in the office of Representative Kevin Yoder (R-KS), developed a video to help the congressman reach out to his deaf constituency that could be a model for others. How can Zach's achievements inspire you to overcome challenges that you face?
Source: MCT via Getty Images

blindness, paralysis, or a mental disorder. As discussed in Chapter 3, many students have some form of learning disability that makes college work a challenge.

People who have physical or learning disabilities want to be treated just as you would treat anyone else—with respect. If a student with a disability is in your class, treat him or her as you would any student; too much eagerness to help might be seen as an expression of pity.

If you have, or think you might have, a learning disability, visit your campus office for students with disabilities for a diagnosis and advice on getting extra help for learning problems. Unlike in high school, students with disabilities need to inform this office if they require accommodations.

Sexuality

The word *sexuality* refers to the people to whom you are romantically attracted. You are familiar with the terms *gay, straight, homosexual, heterosexual,* and *bisexual.* In college you will likely meet students, staff members, and instructors whose sexual orientations may differ from yours. While some people are lucky enough to come from welcoming environments, for many students, college is the first time they have been able to openly express their sexual identity. Sexual orientation can be difficult to talk about, and it is important that you respect all individuals with whom you come in contact. Check to see if your campus has a center for the lesbian, gay, bisexual, or transgendered (LGBT) community. Consider going to hear some speakers, and expand your worldview.

Discrimination, Prejudice, and Insensitivity on College Campuses

You might feel uncomfortable when asked about your views of diversity. We all have **biases,** tendencies against or in favor of certain groups or value systems. Yet it is what we do with our individual beliefs that separates the average person from the racist, the bigot, and the extremist.

Colleges are working to provide a welcoming and inclusive campus environment for all students. Because of acts of violence, intimidation, and stupidity occurring on campuses, college administrations have established policies against any and all forms of discriminatory actions, racism, and insensitivity. Many campuses have adopted zero-tolerance policies that prohibit verbal and nonverbal harassment as well as hate crimes such as physical assault, vandalism, and intimidation.

Whatever form these crimes might take on your campus, it is important to examine your thoughts and feelings about their occurrence. The most important question to ask yourself is this: Will you do something about it, or do you think it is someone else's problem? Commit to becoming involved in making your campus a safe place for all students.

If you have been a victim of a racist, insensitive, or discriminatory act, report it to the proper authorities.

Commit to Coexist

In a college environment, students often learn that there are more commonalities than differences between themselves and others who have been on the opposite side of the fence for centuries. By learning to coexist respectfully and peacefully, students can take the first step toward building a better world.
Source: Jamie Smith-Skinny Genes Photography

YOUR TURN ➤ DISCUSS IT

Think back on your life. Have you ever been harassed or discriminated against for any reason? Have you witnessed someone else being harassed? How did it make you feel? How did you react?

Challenge Yourself to Experience Diversity

Diversity enriches us all, and understanding the value of working with others and the importance of an open mind will enhance your educational and career goals. Your college campus is diverse, and so is the workforce you will be entering.

Challenge yourself to learn about various groups in and around your community, at both school and home. As you build new relationships at your college and workplace, it is important for you to understand and appreciate diversity. Understanding viewpoints different from yours and learning from such differences will help you see similarities where you didn't think they existed. Participate in campus events that include ethnic and cultural celebrations to learn about new and exciting ideas and viewpoints.

Remember that college life is exciting, but it can also be demanding. Be sure to take care of your physical and mental health, manage your emotions well, and expand your relationships, and appreciate the diverse environments in which you'll find yourself. Don't forget that having a strong support system—including your family, friends, instructors, counselors, and supervisors—promotes your success.

MAINTAIN SOME MYSTERY

| THE PROBLEM | *You're open and honest with just about everyone online and when you use mobile apps.* |

| THE FIX | *Carefully manage your online image to ensure it sends the appropriate message to the world.* |

Source: Photo by Glenn Grainger/Zebra Studios. Permission granted by Doggles, LLC.

HOW TO DO IT

1. **Honesty is the best policy, but oversharing is not, especially in the digital age.** This goes double for students. Colleges and employers—present *and* future—can look you up online.

2. **The best way to manage your image online is to be proactive and aware.** Make sure your privacy settings on Facebook are up to par. For instance, allow only your friends to see your page, and if you list your birthday, don't put the year. Be careful about expressing controversial opinions online that could work against you. Encourage your friends to put mobile devices away during activities that shouldn't be recorded and not to share photos or videos that might be harmful to your or someone else's reputation. If you do find yourself tagged in a picture that makes you look reckless or irresponsible, ask that the photo be removed immediately.

   It's not that you can't be yourself, but your online presence should be something you can be proud of. Remember, once you put something online, it is public forever, regardless of your privacy settings. You have very little control over what happens to material after you make it public. This is also the case with mobile apps. For instance, Snapchat allows users to capture videos and pictures that supposedly self-destruct after a few seconds, but there is evidence that such material can indeed be restored. The guiding rule should be never to assume that something that's vanished is truly gone.

3. **Delete old accounts.** If you have MySpace, LiveJournal, Blogger, or any other account that is still open to the public but not being updated, delete it. Not only do old accounts include out-of-date information and possibly tales of your high school crushes, but since you rarely if ever check those sites, you may not notice if your account has been hacked. You don't want a potential employer to find your name associated with spam and question-able promotional links.

4. **Stay one step ahead.** Google yourself regularly, especially when applying for jobs. Make sure you know what potential employers can see. Look into free services like kgb people (**kgbpeople.com**), which can dig up every mention of you online, drawing from regular search engines, social net-works, and other video and photo sites. For more information on protect-ing your virtual reputation, visit **http://blog.kgbpeople.com/**.

OK TO LEAVE FLOATING OUT IN CYBERSPACE
Photos of you looking like an academic superstar.

Source: Monashee Frantz/Getty Images

NOT GOOD
Stuff like this.

Source: Philip Lee Harvey/Getty Images

THINK

If you could make only three recommendations to a new first-year college student about managing his or her college life, what would they be?

1.

2.

3.

WRITE

Describe some of the ways in which your life has changed since you started attending college. How have you handled these changes? What has been the most difficult aspect of your college life so far? Why? Jot down some ideas here and expand on them in a journal, in a notebook, or on your favorite digital device

APPLY

Now that you have read and discussed this chapter, consider how you can apply what you have learned to your academic and personal life. The following prompts will help you reflect on chapter material and its relevance to you both now and in the future.

1. Identify one area in your life in which you need to make changes to become healthier. How do you think becoming healthier will improve your performance in college? What are the challenges you face in becoming healthier?

2. College life offers many opportunities to meet new people and to develop a new support network. But finding friends and mentors you can trust is not always easy. What steps have you taken so far to meet new people and build a network of support in college? What can you do in future to expand your support network?

3. If you are not already involved in on-campus activities and clubs, visit your campus's Web site or student activities office to learn more about the kinds of clubs, organizations, service learning opportunities, sports teams, or volunteer work that are offered. Find at least one activity that seems interesting to you, and learn more about it. When does the group meet and how often? How many students are involved?

4. Check out some of your fellow students' profiles on a social media site such as Facebook or Twitter. What kinds of personal information do they share? What kinds of issues are they writing about? Do you think it is important for college students to be careful about the kind of information they post on social media sites? Why or why not?

5. Use your print or online campus course catalog to identify courses that focus on topics of multiculturalism and diversity. Why do you think academic departments have included these issues in the curriculum? How would studying diversity help you prepare for different academic fields?

AT YOUR COLLEGE

VISIT . . .	*IF YOU NEED HELP . . .*
Counseling Center	thinking and talking about your relationships and making the most appropriate decisions. It is normal to seek such assistance. This kind of counseling is strictly confidential (unless you are a threat to yourself or others) and usually is provided at no charge, which is a great benefit.
Health Center	seeking prevention and/or treatment.
Campus Support Groups	finding support groups led by professionals for dealing with problems related to excessive alcohol and drug use, abusive sexual relationships, and other issues. Your campus counseling center can help you identify support groups at your college or in your community.
Student Organizations	getting into a small group with other students that share the same interests with you.

ONLINE

GO TO . . .	*IF YOU NEED HELP . . .*
Columbia University: http://www.goaskalice.com	getting advice about college student health issues.
American Institute of Stress: http://www.stress.org	dealing with stress.
The American Dietetic Association: http://www.eatright.org	finding information on healthy eating and nutrition.
The American Cancer Society: http://www.cancer.org	finding out how tobacco affects your health and to learn more about the health effects of tobacco.
The Center for Young Women's Health: http://www.youngwomenshealth.org /collegehealth10.html	getting helpful advice on sexual health as well as other issues.
Substance Abuse and Mental Services Administration: http://www.samhsa.gov	finding up-to-date information about substance abuse and mental health.
Drug-Rehab: http://www.drug-rehab.org	finding a private, nonprofit referral service for drug and alcohol rehab treatment.
The Centers for Disease Control and Prevention: http://www.cdc.gov	finding reliable information on disease control.
The National Suicide Prevention Lifeline: 1-800-273-TALK http://www.suicideprevention lifeline.org	answering questions about suicide prevention.

National Eating Disorders Association: http://www.nationaleatingdisorders.org	understanding eating disorders.
U.S. Government's Nutrition Information: http://www.nutrition.gov	accessing nutrition information.
Planned Parenthood Federation of America: http://www.plannedparenthood.org	finding resources for planned parenthood.
The University of Chicago's Student Counseling Virtual Pamphlet Collection: http://www.dr-bob.org/vpc/	solving problems in relationships.
The University of Texas Counseling Center on Healthy Romantic Relationships during College: http://cmhc.utexas.edu/healthyrelationships.html	accessing information that explores the ups and downs of romantic relationships.
The Clery Center for Security on Campus: http://clerycenter.org/campus-sexual-violence -elimination-save-act	finding information on the Campus Sexual Violence Elimination (SaVE) Act.
Diversity Web: http://www.diversityweb.org	finding resources related to diversity on campus.
Tolerance.org: http://www.tolerance.org	accessing resources for dealing with discrimination and prejudice both on and off campus.

MY COLLEGE'S RESOURCES

12 Making the Right Career Choice

PRE-READING ACTIVITY: One of the reasons most students attend two-year colleges is to learn skills that they can apply to a job or career. What kind of job or career do you want to get after you complete your studies? Explain three reasons for your choice.

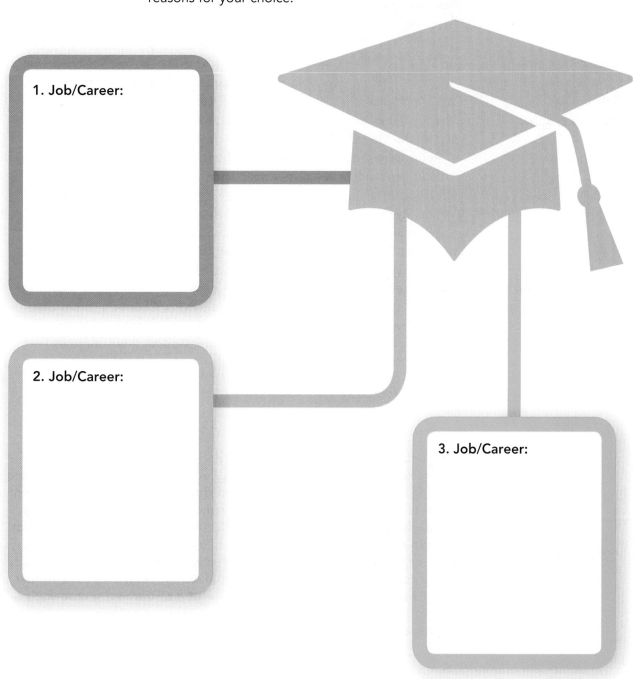

1. Job/Career:

2. Job/Career:

3. Job/Career:

PROFILE

Rebecca Hall, 25
English Major, *Tidewater Community College*

Source: Henrik Sorensen/ Getty Images

Rebecca Hall grew up all over the world, moving with her parents, who were in the military, from state to state and even to countries like France before settling in Virginia. She graduated from high school in 2010 and decided to take time off from academics before heading to college. She began working as a waitress, but after realizing she was losing sight of her career goals, she decided to enroll at Tidewater Community College and study English. She knew she would need a degree to provide for herself, but why English? "My favorite classes so far have been English classes," Rebecca explains. "I love the critical thinking aspects and the ability to write analytically on the topics that are presented in class."

Rebecca has since taken that love of English and writing and transformed the passion into a career goal. She wants to teach English at the high school level. She plans to finish her two-year degree at Tidewater Community College and then transfer to the University of Virginia.

When she is not in school, Rebecca takes a little time out to enjoy hiking and art. She also finds time to work eight hours a week as a peer tutor in the writing center on campus, where she helps students with editing and proofreading their papers.

"Choose a career that you will love for the rest of your life."

Her advice to first-year students is, "Choose a career that you will love for the rest of your life. If you are not happy doing it now, you will most likely not be happy doing it twenty years from now."

Your decision to attend college increases your possibilities for employment and will likely contribute to a great career path. College is a time for gaining academic knowledge and exploring career opportunities to help you grow from a student into a productive member of the global economy.

Some students know what career paths they want to follow before they even begin college. Others enter college to explore career options by taking courses in different subject areas. Even when students choose a major, they may not be clear on how their selected majors relates to their future careers. This chapter provides you with tips and resources for career planning. Visiting your college career center can help you to build on the material in this chapter, so be sure to use these valuable resources.

CAREERS AND THE NEW ECONOMY

For some people, the reason for attending college is to get a good job. For others, the reason is to fulfill the dream of getting a college education. For many students who are first in their families to attend college, it's both. Two-year colleges help students to get better jobs by preparing them for continuing their studies at a four-year college or university, improving their critical thinking and problem-solving skills, and changing their societal status to college-educated individuals.

Over the past few years, the global economy has experienced extreme ups and downs. Economic uncertainty is a reality, and although earning a college degree is one of the best ways you can increase your chances of gaining employment, it is important to make decisions about your major and career path based on information about yourself and the long-term demands of the job market.

YOUR TURN › DISCUSS IT

Discuss with another student how the current state of the economy affects your thinking about your future career.

Characteristics of Today's Economy

The following characteristics define today's economy:

- **Global.** Many corporations are multinational; they look for cheap labor, capital, and resources both within and outside the United States. Competition on a global level presents challenges for American workers. College graduates in the United States now compete for jobs with others around the world, particularly in industries that involve the fields of science, technology, engineering, and mathematics (STEM).
- **Unstable.** In late 2008, the world economy began suffering from a series of events that led to bankruptcies, foreclosures, failing businesses, downturns in stock markets, and lost jobs. The nation's economic situation has gradually improved since then, but that may or may not be true by the time you graduate. Economic instability is troubling, but having a college education gives you a great advantage over those without degrees. Attending a two-year college to earn a degree or certificate in a relatively short time, allows you flexibility in an uncertain job market.

Stiff Competition
The information and strategies in this chapter will help you prepare for job interviews so that when it's your turn, you can walk in with confidence.
Source: © Lynne Sladky/AP/Corbis

- **Innovative.** The economy has always depended on creativity to generate consumer interest in new products and services around the world. The United States, as a leader in industry innovation, needs college graduates who possess creativity and imagination and a desire to move forward.
- **Boundaries.** In almost every organization, teams need to work together. You might be an accountant and find yourself working with the public relations division of your company, or you might be a nurse who does staff training. The ability to work outside of traditional boundaries while expanding your skills, abilities, and knowledge will be essential to your professional success.
- **Ever changing.** As we rebuild our economy, new jobs in nearly all industries will demand more education and training. As you previously learned in this book, the most important skill you need to learn in college is how to keep learning throughout your life. To give yourself the best chance at avoiding a negative employment situation, it's important to adapt your skills to the job market that exists. Doing so requires flexibility and the desire to continue to develop yourself.
- **Social.** Technology has allowed us to stay more connected than ever in our personal lives and in business; however, it has also decreased our need for face-to-face social interactions (or so we think—the long-term effects of less face-to-face contact have not been definitively measured). Employers rank the following abilities as the most important skills or qualities they look for in job candidates: the ability to work in a team structure; the ability to make decisions and solve problems; the ability to plan, organize, and prioritize work; and the ability to verbally communicate with people inside and outside the organization.[1] In this world of increasing technology advancements, the ability to be a team player is the top asset organizations look for when hiring new employees.

---

[1]National Association of Colleges and Employers, *Job Outlook 2014* (Bethlehem, PA: National Association of Colleges and Employers, 2013).

These characteristics of the economy—global, unstable, innovative, without boundaries, and social—should provide a road map for you as you make decisions throughout your college experience.

Building the Right Mind-set for the Future

Even after you have landed a job, you will be expected to continue learning and developing yourself. Whether you are preparing to enter a career for the first time or to change careers after many years on the job, keep in mind the following:

- **A college degree does not guarantee employment.** Consider what it will be like competing with hundreds of other two-year college graduates earning the same degree as you and graduating at the same time! With a college degree, however, more opportunities will be available, financially and otherwise, than if you did not have a degree. For those who start an associate's degree and complete it, the reward is considerable. If you transfer to a four-year college or university after you graduate from your two-year college, the payoff is even greater. Just because you want to work for a certain organization or in a certain field, though, doesn't mean that a job will always be available for you there.

- **You are more or less solely responsible for your career.** Career development is a lifelong process, controlled only by you! Although employees at all levels require some degree of training, they might assist you with information on available positions in the industry. However, the ultimate task of creating a career path is yours. Students who realize they are responsible for managing their careers actively throughout their lifetime will be more successful and more satisfied than those who think someone else will come along to manage things for them.

Thinking Things Through

When you're asked about your plans for employment after college, do you feel clueless? If so, you're not alone. Many students come to college without firm career plans. This chapter will give you some new ways to think about your career choices. Your experiences in college will help you make thoughtful decisions about your future.

Source: Blend Images/Peathegee Inc.

- **To advance your career, you must accept the risks that accompany employment and plan for the future.** As organizations grow or downsize in response to economic conditions, you must do your best to prepare for the unexpected. As we have stated at several points in this book, perhaps the most vital skill you can gain in college is learning how to learn. Lifelong learning will help keep you employable and can provide you with many opportunities regardless of the economy.
- **Career choice is not permanent.** College students often view the choice of a career as a big and permanent decision. This is not correct. A career is based on your professional development decisions over a lifetime. In fact, many students with jobs attend two-year colleges to change their careers because of professional or personal reasons. There is no one right occupation just waiting to be discovered. Rather, there are many career choices you might find satisfying. The question to consider is this: What is the best choice for me now?

Now the good news: Hundreds of thousands of graduates find jobs every year, even in difficult economic times. It might take them longer to get where they want to be, but persistence pays off. If you start preparing now and continue to do so while in college, you'll have time to build a portfolio of academic and **other** learning experiences (e.g., on-campus clubs and groups, cooperative (co-op) programs, internships, work-study jobs) that will begin to add to your career profile.

YOUR TURN > WORK TOGETHER

Ask another student about his or her career goals. Why has she or he chosen that career path? Does that person seem passionate about this career? Why or why not?

12.2 SELF-EXPLORATION IN CAREER PLANNING

Are you confident in your skills and abilities? Do you know exactly what you want or can accomplish? How well you know yourself and how effectively you can do the things you need to do are central to your success not only as a college student but also as a person. **Self-assessment** is the process of gathering information about yourself in order to make informed decisions.

Self-assessment is a good first step in setting your academic and career goals. While you might know what you like to do and what you are good at doing, you may lack a clear idea of how your self-knowledge can help you explore different career possibilities. Factors that can affect your career choices include your values, skills, aptitudes, personality, life goals, work satisfaction, and interests.

A Passion for the Outdoors?

Are you interested in American history? Do you enjoy talking with the public? Do you value education? Do you value the preservation of our natural resources and historical landmarks? People who answer yes to these questions might find that a career as a park ranger suits them. How does the career you are planning to pursue align with your values, interests, and personality? If you cannot answer these questions, you might want to reconsider your plans.
Source: The Washington Post/Getty Images

Values

Your values, formed through your life experiences, are those things you feel most strongly about. For career planning, values generally refer to what you most want in a career in relation to how you want to live. For example, some people value job security, money, and a regular schedule. Others value flexibility, excitement, independence, variety, and particular work environments, such as the outdoors. Some career choices pay higher salaries than others but may require hard work and long hours.

Thus, knowing your personal wishes and needs in relation to your values is important. You might find that what you value most is not money but rather the chance to work for a specific cause or the opportunity to have a particular lifestyle. In general, being aware of what you value is important because a career choice that is closely related to your core values is likely to be the best choice.

Skills

The ability to do something well can usually be improved with practice. You may bring different skills to different situations, and it is important to know both your strengths and weaknesses. Skills typically fall into three categories:

1. **Personal.** Some skills come naturally or are learned through personal experience. Examples of these skills are honesty, punctuality, teamwork, self-motivation, and conflict management.
2. **Workplace.** Some skills can be learned on the job; others are gained through training designed to increase your knowledge or expertise in a certain area. Examples include designing Web sites, bookkeeping, and providing customer service.

3. **Transferrable.** Some skills gained through your previous jobs, hobbies, or even everyday life can be transferred to another job. Examples include planning events, motivating others, paying attention to detail, and organizing workspaces.

By identifying your skill set, you can turn your current skills into career possibilities.

Aptitudes

Aptitude is your natural or acquired proficiency in a particular area, which makes it easier for you to learn or to do certain things. Shine a light on your aptitudes and discover a path in which your strengths become your best intellectual assets.

Personality

Your personality makes you who you are and can't be ignored when you make career decisions. The quiet, orderly, calm, detail-oriented person will probably make a different work choice than the aggressive, outgoing, argumentative person will. The chapter on Discovering How You Learn, discussed the Myers-Briggs Type Indicator, one of the best-known, most widely used personality inventories. This assessment can help you understand how you make decisions, perceive the world, and interact with others.

Life Goals and Work Satisfaction

Each of us defines success and satisfaction in our own way. The process is complex and personal. Two factors can change how we feel about our success and happiness: knowing that we are achieving the life goals we've set for ourselves and finding that we gain satisfaction from what we're receiving from our work. If your values are not in line with the values of the organization where you work, you might be in for trouble.

Interests

From birth, we develop interests. These interests help shape, and might even define, our career paths. Good career exploration begins with considering what you like to do and relating that to your career choices. For example, because you enjoyed writing for your high school paper, you might be interested in writing for the college newspaper with an eye on entering a career in journalism. On the other hand, you might enroll in Psychology 101 with a great interest in human behavior and realize halfway through the course that psychology is not what you imagined and that you have no desire to become a psychologist. Because your interests are unique to you, you are the only person who should determine what you want to do in the future.

> **YOUR TURN › WORK TOGETHER**
>
> Work with a classmate and discuss the jobs you have had, either for pay or as a volunteer. Which of your jobs was your favorite? Which did you dislike? Be prepared to discuss your ideas in class and to offer thoughts about what your previous work experiences tell you about your preferences for work in the future.

PLANNING FOR YOUR CAREER

12.3

The process of making a career choice begins with creating a career plan, and college is a good time to start, if you haven't already. Here are some important steps to take:

- **Take a variety of classes.** You'll want to to be introduced to various topics of study.
- **Visit your college's career center in person, and explore its Web site.** You'll find listings for part- and full-time positions, internships, co-op programs, and seasonal employment. You'll also find on-campus interviewing opportunities for internships and for full-time employment after graduation. Attend workshops on advanced résumé writing, internship placement, interviewing, and other job search skills. Participate in mock interview activities to improve your interviewing skills.
- **Take as many self-assessments as possible.** Talk to a career counselor about your skills, aptitudes, interests, and career plans. Research possible occupations that match your skills, interests, and academic major (see the Tech Tip at the end of this chapter).
- **Prepare a draft of your résumé and have it reviewed by a career counselor or a professional in your desired field.** These individuals can provide you with useful feedback to improve your résumé.
- **Create professional profiles on professional sites, such as LinkedIn.** Share your skills and experience with potential employers and make professional connections.
- **Get involved in clubs and organizations.** Take on a leadership role in clubs and organizations.
- **Attend your college's career fair.** Employers in the area visit your campus to hire students. Get to know more about the employers who hire graduates in your major. Some career fairs may be specific to disciplines such as health care, information technology, or business.
- **Build on your strengths and develop your weaker skills.** Whether in or out of class, find ways to practice what you are good at and get help with what you need to improve.

- **Network.** Connect with instructors, family members, and friends to find contacts in your fields of interest so that you can learn more about those areas. Participate, if possible, in mentoring programs hosted by alumni (past graduates of your college). Spend the summer completing internship, service-learning, and co-op experiences.
- **Volunteer.** Whether you give of your time to a nonprofit organization, a school, or a business, volunteering can help you explore careers and get some experience in an area that interests you.
- **Do occupational and industry research for your field or for geographic areas that interest you.** Look for all the career options within and beyond your field.
- **Visit work environments in person.** Explore career options through informational interviews (interviewing to find out about a career) and job shadowing (observing someone at work with their permission).
- **Get a job.** Many students already have jobs when they enter college. Holding a job, especially one related to your major, can add to your classroom learning. Even a part-time job will develop your skills and might help you to make decisions about what you like and don't like in a work environment. In any job, you learn essential skills such as teamwork, communication, and time management which are important to employers!
- **Conduct a social media audit of your own online presence.** Make sure nothing inappropriate in posted about you on Facebook, Instagram, Twitter, or other social media.

You can complete these steps at a different pace or in a different order than your friends do. What you want is to develop your qualifications, make good choices, and take advantage of opportunities on and off campus to learn more about your career preferences. Keep your goals in mind as you select courses and look for employment, but also keep an eye out for special opportunities. The route you think you want to take might change as you grow.

YOUR TURN > ON YOUR OWN

Have you explored your college's career center? What did you learn? What other benefits did you gain as a result of your visit? If you haven't made a visit, when in your college experience do you think going to the career center will be most important? Why? List the reasons here:

Industry Research

Throughout this book, you've obtained knowledge about yourself and information on how to be a successful college student. Similarly, the more knowledge you have about your field, the better your chances of making a good career decision. You can gain an edge over other job applicants by taking the steps below to do industry research.

Steps to Doing Industry Research

Step 1.	Figure out what industries interest you.
Step 2.	Continue your research to identify your desired role within your chosen industry. Large industries offer many career possibilities.
Step 3.	Identify companies or organizations of interest within a larger industry. The federal government alone, for example, has approximately 575 departments and agencies! Because you have so many choices, this part of your research depends on your own expectations and wants.
Step 4.	Do research on each individual employer of interest. How well does the organization pay compared to others in the same industry? Does this employer require long hours or frequent travel? Set up an informational interview to talk to people who are already working within the organization.

Finding out all you can about organizations you want to work for early on can help you make a career decision based on fit. The Tech Tip at the end of this chapter walks you through the process.

YOUR TURN › DISCUSS IT

Go online to the Bureau of Labor Statistics' *Occupational Outlook Handbook* (**www.bls.gov/ooh**) to begin your industry research. Search for occupations related to your major. Discuss in class what you found.

GETTING EXPERIENCE

12.4

Now that you have developed a career plan, gotten a handle on your interests, and done your industry research, it's time to test the waters. But since employers prefer to hire people with experience, how can you gain experience if they won't hire you without any? The answer is that there are several ways to gain some experience while you are in college. Engaging in experiential learning opportunities such as service learning, volunteer activities, internships, co-op programs, and competitions and projects designed for students, can help you gain some experience while you are in college.

Experiential Learning Opportunities

Gaining experience in your field while in college can help you meet people who may later serve as important references for employment. That experience can also teach you things you won't learn in the classroom. Here are a number of ways to pursue such experience:

- **Service learning/volunteer activities.** Service learning allows you to apply what you learn in class to actual practice. Some instructors build service learning into their courses, but if this option isn't available, consider volunteering! A little time spent each week can provide many personal and professional rewards, allowing you to continue learning about yourself, your interests, and your abilities.
- **Internships and co-ops.** What you learn in the classroom can be applied to the real world through internships and co-ops. An *internship* is a short-term, structured method of on-the-job training. As an intern, you are not likely to be paid, but you might be able to receive academic credit. Check with your academic department and career center to find out what internships are available in your major. Remember that with one or more internships on your résumé, you'll be a step ahead of students who ignore this valuable experience. A *co-op program* allows you to alternate work experience and classes. As a co-op student, you can also have paid work assignments that provide you with an opportunity to apply what you learn to the workplace.
- **Student projects/competitions.** In many fields, students engage in competitions based on what they have learned in the classroom. They might compete against teams from other colleges. In the process, they learn teamwork, communication, and problem-solving skills.

Trash or Treasure?

This student intern in the campus recycling department empties a bin of food into a container that will be sent to an off-campus composting center. Imagine what he is learning about the business of recycling, composting, and food waste reduction with regard to an academic area like environmental or sustainability studies.

Source: MCT via Getty Images

Working in College

Among the many benefits of working while taking classes are the following:

- Gaining professional experience
- Earning money for tuition, books, and living expenses
- Networking/making connections
- Learning more about yourself and others
- Developing key skills, such as communication, teamwork, problem-solving, work ethic, and time management

Your first decision will be whether to work on campus or off. If you choose to work on campus, look for opportunities as early in the semester as you can. You might be pleasantly surprised to learn how varied on-campus opportunities are, such as tutoring in the writing or math center, being an attendant in the fitness center, or serving as a student ambassador for the admissions office or career center.

One benefit of on-campus employment is that the work schedules are often flexible. Another benefit is that you might be able to connect with instructors and administrators you can later consult as mentors or ask for reference letters. Plus, your boss will understand that you occasionally need time off to study or take exams. Finally, students who work on campus are more likely to graduate from college than are students who work off campus; keep this fact in mind as you think about mixing college and work.

Some on-campus jobs are reserved for work-study students. The federal work-study program is a form of government-sponsored financial aid that provides part-time employment to help with college expenses. Once you accept the work-study award on your financial aid notification, you will be sent information regarding the steps you should take for getting a job within the program. Keep in mind that your work-study award will be limited to a certain amount each term; once you reach your limit in earnings, you can no longer work until the next term begins. Generally, you will have to interview for a work-study position whether on or off campus. Check with your college's financial aid office or career center to get a list of available jobs and to get help preparing your application materials and getting ready for the interview.

Work-Study

Often you will see students on campus who are studying while they work.

As a college student, you may decide that you would rather work off campus. An off-campus job might pay better than an on-campus one, or be closer to your home, or be in an organization where you want to continue working after you finish college. The best place to start looking for off-campus jobs is your campus career center, which might have listings or Web sites with off-campus employment opportunities. Feel free to ask a career counselor for suggestions.

Whether you choose to work on or off campus, keep in mind that overextending yourself can interfere with your college success and your ability to attend class, do your homework, and participate in many other valuable parts of college life, such as group study. Take some time to determine how involved you are able to be, and stay within reasonable limits. Students who work in paid jobs more than fifteen hours a week have a lower chance of success in college.

JOB-SEARCH STRATEGIES

12.5

To find a job, whether while you are in college or after you graduate, you can apply the following job-search strategies:

- Learn the names of the major employers in your college's geographic area: manufacturers, service industries, resorts, and so on. Once you know who the major employers are, check them out, visit their Web sites. If you like what you see, visit your career center to arrange an informational interview or job-shadowing opportunity.

- Visit online postings, and look at the classified ads in the local newspaper, either in print or online.
- Check your college's student newspaper. Employers who favor hiring college students (such as UPS) often advertise there. Be cautious about work opportunities that seem unrealistic, such as those offering big salaries for working at home or those that ask you to pay an up-front fee for a job. When in doubt, ask your career center for advice.
- Be aware that many job openings are never posted. Employers usually prefer to hire people who are recommended to them by current employees, friends, or the person leaving the position. Realize that who you know is important. Your friends who already work on campus or who have had an internship can be the best people to help you when you are ready to search for your job.

Market Yourself

Some people think that marketing yourself is what you do when you need a job, but in fact that's not the case at all. Marketing yourself is actually about developing a presence at your college and within your industry. If you can create a name and reputation for yourself, you can shape your own future. Here are a few points to consider:

- **If you don't do it, no one else will.** Taking control of your own image is your responsibility. There is no one better to portray *you* as accurately as *you*. Remember to share your career goals with instructors, advisers, friends, and family; they can't help market you if they don't know you! The more others know about your professional goals, the more they are able to help you make professional connections.
- **Get an edge over your competition.** You need to stand out from your peers if you want to go far in your career. Think carefully about what you are doing to advance yourself professionally outside the classroom, such as becoming a co-op student, an intern, or a volunteer.

YOUR TURN ❯ WORK TOGETHER

Discuss with your classmates what strategies you could use to market yourself to a potential employer? Which of your characteristics or aptitudes would you emphasize? What do your peers plan to do to market themselves?

Build a Résumé

A good résumé is an excellent and necessary way of marketing yourself. Before you finish college, you'll need a résumé, whether it's for a part-time job, an internship or co-op position, or to show to an instructor who agrees to write you a letter of recommendation. There are two résumé formats: chronological and skill focused. Figure 12.1 shows a chronological résumé. Generally, choose the chronological format to list your jobs and other experiences from the most to least recent). Choose the skills résumé if you can group skills from a number of jobs or projects under several meaningful categories. Your career center can help you choose the format that is right for you based on your experience and future goals.

The average time an employer spends screening résumés for the first time is 7 to 10 seconds. Many employers also use résumé-scanning software to identify key terms and experiences of the applicant that are most important to the employer. If you are a new professional, a one-page résumé is appropriate. Add a second page only if you have truly outstanding skills or work experiences that won't fit on the first page, but consult with your career center for guidance on this point. If you are in college to get retrained and change your career, make sure to update your information on your résumé.

Write a Cover Letter

A cover letter is *more important* than a résumé and much harder to write well. When sending a cover letter, think about who will receive it. Different fields will have different requirements. Your academic adviser or career counselor can help you address your letter to the right person; so can the Internet. Never write, "To whom it may concern." Use the proper formats for date, address, and salutation (Dear _____:). These are details that employers pay attention to, and a mistake in your letter may cost you an interview. And make sure to ask someone whose writing ability you trust to proofread your cover letter.

A cover letter, written to explain how hiring you will benefit the organization, is an excellent way of marketing yourself to a potential employer. It is important to review the organization's Web site and find out what skills and experience its employees have. Use the cover letter to highlight your skills for every requirement of the position. Your career center can help you write a cover letter that talks about your education and your experience related to the position. Spending time on writing an excellent cover letter also prepares you for the interview by allowing you to think about how your background matches the needs of that position and the organization. Figure 12.2 (see page 278) provides a sample cover letter.

Interviewing

The first year of college might not seem like a time to be concerned about interviews. However, students often find themselves in interview

FIGURE 12.1 ❯ Sample Résumé

Sandra Sanchez
1322 8th Avenue, Apt. # 8A
Jersey City, NJ 07087
Cell: 201-555-1212
ssanchez@yahoo.com

Objective

To obtain a position as an IT intern

Qualifications

Dedicated individual with the ability to identify problems, provide solutions, plan and organize tasks, and work in groups

Work Experience

September 2012- September 2014

Computer Lab Assistant Hudson County Community College
- Assisted students with their computer problems in the lab
- Maintained the computer stations by updating software programs
- Helped to provide an organized learning environment
- Labeled and displayed materials and information related to the lab

August 2010- December 2012
Import/Export Clover Company

Secretary
- Answered telephone calls
- Assisted the manager with correspondence
- Managed filing, faxing, copying, and other clerical tasks
- Use Outlook calendar function to make appointments and organize events
- Maintained the database

Education

Hudson County Community College, Jersey City, NJ
September 2012- Present
Associate Degree in Computer Science

Union City High School
September 2008 - June 2012
Diploma

Languages

English, Spanish

References

Furnished upon request.

situations soon after arriving on campus. You might be looking for positions in student government, finding an on-campus job, competing for a second-year scholarship, choosing a summer job opportunity, or applying for an internship. Preparing for an interview begins the moment you arrive on campus because, as a first-year student, the interview will be about you and how college is changing you. Students who have taken only a little time to think about who they are and how they have changed can feel lost in an interview. Luckily, the chapters in this book have begun preparing you for the interview process.

The purpose of the interview is to exchange information; the goal is to assess your abilities and competencies. For you, the interview is an opportunity to learn more about the employer and whether the position would be a good fit with your abilities and preferences. Ideally, you want to find a match between your interests and abilities and the position or experience you are seeking. It is important to research the organization and the people you may be working with prior to any interview. Doing so will help prepare you for the interview and help you know what questions to ask. The following explains how you can go about doing this research:

1. **Start with the company Web site.** This is usually the single best resource. Scroll through the entire site. Note details you can use to develop good questions to ask in your interview and prepare relevant answers to anticipated interview questions. If the company does not have its own Web site, go to other sites, such as Hoovers.com, which provide extensive information about companies and industries.
2. **Ask for advice.** Ask your instructor or your career center about the organization.
3. **Use your library.** Find articles in business publications and industry trade magazines.
4. **Note the employer's goals and values.** This tells you about the organizational culture. Use this information to decide whether you would be a good fit.
5. **Research details on the employer's products and services.** Being able to talk a company's language shows that you have prepared yourself.
6. **Take your research with you to the interview.** It is recommended that you show how you have taken the time to find out about the company prior to the interview.

After you've done your research, the next step is to practice interviewing *before* the actual interview. Check with your career center to find out whether you can participate in a mock interview. Mock interviews help students feel comfortable in real interview situations. Your counselor might ask you for a position description, your résumé, and an organization profile before the interview. Career counselors use these materials to create a situation similar to an actual interview. Many career centers also have practice interview software such as InterviewStream, which is a popular program that allows you to record answers to interview questions asked by the computer for replay and review. You can record your answers multiple times as you try to perfect your response; you can send your recorded interview to instructors or others for feedback; and because

FIGURE 12.2 ❯ Sample Cover Letter

Sandra Sanchez
1322 8th Avenue, Apt. # 8A
Jersey City, NJ 07087
Cell: 201-555-1212
ssanchez@yahoo.com

September 05, 2014

International Business Consultants
Department of Human Resources

Dear Madam/Sir

Attached please find my resume for the IT internship position posted on your company Web site on August 27, 2014.

I have two years of experience working as a computer lab assistant at Hudson County Community College. In this position, I have demonstrated my knowledge of different software programs and have been able to work effectively in a fast-paced environment. As a student at the College, I have had the opportunity to work independently and with others and improved my communication and organizational skills.

Based on my education and experience, I am a strong candidate for this position. If you have any questions, please call me at 201-555-1212, or email me at ssanchez@yahoo.com.

Thank you for considering my application.

Sincerely,

Sandra Sanchez

First Impressions

A critical step on the way to any job is the personal interview. This is your chance to put your best foot forward. Remember to be on time, dress professionally, offer a firm handshake, answer questions honestly, and smile!

the interview is recorded using a webcam, you can review not only your words but also your body language! Nonverbal communication is often more important than what you actually say in the interview. Even if a mock interview session is not available, the career center can offer tips on handling an interview situation. Check your career center Web site for sample interview questions so that you can practice before an interview.

If you are changing your career and have been interviewed before, make sure to think about the best and worst interviews you have had and try to avoid repeating the mistakes you made in the past; more important, build on the positive interview strategies you used in previous successful interviews.

Appropriate Interview Conduct In an interview situation, any of the following might be a deciding factor in whether you are hired for the position:

- **Dress appropriately.** First impressions matter, so always dress neatly and appropriately. You can be somewhat casual for some types of employers, but it is better to dress too professionally than too informally. Check with your career center to get advice about proper dress. Also, many two-year colleges have suits to loan to students who cannot yet afford to buy expensive clothes for an interview.
- **Arrive on time to the interview.** If your interview is off campus, carefully estimate how long it will take you to travel to the interview site before the day of your interview. Be mindful of traffic volume at certain times of the day, and if you are driving, make sure you know where to park. The interviewer expects you to be on time, regardless of the weather or your commuting time.

- **Follow up.** It is important to follow up any interview with a thank-you e-mail. Many times, the person to whom you addressed your cover letter is not the person with whom you actually interview. Prior to leaving the interview, ask for business cards of the professionals you met with so that you have their contact information. Send a thank-you to every person who interviewed you. In your follow-up, you can once more highlight how your skills and experience match with the organization's goals.

12.6

SKILLS EMPLOYERS SEEK

One of the many important purposes and outcomes of your college experience is gaining a combination of knowledge and skills. Two types of skills are essential to employment and to life: content skills and transferable skills. **Content skills** are intellectual, or "hard," skills you gain in your academic field. They include writing proficiency, computer literacy, and foreign language skills. Computer literacy is now a core skill like reading, writing, and mathematics. You can apply content skills to jobs in any field or occupation.

Certain types of employers expect extensive knowledge in your academic major before they consider hiring you; for example, to get a job in accounting, you must have knowledge of QuickBooks or of Microsoft

Making Connections

Some career fairs may be specific to disciplines such as health care, information technology, or business. Others may be specific to the audience, such as this career fair for military veterans. Attending events like these is part of planning for your career. Career fairs give job candidates the opportunity to make a strong first impression with potential employers.
Source: © Sandy Huffaker/Corbis

Excel's advanced features. Employers will not train you in basic applications or knowledge related to your field, so remember to be prepared to speak of your qualifications during the interview process. Remember for most college students, it's sufficient to have some fundamental knowledge. You will learn on the job as you move from entry-level to advanced positions.

Transferable skills are general skills that can be applied in a lot of settings. Some transferable skills are listed and described below:

Skills	Abilities
Communication	-Being a clear and persuasive speaker
	-Listening attentively
	-Writing well
Presentation	-Justifying
	-Persuading
	-Responding to questions and serious critiques of presentation material
Leadership	-Taking charge
	-Providing direction
Teamwork	-Working with different people while maintaining control over some assignments
Interpersonal	-Relating to others
	-Motivating others to participate
	-Easing conflict between coworkers
Personal traits	-Showing motivation
	-Recognizing the need to take action
	-Being adaptable to change
	-Having a strong work ethic
	-Being reliable and honest
	-Acting in an ethical manner
	-Knowing how to plan and organize multiple tasks
	-Being able to respond positively to customer concerns
Critical thinking and problem solving	-Identifying problems and their solutions by combining information from different sources and considering options

Transferable skills are valuable to many kinds of employers and professions. They give you flexibility in your career planning. For example, volunteer work, involvement in a student professional organization or club, and having hobbies or interests can all build teamwork, leadership, interpersonal skills, and effective communication abilities. Internships and career-related work can offer you valuable opportunities to practice these skills in the real world.

JOB CANDIDATE SKILLS/QUALITIES RANKED AS VERY IMPORTANT OR EXTREMELY IMPORTANT BY EMPLOYERS

Ability to work in a team structure

Ability to make decisions and solve problems

Ability to plan, organize, and prioritize work

Ability to verbally communicate with persons inside and outside the organization

Ability to obtain and process information

Ability to analyze quantitative data

Technical knowledge related to the job

Therefore, the ideal candidate is a team player and good communicator who can make decisions and solve problems and prioritize.

Source: National Association of Colleges and Employers, *Job Outlook 2014* (Bethlehem, PA: National Association of Colleges and Employers, 2013).

12.7

STAYING ON THE PATH TO SUCCESS

Because so much research has been done on first-year students like you, we can confidently tell you that successful completion of this course is a good predictor for overall success in college. When you finish any of your college courses, take some time to step back, think, ask yourself the following questions, and perhaps even record your answers:

- What did I learn in this course?
- How can I apply what I have learned to other courses or to my current job?
- How will I use what I learned both in and out of class?
- What did I learn that I am most likely to remember?
- Do I want to stay in touch with this instructor?
- Did I improve my basic skills?
- How do I feel about what I accomplished?
- Did I do better than I thought I would?
- What did I do that helped me progress, and how can I repeat those kinds of successful efforts in other courses?
- What challenges do I still face?

Celebrate!

Before you know it, you'll be a college graduate, equipped with all the knowledge and skills you have acquired and on your way to a successful career and a bright future.
Source: © Corbis

Whether you are finishing this course at the end of your first term or first year in college, you have learned many success strategies that can help you throughout your entire college experience.

For many students, the first year is by far the most challenging, especially in terms of adjusting or readjusting to college life. Once you complete your first year, you will have many decisions and opportunities, and you need a set of strategies to succeed beyond the first year.

CONDUCTING INDUSTRY RESEARCH

In the world of business, anything older than six months is considered ancient. Today, information about industries and the companies that represent them is essential for anyone who wants to get a sense of how careers are trending, what the coolest sectors are, which college majors are in or out, where the money is, and who's hiring.

THE PROBLEM

You have no idea where to begin your industry research—all the options leave you dizzy.

THE FIX

Start with tried-and-true comprehensive resources: O*NET, the U.S. Bureau of Labor Statistics' Occupational Outlook Handbook, and a targeted hunt.

HOW TO DO IT

1. Visit O*NET OnLine (**onetonline.org**) and use the Find Occupations option at top of the page to begin your search.

2. Search occupations by keyword, or choose from the occupational categories:

   a. **Career Cluster.** These are occupations in the same field of work that require similar skills. You can use Career Clusters to help focus your education plans toward obtaining the necessary knowledge, competencies, and training for success in a particular career path.

   b. **Industry.** These are broad groups of businesses or organizations with similar activities, products, or services.

   c. **Job Zone.** These zones group occupations into one of five categories based on levels of education, experience, and training necessary to perform the occupation.

   d. **Bright Outlook.** These are occupations that are new and emerging, are expected to grow rapidly in the next several years, and are expected to have large numbers of job openings.

   e. **Green Economy Sector.** These are occupations in fields related to environmental protection and sustainable energy.

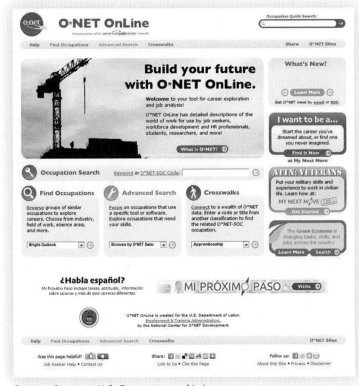

Source: Courtesy U.S. Department of Labor

    f. **Job Families.** These are groups of occupations based on skills, education, training, credentials, and work performed.

    g. **STEM Disciplines.** These are occupations that require education in science, technology, engineering, and mathematics (STEM) disciplines.

3. The **search results** for your particular occupation are listed in a rank order calculated on relevance of the occupational title, alternate titles, description, tasks, and detailed work activities associated with the keyword you entered.

4. Select the **Relevance Score** to view the specific items matched by your search within the occupation.

5. Review **Occupational Report** associated with each desired occupation to find the following information related to each occupation:

Tasks | Tools & Technology | Knowledge | Skills | Abilities | Work Activities | Work Context | Job Zone | Education | Interests | Work Styles | Work Values | Related Occupations | Wages & Employment | Additional Information

6. Use this **Summary Report** to make more informed decisions about your professional, academic, and career-related choices.

A FEW SITES WE LIKE

Web Site	Internet Address
O*NET OnLine	onetonline.org
Market Research	marketresearch.com
Wall Street Journal	executivelibrary.com/Research.asp
First Research	firstresearch.com/Industry-Profiles.aspx
Market Watch	marketwatch.com/tools/industry
Hoovers	hoovers.com
Occupational Outlook Handbook	bls.gov/ooh
Indeed.com	indeed.com
Job.com	job.com
Job Bank USA	jobbankusa.com
JobWeb	jobweb.com
Simply Hired	simplyhired.com
USA Jobs	usajobs.gov
Volunteer Match	volunteermatch.org
Yahoo! Hot Jobs	hotjobs.yahoo.com

SOMETHING YOU SHOULD EXPLORE:

What kinds of jobs jump out at you? Although you're still in college, it's wise to read up on job descriptions and look into internships in fields that interest you. An internship gives you something impressive to put on your résumé and is also one of the fastest ways to find out if you *don't* like a job.

ONE STEP FURTHER

Create an Online Profile on LinkedIn.com. Remember: Your online profile should be professional and include your résumé and only the information you'd like potential employers to know.

Source: O*NET OnLine (www.onetonline.org), and the Bureau of Labor Statistics, *Occupational Outlook Handbook* (www.bls.gov/ooh).

12

THINK
WRITE
APPLY

As a first-year student, you do not have to know exactly what you want to do when you graduate from college. What is important, however, is to take advantage of the resources and support available. List three strategies that can help you make the right career choice.

1. _____

2. _____

3. _____

WRITE

Choosing a career can be a challenge. Of the topics covered in this chapter, which would you like to learn more about? Jot down some thoughts here, and expand on them in a journal, in a notebook, or on your favorite digital device.

_____

_____

_____

_____

_____

APPLY

1. Almost every two-year college has a career center where you can obtain free counseling and information on different careers. A career professional will work with you to help you define your interests, interpret the results of any assessment you complete, coach you on interview techniques, and critique your résumé. Schedule an appointment with a career counselor who is responsible for your academic major or interests. Ask about opportunities for internships and interview practice. Find out as much as possible about the education and training required for a specific career in the field. Ask about the skills that are necessary to succeed and the outlook for the future. In the following table, list what you need to do each term to prepare for your job or career of choice when you graduate:

Timeline	To Do
First Term	
Second Term	
Third Term	
Fourth Term	

2. Now that you have a better understanding of your possible career, identify a person whose job you wish to have in future. Make an appointment with this person to interview him or her. Create a list of questions you would like to ask during the interview. For example, you can ask about college degrees, training, and previous jobs. You can also seek advice on how to prepare for a job similar to the one this person has.

WHERE TO GO FOR HELP

AT YOUR COLLEGE

VISIT . . .	IF YOU NEED HELP . . .
Career Center	learning about specific jobs and careers, how to prepare an effective résumé and cover letter, and prepare for an interview.
Academic Advising/First-Year Counselors	finding supportive networks to connect academic learning to co-curricular and extracurricular learning.
Instructors	connecting your academic interests to careers. Instructors can recommend specific courses that relate to a particular career. Some instructors have direct contact with companies and serve as contacts for internships.
Library	finding information on careers.
Upperclass Students	navigating courses and finding important resources. Many two-year colleges have established peer mentoring programs that connect you to upperclass students for one-on-one guidance. Upperclass students might also have practical experience gained from internships and volunteering.
Student Organizations	finding leadership development opportunities.

ONLINE

GO TO . . .	IF YOU NEED HELP . . .
Occupational Information Network: onetcenter.org	getting information on occupations, skill sets, and links to professional sites for selected occupations.
Mapping Your Future: mappingyourfuture.org	exploring careers.
The Riley Guide: rileyguide.com	finding tips for interviewing and job search strategies.

MY COLLEGE'S RESOURCES

Glossary

abstract   A paragraph-length summary of the methods and major findings of an article in a scholarly journal.

academic calendar   Calendar which shows all the important dates that are specific to your campus such as financial aid, registration, and add/drop deadlines; midterm and final exam dates; holidays; graduation deadlines; and so forth.

active learning   Learning through participation—talking with others, asking questions in class, studying in groups, and going beyond the lecture material and required reading.

active reading   Participating in reading by using strategies, such as highlighting and taking notes that help you stay focused.

adjuncts   Instructors who teach part-time at your college.

annotate   To add critical or explanatory in the margins of a page as you read.

annotations   Notes or remarks about a piece of writing.

appendixes   Supplemental materials at the end of the book.

aptitude   Your natural or acquired proficiency in a particular area, which makes it easier for you to learn or to do certain things.

argument   A calm, reasoned effort to persuade someone of the value of an idea.

balance   A state in which different things occur in proper amounts.

biases   Some tendencies against or in favor of certain groups or value systems.

bloom's taxonomy   A system of classifying goals for the learning process, now used at all levels of education to define and describe the process that students use to understand and think critically about what they are learning.

budget   A spending plan that tracks all sources of income (financial aid, wages, money from parents, etc.) and expenses (rent, tuition, books, etc.) during a set period of time (weekly, monthly, etc.).

citation   A reference that enables a reader to locate a source based on the information such as the author's name, the title of the work, and the publication date.

collaboration   Working with others.

content skills   Intellectual or "hard" skills you gain in your academic field which can include writing proficiency, computer literacy, and foreign language skills.

cornell format   One of the best-know methods for organizing notes which uses two columns—one column is used for note taking during class and the other is designated as a "recall" column where you can jot down main ideas and important details.

credit score   A single number that comes from a report that has information about accounts in your name such as credit cards, student loans, utility bills, cell phones, car loans, and so on.

critical thinking   A search for truth that requires asking questions, considering multiple points of view, and drawing conclusions supported by evidence.

culture   Those aspects of a group of people that are passed on or learned.

database   An organized and searchable set of information often organized by certain subject areas.

deep learning   Understanding the why and how behind the details.

discipline   Areas of academic study.

diversity   The set of difference in social and cultural identities among people living together.

emotional intelligence (EI)   How well you recognize, understand, and manage moods, feelings, and attitudes.

engaged students   Those who are fully involved with the college experience and spend the time and the energy necessary to learn, both in and out of class.

essay exams   Exams which include questions that require students to write a few paragraphs in response to each question.

ethnicity   The identity that is assigned to a specific group of people who are historically connected by a common national origin or language.

evidence   Facts supporting an argument.

experiential learning   Learning by doing and from experience.

fill-in-the-blank   Test questions which consist of a phrase, sentence, or paragraph with a blank space indicating where the student should provide the missing word or words.

forgetting curve   The decline of memory over time.

foreword   An endorsement of the book written by someone other than the author.

freewriting   Writing without worrying about punctuation, grammar, spelling, and background.

glossary   A list of key words and their definitions.

humanities   Branches of knowledge that investigate human beings, their culture, and their self-expression, such as philosophy, religion, literature, music, and art.

hybrid course   A course that uses both face-to-face and online instruction.

identity theft   A crime that occurs when someone uses another person's personal information.

idioms   Phrases that cannot be understood from the individual meanings of the words.

independent learner   A learner who does not always wait for an instructor to point him or her in the right direction.

interlibrary loan   A service that allows you to request an item at no charge from another library at a different college or university.

introduction   The part of a book which reviews the book's overall organization and its contents, often chapter by chapter.

keyword A word or phrase that tells an online search tool what you're looking for.

knowledge The bottom level of Bloom's Taxonomy which refers to remembering previously learned material and includes arranging, defining, memorizing, and recognizing.

learning disabilities Conditions that affect people's ability to either interpret what they see and hear or connect information across different areas of the brain.

learning objectives The main ideas or skills students are expected to learn from reading the chapter.

logical fallacies Mistakes in reasoning that contain invalid arguments or irrelevant points that undermine the logic of an argument.

long-term memory The capacity to retain and recall information over the long term, from hours to years.

major An area of study like psychology, engineering, education, or nursing.

mapping A preview strategy of drawing a wheel or branching structure to show relationships between main ideas and secondary ideas and how different concepts and terms fit together; it also helps you make connections to what you already know about the subject.

marking An active reading strategy entailing making marks in the text by underlining, highlighting, or making margin notes or annotations that helps you focus and concentrate as you read.

matching questions A type of exam question which is set up with terms in one column and descriptions in the other, and you must make the proper pairings.

mind map A visual review sheet that shows the relationships between ideas whose visual patterns provide you with clues to jog your memory.

mnemonics The different methods of tricks to help with remembering the information.

multiple intelligences A theory developed by Dr. Howard Gardner which suggests all human beings have at least eight different types of intelligence including: verbal/linguistic, logical/mathematical, visual/spatial, bodily/kinesthetic, musical/rhythmic, interpersonal, intrapersonal, and naturalistic.

multiple-choice questions Questions which provide any number of possible answers, often between three and five. The answer choices are usually numbered (1,2,3,4...) or lettered (a,b,c,d...), and the test-taker is supposed to select the correct or the best one.

multitasking Doing more than one thing at a time.

myers-briggs type indicatory (MBTI) One of the best known and most widely used personality inventories to describe learning styles that examines basic personality characteristics and how those relate to human interaction and learning.

nontraditional student Someone who is not an eighteen year old recent high school graduate and may have a family and a job.

office hours The posted hours when instructors are in their office and available to students.

outline A method for organizing notes which utilizes Roman numerals to represent key ideas. Other ideas relating to each key idea are marked by uppercase letters (A,B,C, etc.), numbers (1,2,3, etc.), and lowercase letters (a, b, c, etc.) in descending order of importance or detail.

overextended Having too much to do given the resources available to you.

peer-reviewed A term meaning that other experts in the field read and evaluate the articles in the journal before it is published.

periodical A resource such as a journal, a magazine, or a newspaper that is published multiple times a year.

plagiarism Taking another person's ideas or work and presenting them as your own.

preface A brief overview near the beginning of a book which is usually written by the author (or authors) and will tell you why they wrote the book and what material the book covers; it will also explain the book's organization and give insight into the author's viewpoint.

previewing The step in active reading when you take a first look at assigned reading before you really tackle the content.

primary sources The original research or documents on a topic.

prioritize Putting your tasks, goals, and values in order of importance.

procrastination The habit of delaying something that needs your immediate attention.

punctuality Being on time.

race The biological characteristics that are shared by groups of people, including skin tone, hair texture and color, and facial features.

religion A specific fundamental set of beliefs and practices generally agreed upon by a number of persons or sects.

reviewing The process of looking through your assigned reading again.

review sheets Lists of key terms and ideas that you need to remember.

research A process of steps used to collect and analyze information to increase understanding of a topic or issue. Those steps include asking questions, collecting and analyzing data related to those questions, and presenting one or more answers.

self-assessment The process of gathering information about yourself in order to make an informed decision.

sexual harassment Any kind of unwanted sexual advances or remarks.

scholarly journals Collections of original, peer-reviewed research articles written by experts or researchers in a particular academic discipline.

short-term memory How many items you are able to understand and remember at one time.

social sciences Academic disciplines that examine human aspects of the world, such as sociology, psychology, anthropology, economics, political science, and history.

stacks The area of a library in which most of the books are shelved.

stereotype A generalization usually exaggerated or over-simplified and often offensive, that is used to describe or distinguish a group.

summary Provides the most important ideas in the chapter.

summary paragraphs A note-taking format in which you write two or three sentences that sum up a larger section of material.

supplemental instruction (SI) Opportunities outside class to discuss the information covered in class.

synthesis An activity which involves accepting some ideas, rejecting others, combining related concepts, assessing the information, and pulling it all together to create new ideas that other people can use.

thesis statement A short statement that clearly defines the purpose of the paper.

transferable skills General skills that can be applied in a lot of settings.

true/false Questions which ask students to determine whether the statement is correct or not.

VARK inventory A sixteen-item questionnaire which focuses on how learners prefer to use their senses (hearing, seeing, writing and reading, or experiencing) to learn.

vocabulary A set of words in a particular language or field of knowledge.

Index